Internment in Switzerland during the First World War

Also available from Bloomsbury

Internment during the Second World War: A Comparative Study of Great Britain and the USA, Rachel Pistol
The Great War: Myth and Memory, Dan Todman

Internment in Switzerland during the First World War

Susan Barton

BLOOMSBURY ACADEMIC
LONDON • NEW YORK • OXFORD • NEW DELHI • SYDNEY

BLOOMSBURY ACADEMIC
Bloomsbury Publishing Plc
50 Bedford Square, London, WC1B 3DP, UK
1385 Broadway, New York, NY 10018, USA
29 Earlsfort Terrace, Dublin 2, Ireland

BLOOMSBURY, BLOOMSBURY ACADEMIC and the Diana logo are trademarks of
Bloomsbury Publishing Plc

First published in Great Britain 2019
This paperback edition published in 2021

Copyright © Susan Barton, 2019

Susan Barton has asserted her right under the Copyright, Designs and Patents Act,
1988, to be identified as Author of this work.

For legal purposes the Acknowledgements on p. vii constitute an extension of this
copyright page.

Cover image: British prisoners interned at Mürren, Switzerland, enjoying winter sports.
Q 64090. (© Imperial War Museum)

All rights reserved. No part of this publication may be reproduced or transmitted in any
form or by any means, electronic or mechanical, including photocopying, recording, or
any information storage or retrieval system, without prior permission in writing from the
publishers.

Bloomsbury Publishing Plc does not have any control over, or responsibility for,
any third-party websites referred to or in this book. All internet addresses given in this
book were correct at the time of going to press. The author and publisher regret any
inconvenience caused if addresses have changed or sites have ceased to exist,
but can accept no responsibility for any such changes.

A catalogue record for this book is available from the British Library.

A catalog record for this book is available from the Library of Congress.

ISBN: HB: 978-1-3500-3773-1
PB: 978-1-3502-0159-0
ePDF: 978-1-3500-3774-8
eBook: 978-1-3500-3775-5

Typeset by Deanta Global Publishing Services, Chennai, India

To find out more about our authors and books visit www.bloomsbury.com and
sign up for our newsletters.

Contents

Figures		vi
Acknowledgements		vii
1	Introduction	1
2	Negotiations and agreements between the belligerents and Switzerland	13
3	Arrival and welcome	33
4	Conditions of internment	53
5	Work, education and training	77
6	Sport and internment	99
7	Entertainment, relaxation, intellectual and spiritual well-being	141
8	Family life and relatives' visits	165
9	Going home and conclusion	199
Bibliography		213
Index		218

Figures

2.1　Exchange document for Private Jack Taylor 25
3.1　German internees arrive in Davos 34
3.2　Montreux hotel decorated to welcome British internees 39
3.3　British internees welcomed in Chateau d'Oex 41
3.4　Mürren welcomes British internees 43
4.1　British internees at the Hotel Edelweiss, Mürren 55
4.2　British internees in Mürren 58
4.3　A ward in Fribourg Allies Hospital 62
4.4　Operating theatre in Fribourg Allies Hospital 63
4.5　German internees involved in rescue work after an avalanche derails a train near Davos 66
4.6　German internees visit the Weber Bakery, Davos, 1917 68
5.1　German internee's carpentry workshop 87
5.2　German internees in an art class, Davos, 1918 91
5.3　Certificate awarded to Private Jack Taylor 95
6.1　Boxing match between French internees 113
6.2　French and Belgian internees line up to start a race, Engelberg, 1916 114
6.3　French internees with a bobsleigh, skis and toboggan 125
6.4　British officers curling in Mürren 129
7.1　German internees' theatrical group 145
7.2　Christmas in Chateau d'Oex 151
7.3　Souvenir photo booklet presented as a gift to British internees 152
7.4　German internees celebrating at Schatzalp Sanatorium, Davos, 1917 153
7.5　German internees relax with friends, a drink and a smoke 156
8.1　The wedding of Jack Taylor and Agnes Atkinson, Mürren, May 1917 181
8.2　Wedding reception for six British couples, Palace Hotel, Mürren, May 1917 182
8.3　Internees and some wives in Mürren 188
8.4　German internees, accompanied by women and children, enjoy an outing 192
9.1　Programme of homecoming ceremony for Leicester prisoners of war and internees, February 1919 206

Acknowledgements

I would like to thank Switzerland Tourism in London, Timothy Nelson, Dokumentationsbibliotek Davos; Nicole Eller Risi, Talmuseum Engelberg; Pascale Simond, Musée de Montreux; Patricia and Mark Esling; Guy Girardet.

1

Introduction

Studies of tourism history either come to an abrupt end with the outbreak of war in 1914 or skip over the four years of conflict between the *belle époque* and what is termed the 'inter-war years'. Research into the history of the Swiss tourism industry revealed that visitor numbers had increased steadily since the 1880s in the increasingly fashionable alpine resorts. Communities and hoteliers had invested heavily in capital infrastructure projects, including new hotels and sanatoria, to meet the demands of both health and pleasure seekers. The 1900s saw even greater growth in visitors as winter sports began to attract a wider section of the European elite and hotel owners extended or upgraded their facilities, often with the aid of loans, with the result that the year 1913 to 1914 brought record numbers of visitors to Switzerland, over 2 million annually, about 24 per cent of them British.[1] This raised the question of how the tourism industry survived the war and what did those involved in the business do during the years when there were few or no visitors.

In the *Dokumentationsbibliothek* in Davos, newspapers produced for visitors who remained there during the war years told of the preparations for and arrival there of wounded German prisoners from France during January 1916. Simultaneously, French prisoners were also arriving in Switzerland from German prisons. Curiosity aroused, the research for this book about the internment of wounded prisoners of war in Switzerland eventually followed. What was discovered was an unusually positive and little-known First World War story, a contrast to the plethora of works focusing on the tragic waste of human life, the causes of the war, its conduct, military history, the home front and individual biographies. Switzerland is an interesting case to study as it demonstrates the impact of the First World War on a neutral state and the humanitarian role such nations can play.

Although Switzerland was a neutral nation and managed to stay out of the fighting, the country was still adversely affected by the war. War meant rationing and inflation causing hardship, particularly to the poorest. Being dependent on imports of food, coal and other necessities, it was essential to keep cross-border transport routes open. At the beginning of the war Swiss men of military age were mobilized to defend the borders and ensure there was no breach of neutrality by foreign armies crossing into Swiss territory. This suited the belligerents who had no wish to open another front. The men's absence left a serious labour shortage. Horses were requisitioned for military use, including farm horses, making agricultural work difficult for the women and older men left behind to manage alone, particularly at ploughing and harvest time. In the tourism resorts, many hotels were heavily mortgaged and the sudden decline in visitor numbers and associated revenue caused cash-flow problems and debt, although some resorts, like Davos, continued scaled-down summer and winter sports seasons. The possibility of interning wounded prisoners of war transferred from prison camps in the belligerent nations offered them a financial lifeline.

Switzerland had some previous experience of interning foreign military personnel and civilian refugees when, following the Franco-Prussian War in 1871, around 87,000 French soldiers of General Bourbaki's Eastern French Army crossed the border into Switzerland where they were interned for six weeks.[2] This event became ingrained in Swiss popular culture by the huge 110-metre-long panoramic painting of the scene by Red Cross volunteer, Edouard Castres, who witnessed the events first hand. The giant *Bourbaki Panorama* was installed in 1889 in a circular gallery to be viewed by visitors to Lucerne's Tourist Mile.[3]

The subject of this book is not one that has been examined in detail in a monograph-length study. There are few, if any publications that investigate internment of wounded prisoners in Switzerland written in English, French or German. There have been some publications in English that look at themes relating to military prisoners of war and civilian internment in both the First and Second World Wars. None look at their transfer to Switzerland and what happened to them while they were there. What these publications have in common with this work is the emphasis placed on the importance of routine and the role of work, sport, entertainment and the development of individual interests as means of discipline and to maintain morale and mental survival. Oliver Wilkinson, for instance, in *British Prisoners of War in First World War Germany* writes, 'Inmates in many camps in Germany exercised semi-autonomous government, and structured their captive world in a way which imitated their previous round of life within an organised military regime.'[4] He also notes that non-officers had the routine of work and drill that created continuity with pre-captive military life. 'They were kept occupied, which reduced their free time and so maintained discipline.'[5] Prisoners had sport in the afternoons after fatigues. The structured life of prisoners was reproduced in civilian internment camps where men deemed to be aliens were held to prevent them leaving to join enemy armies. Panikos Panayi in *Prisoners of Britain* describes how German civilians and also military captives interned in Britain between 1914 and 1918 created their own routines which included work, education, organized sport, musical and intellectual activities. Their opposite numbers, British civilian men interned in Berlin at Ruhleben camp, did the same, creating their own prison camp societies, the title of Canadian psychologist J. David Ketchum's posthumous account of his personal experience of internment during the First World War, *Ruhleben: A Prison Camp Society*.[6] One group interned in Ruhleben, the musicians is discussed in the paper *In Ruhleben Camp* by Lewis Foreman, based on the camp's journal of the same name *In Ruhleben Camp*.[7] The importance of routine and occupation to prisoners is also emphasized by Clare Makepeace in *Captives of War, British Prisoners of War in Europe in the Second World War*. Routines that included classes, reading, writing, walking round a field for exercise, perhaps an evening lecture or concert, followed by bridge in their rooms, kept prisoners of war (POWs) disciplined, active and occupied, in what Makepeace describes as a 'Kriegie Way of Life'. Kriegie is short for *Kriegsgefangener*, German for prisoner of war.[8] Orchestras, bands, concerts, art and sports, such as football, boxing, cricket and rugby, were part of the POW experience in the Second World War, just as they were in the First, a theme pursued by historian Midge Gillies's monograph *The Barbed-Wire University, the Real Lives of Allied Prisoners of War in the Second World War*. Gillies devotes a chapter to sport and looks in depth at the role of the arts, that provided mental escape through creativity. Learning a new skill or uncovering a new talent was a way of stealing back some of the time the war had taken away.[9] Lena Radauer, in her PhD research on prisoners of war held in Russia, looks at the experiences of captives of the Russians within military internment facilities in Siberia, who developed similar artistic and cultural pastimes as survival strategies.[10] These routines and activities were important to the lives of wounded prisoners interned in Switzerland. Because they were not living in a closed homosocial environment those interned in Switzerland could extend their activities to include civilians and females while sport created opportunities to travel to other communities to compete with other nationalities.

In his paper *Diluting Displacement, Letters from Captivity* Wilkinson emphasizes how keeping in touch with home, through letters and parcels, helped maintain close relationships with family and wives, contacts that were important psychologically.¹¹ Letters from family were important to civilian internees too. Panayi recognizes that the post played a central role in the mood of the camps and quotes an internee, Gunther Plüschow, who wrote of his experience: 'The post was the Alpha and Omega of our existence. We divided our whole day according to its delivery, and the temper of the camp was regulated by it.'¹² Makepeace's research on the Second World War also emphasizes the importance of letters as a connection with home, a place that prisoners would often fantasize about.¹³ This recurring theme is also central to Michael Roper's psychological history *The Secret Battle, Emotional Survival in the Great War*. Roper looks beyond the walls of prison camps and identifies that connections between home and war fronts were a central part of the experience of battle.¹⁴ Letters were eagerly awaited by soldiers in the trenches. However, Roper is concerned that the importance of home links may be overstated as young men at the front were reluctant to engage honestly with their wives or mothers about the horror they faced and perhaps their very protestation of good spirits suggested that all was not well.¹⁵ Realizing that people at home could not understand what conditions were really like could emphasize isolation rather than bring closeness. For Roper, the mother and son relationship was the primary one for most young working-class soldiers. For internees in Switzerland letters and postcards also played an important role. Postage was free during the early stages of the internment scheme and was enthusiastically made use of. The first thing most internees did on arrival in Switzerland was send a postcard home showing their new address. The postcards were then followed up by letters. As prisoners, men formed close relationships with each other and so picture postcards and letters helped maintain friendships with comrades from whom they were separated. For those interned in Switzerland, family links could be maintained by stronger means than a letter as officers' wives, mothers and children could come over to stay in the internment centres for the duration of the war. For the ordinary soldiers on low incomes their wives or mothers could visit for a fortnight, supported by public subscription. The fact that these visits were officially sanctioned and encouraged demonstrates how important maintaining family links was judged to be by both governments and the public.

The history of prisoners of war is mainly written from two perspectives, argues Makepeace, the first being the policies of governments and neutral observers, such as the International Committee of the Red Cross (ICRC) or a protecting power, a neutral state nominated by a belligerent government, who visited prisoners and monitored their incarceration. The second perspective is that of the prisoners, what they went through and what POW life was like.¹⁶

Makepeace distinguishes her own work on POWs in the Second World War from these perspectives by adopting a cultural approach, explaining how POWs made sense of their experiences as men, in a gendered environment, linked to concepts of masculinity. She also points out that prisoners' families are rarely discussed by historians.

So far the discussion has focused solely on wartime internees, men who had no choice about where they were or how long they would be forced to stay. The strict regime of the prison camp had some similarities with the routines of colonies of health seekers, mountaineers and winter sports enthusiasts in Switzerland during the forty years or so leading up to the First World War. These groups of visitors created their own entertainment of concerts, theatricals and dances and formed clubs to organize winter sports, a particularly British habit.[17] These people were free to leave whenever they chose, except when medical advice dictated otherwise, but there were many parallels with the lives of the internees who replaced them in the hotels they vacated in 1914.

In *Wounded Prisoners of War Interned in Switzerland* a variety of approaches and historical methods are incorporated to create a broad perspective: diplomacy, the effect on the Swiss hosts, what internee life was like, how they occupied their time, how internment affected women and families. The book overlaps a number of thematic areas of historical study including gender and sports history. Although it is about prisoners of war the work does not look at prison camps and although there were similarities with both military and civilian internment, there were significant differences. There were also similarities to the routines of pre-war hotel guests and sanatoria patients, the main difference being that the internees could not choose to leave. These similarities can be explained by comparison with closed communities where structure and familiarity are important to emotional survival.

As this book is about soldiers who were wounded or ill, Joanna Bourke's *Dismembering the Male* was invaluable background reading to the project.[18] Its focus on the male body during the First World War clarified some of the contemporary social, cultural attitudes towards disability and disfigurement and the psychological impacts on individuals. Every prisoner who went to Switzerland was seriously ill or maimed in some way: some with disfiguring facial injuries and others walked with crutches or a stick or had lost limbs. Life-changing injuries brought into question what Makepeace describes as the '3 "P"s of the manly role – procreator, provider and protector'.[19] Their stay in Switzerland gave the wounded a time of seclusion to recover and adjust to their changed circumstances and learn appropriate new skills before returning home, to give them a chance to restore or renegotiate their masculinity and create an independent life, hopefully as a wage earner.

Another important work on the history of POWs in the First World War is Heather Jones's *Violence against Prisoners of War* in which she describes a radicalization of violence against unarmed captives in France, Germany and Britain. Prisoners told stories of abuse from their captors and civilians during transit to prison camps and during captivity, stories which in turn were used in propaganda and justified retaliation.[20] *Internment in Switzerland during the First World War* shows an opposite dynamic, of the contrast between the violence of being taken into captivity and the kindness, warm welcome and generosity shown on their arrival in Swiss communities. What Jones's work shares with this book is a comparative approach, investigating the experiences of British, French and German prisoners.

Books about the First World War or military prisoners tend to be written from the point of view of one nation only. Another of the few books that adopt a comparative approach to a war time study is Susan Grayzel's *Women and the First World War*. In *Internment in Switzerland during the First World War* efforts have been made to include the experiences of internees of all nations involved. To accomplish this, research visits were made to several regions of Switzerland where wounded prisoners of different nationalities were interned, in French and in German-speaking areas. Local histories of internment in particular communities demonstrate how internment affected individuals and villages. The internees themselves and their leaders have been given a voice through the magazines produced by and for them: *British Interned Mürren/Magazine, Journal des Internés Français* and *Deutsche Internierten Zeitung* gave an insight into the preoccupations, interests, activities, occupations and social life of the communities of internees. Rather than showing differences that could be compared, the magazines show that the internees had more interests in common than differences. The private papers and letters of mostly British men who experienced internment, held at the Imperial War Museum in London, give further insight into the internees' perspectives. Another key source was the British Foreign Office records in the National Archive which contain material from the POW section of the War Office. Swiss archives provided documentation on French and German internment.

Important to the understanding of internment and why and how it took place are the negotiations between the warring countries and the Swiss to reach agreements on the transfer of sick and wounded prisoners from prison camps in Germany, France and Britain to Switzerland. The first agreement was for the transfer of tuberculosis sufferers held in camps in Germany and France. This agreement between France, Germany and the Swiss took effect from early January 1916. A few months later, the categories of illness or injury eligible for internment were extended to include those seriously wounded but who were expected to eventually recover. Internment in Switzerland would prevent them making a useful contribution to the war effort should they return home. The British were hesitant and not involved in these negotiations until a few months later when eventually agreements were reached between Great Britain, Germany, Switzerland and also France which had to be crossed by any prisoners travelling from Britain. Swiss historians, Thomas Bürgisser, Christophe Vuilleumier, Cédric Cotter and Irène Herrmann have studied the diplomatic and political aspects of internment. Bürgisser and Vuilleumier from a diplomatic and Swiss governmental perspective while Cotter and Herrmann examine the important role played by the ICRC in Geneva which had close links with the government. For Vuilleumier, welcoming wounded prisoners played an important role for the image, economy and identity of Switzerland.[21] The 2014 doctoral thesis of German historian Marcelin Oliver Draenert, *Kriegschirurgie und Kriegsorthopädie in der Schweiz zur Zeit des Ersten Weltkrieges*, investigates Swiss medical history during the time of internment and the opportunities this created for surgeons to develop their skills.[22] In comparison with the internment of the French, Belgians and British, a story which is relatively well known in Switzerland, Vuilleumier acknowledges that internment of Germans is hardly studied. This book will address that by investigating the conditions of internment for Germans, as well as the other nationalities. Bürgisser emphasizes that internment is a small but growing area of study of a topic of great importance to Switzerland's self-perception during the Great War.[23]

Cotter and Herrmann's study discusses the role of the ICRC in diplomacy, repatriation of the seriously wounded, and as an intermediary between belligerents.[24] They investigate the positive impact of internment on national cohesion between French- and German-speaking cantons and how humanitarianism became an aspect of Swiss identity at a time when it was threatened by doubts about the viability of neutrality, with different linguistic regions taking opposing sides.[25] The transport, hospitalization and care of sick and wounded internees provided employment for some of the Swiss medical staff left unemployed at the start of the war as spas and sanatoria were forced to close.[26]

This work seeks to investigate and analyse a number of aspects regarding internment of wounded military prisoners in the neutral state of Switzerland.

In what ways did internment in a neutral country differ from imprisonment in a military-run prisoner-of-war camp or a civilian internment camp? A thematic approach has been adopted as the research highlighted a number of themes, all integral to the experience of internment. A focus on the negotiations to enable internment to take place comes from the rich source of the records of the British Foreign Office and the War Office in the National Archives, which document the process leading up to the agreement for the exchange and transfer to Switzerland of British and German wounded prisoners. Light is cast on the reason why this took place after the exchange between France and Germany was already implemented. Why internment of foreign wounded prisoners within the borders of their neutral nation was important to the Swiss is discussed looking at international research on this theme and contemporary documents. How did internment affect Switzerland politically, economically and also socially is another theme to discuss. The impacts on the internees themselves are investigated by looking at their experiences of transfer and arrival in Switzerland, how they were occupied by employment, education, training, sport and entertainment and leisure activities, both as participants and as observers. How these experiences were related to similar themes in civilian internment, the military and military-run prisoner-of-war camps will be explored. A major difference between military and civilian internment and neutral internment was that internees were able to associate and socialize with females, both native Swiss and their own wives, mothers and fiancées who could come and stay or visit. In neutral countries the wounded soldiers and officers were not enemies and so were not kept in confinement, unless they had committed a crime. Even so, they were subject to military discipline according to their rank and status within their own military hierarchy and also under the supervision of the Swiss Army. In contrast to a military or civilian camp, the internees enjoyed relative freedom.

Sources used to explore the internees' experiences include the magazines they produced that reported on all aspects of internment life in Switzerland: comings and goings, sport, concerts, cultural pursuits, festive celebrations, weddings, births, funerals and repatriation. These magazines were produced regularly by and for British, French and German internees. Other sources were discovered in Swiss archives and collections in the regions of internment. These include regulations that internees had to abide by, rations supplied, photographs and artefacts. Particularly helpful were the museum archives in Montreux and Engelberg, the cantonal archive in Fribourg and the Documentation Library in Davos. Swiss local histories of life in the First World War were also important sources. The frequent reports sent to the War Office in London from Lieutenant

Colonel Picot, in overall charge of the British internees, and the senior British officers in the centres of internment give an insight into the management and some of the problems and concerns of internment. Another valuable source of information about internment life are the many reports in regional newspapers about local men transferred to Switzerland and some of the women who went out to visit them. The Imperial War Museum in London contains personal papers, including letters and photographs belonging to some of the interned soldiers which provide individual, sometimes intimate, accounts not available in more public documents. The Red Cross papers and records are another source of information. For information on the development of winter sports, the Ski Club of Great Britain archive, housed among De Montfort University's Special Collections was consulted.

Heather Jones and others have estimated there were around 9 million prisoners of war around the world during the First World War.[27] Germany held the highest number of captives, an estimated 2.5 million of them by the war's end. Of these 185,329 were British military prisoners imprisoned in Germany.[28] The nearly 68,000 or so, of all sides, that came to Switzerland was only a tiny minority of up to 9 million imprisoned, including an estimated 2.4 million held in the Russian Empire.[29] The scope of this work does not cover refugees, deserters, war resisters or civilian internees, who were in Switzerland, many of whom were less welcome than the wounded POWs. Prisoners of war were also interned in neutral Holland, which is not discussed in this book but worthy of a comparative study in its own right.

Notes

1 Laurent Tissot, *Naissance d'une industrie touristique: Les Anglais et la Suisse au XIXe siècle*, Lausanne, 2000.
2 Thomas Bürgisser, 'L'humanité comme raison d'Etat: l'internement des prisonniers de guerre étrangers en Suisse pendant la Première Guerre Mondiale', in Roman Rossfield, Thomas Buomberger and Patrick Kury (eds), *14/18 La Suisse et la Grande Guerre*, Baden, 2014, p. 269.
3 Andreas Bürgi, 'Die Tourismusmeile in Luzern, Essen und Trinken unterwegs', *Wege und Geschichte*, 1, 2013, pp. 39–42, p. 39.
4 Oliver Wilkinson, *British Prisoners of War in First World War Germany*, Cambridge, 2017, p. 77.
5 Ibid., pp. 84–5.

6 J. David Ketchum, *Ruhleben, A Prison Camp Society*, Toronto, 1965.
7 Lewis Foreman, 'In Ruhleben Camp', *First World War Studies*, 2:1, 2011, pp. 27–40, DOI: 10.1080/19475020.2011.555470.
8 Clare Makepeace, *Captives of War, British Prisoners of War in Europe in the Second World War*, Cambridge, 2017, p. 69.
9 Midge Gillies, *The Barbed-Wire University, the Real Lives of Allied Prisoners of War in the Second World War*, London, 2011.
10 Lena Radauer, 'Seite an Seite mit dem Feind – Deutsche Kriegsgefangene in Russland vor und nach 1917/1918', *Jahrbuch des Bundesinstituts für Kultur und Geschichte der Deutschen im Östlichen Europa*, Band 25, Oldenburg, 2017, pp. 219–34.
11 Oliver Wilkinson, 'Diluting Displacement: Letters from Captivity', in Sandra Barkhof and Angela K. Smith (eds), *War and Displacement in Twentieth Century Global Conflicts*, London, 2014, pp. 70–88.
12 Panikos Panayi, *Prisoners of Britain, German Civilian and Combatant Internees during the First World War*, Manchester, 2012, p. 146.
13 Makepeace, *Captives of War*, p. 136.
14 Michael Roper, *The Secret Battle – Emotional Survival in the Great War*, Manchester, 2009.
15 Ibid., p. 12.
16 Makepeace, *Captives of War*, p. 6.
17 Susan Barton, *Healthy Living in the Alps – The Origins of Winter Tourism in Switzerland 1860-1914*, Manchester, 2008.
18 Joanna Bourke, *Dismembering the Male: Men's Bodies, Britain and the Great War*, London, 1996.
19 Makepeace, *Captives of War*, p. 153.
20 Heather Jones, *Violence against Prisoners of War in the First World War: Britain, France and Germany, 1914-1920*, Cambridge, 2011.
21 Christophe Vuilleumier, 'Dossier: La Suisse, asile de l'Europe, Dossier: Les Internés de la Grande Guerre', *Passé Simple*, No. 21, January 2017, p. 2.
22 Marcelin Oliver Draenert, *Kriegschirurgie und Kriegsorthopädie in der Schweiz zur Zeit des Ersten Weltkrieges*, Inauguraldissertation zur Erlangung der Doktorwürde der Philosophischen Fakultät der Universität Heidelberg, 2014.
23 Thomas Bürgisser, 'Internees (Switzerland)', in Peter Gatrell, Oliver Janz, Heather Jones, Jennifer Keene, Aalan Kramer and Bill Nasson (eds), *1914-1918-online: International Encyclopedia of the First World War*, Berlin: Freie Universität Berlin, 29 September 2015. DOI: 10.15463/ie1418.10735.
24 Cédric Cotter and Irène Herrmann. 'Quand secourir sert se protéger: la Suisse et les ouvres humanitaires', in Roman Rossfeld, Thomas Buomberger and Patrick Kury (eds), *14/18 La Suisse et la Grande Guerre*, Baden, 20 August 2014, pp. 240–65.

25 Ibid., p. 250.
26 Ibid., p. 257.
27 Jones, *Violence against Prisoners of War in the First World War*, p. 2.
28 Wilkinson, *British Prisoners of War in the First World War in Germany*, p. 1.
29 Reinhard Nachtigal, 'Zur Anzahl der Kriegsgefangenen im Ersten Weltkrieg', *Militärgeschichtliche Zeitschrift*, 67:2, 2008, pp. 345–84.

2

Negotiations and agreements between the belligerents and Switzerland

The decisions by the Swiss government and the warring nations to allow some prisoners of war to exchange their place of incarceration for a Swiss hotel came about after lengthy and complex negotiations. As a neutral state, Switzerland was unable to take sides, but with war raging all around them, the Swiss could not ignore what was happening to their neighbours. The Swiss Army had conscripted men of military age and requisitioned farm horses, in order to build a force it was hoped would be capable of defending Switzerland's borders and preventing any combatants violating its neutrality by intruding onto its territory, risking opening another front. There were also fears that Italy might attempt to annexe Ticino.[1] Swiss neutrality was therefore desirable for the belligerents. Another threat to neutrality was partisanship: it was a concern that people in the eastern part of the country, where the majority spoke German dialects, might favour the Central Powers, led by the German Empire whose Kaiser Wilhelm II had received a triumphal welcome when he visited Switzerland only two years earlier. German-speaking Swiss politicians had studied at German universities and so had links with Germany. Inhabitants of French-speaking areas, *Suisse Romande*, favoured the Entente allies, especially after the invasion of Belgium. For the Swiss, observing the suffering and chaos surrounding their island of peace was problematic and also caused division and doubts about the viability of neutrality.[2] Some of this was due to the influence of the media. Swiss from the different linguistic communities would naturally read newspapers written in their own language with information originating from German or French sources. This meant that readers received information biased to the different sides of the conflict.[3] The media waged war with the weapon of public opinion, disseminated to serve the needs of the belligerent governments who had 'the exclusive monopoly of imparting news from the front. Different nations received entirely conflicting versions of the same event that followed the boundaries of languages and dominant intellectual influences.'[4] As Charles Borgeaud, a professor at the University of Geneva in 1914, wrote of the effect on neutrals of differing versions of the news from different national sources, it had 'the nefarious effect of extending the action of war across their boundaries by encroaching on the battle-field of thought, upon their declared neutrality'.[5] Action was needed from the Swiss government to prevent any divisions becoming a political danger. What was needed was an initiative to unite the Swiss as one nation with a common purpose and identity. The federal government issued an *Appeal to the Swiss People*, signed by President Hoffmann, on 1 October 1914 urging citizens to refrain from any partiality in order to preserve Switzerland's obligations as a neutral state and to maintain good relationships with other countries. Hoffmann called on Swiss journalists and citizens of all parties and languages to show moderation rather than sew division by taking sides.

> We see the ideal of our fatherland in a community of culture which rises above races and tongues. First of all we are Swiss, and only secondarily Latins or Germans. Above all sympathies for the nations to which we feel tied by common descent, we place the welfare of Switzerland, our common good. To that welfare we must subordinate all the rest.[6]

To bring the country together as one nation with a common aim, the federal government looked to the Swiss role in the founding of the ICRC and the Geneva Convention. The ICRC originated in the experiences of Henry Dunant (1828–1910) who witnessed the dreadful suffering of wounded soldiers after the Battle of Solferino in Italy in 1859. Dunant was appalled by the complete lack of appropriate medical care which meant the injured were just abandoned to die or left dependent on the kindness of local people. Dunant wrote about his traumatic experiences of the aftermath of the battle in his book *A Memory of Solferino* published in 1862. At the end of the book he made two practical proposals that he believed might prevent future neglect of injured combatants. One of these was the founding of relief societies during peacetime, made up of civilians in every country, with the purpose of aiding wounded soldiers. If war were to break out the volunteers would move into action to support the army's medical provision. The second proposal was that European governments sign up to a binding international agreement or convention which would provide the basis for organizations or societies to offer relief to the wounded in the different countries.[7] Inspired by this, Gustave Moynier (1826–1910), the chairman of the Geneva Society for Public Welfare, was determined to put these proposals into action. Moynier created a committee of five members from the Society of

Public Welfare, which included Dunant and himself, in February 1863. At its first meeting this group declared itself to be an international and permanent committee. It was known as 'the International Committee for Relief to Wounded Soldiers' until its name was changed in 1875 to the ICRC. At a conference in Geneva in October 1863, the new organization secured a commitment from sixteen countries to set up national committees to provide relief for wounded soldiers, staffed by voluntary medical personnel who would be identified by wearing an armband with a red cross on a white background, or a red crescent in the Ottoman Empire. Individual states had their own Red Cross Societies, independent from the ICRC which acted as a co-ordinator.

At a diplomatic conference organized by the Swiss government in collaboration with the new ICRC in August 1864, a treaty was drawn up, the Convention for the Amelioration of the Condition of the Wounded Armies in the Field, commonly known as 'the first Geneva Convention'. The signatories agreed that in the event of war, medical workers, ambulances and hospitals would be considered neutral, and the wounded would be cared for without regard to nationality.[8] This was the Swiss foundation of modern international humanitarian law. The ICRC played an important role in the Franco-Prussian War of 1870 to 1871 when it realized the importance of not only dealing with wounded prisoners of war but also helping families trace uninjured ones too. By 1914, the ICRC had grown from five members to nine, still a small voluntary organization led by Gustave Ador, its president since 1910, with part-time volunteer members, all upper-class Geneva protestants.[9] Despite being president of both the ICRC and of the Swiss Federal Council, bound to strictly adhere to neutrality, Ador, in common with many of his fellow *Suisse-Romandes*, was a Francophile who hoped to minimize pro-German feelings among Swiss-Germans, something feared by the French.[10]

The ICRC, with its nine part-time members, was completely unprepared for the scale of need the Great War would bring. Initially the Committee tried to do all the work by itself but was soon overwhelmed by the volume of letters seeking information about missing men, the wounded and prisoners. Within two months of the outbreak of war, the ICRC had increased its staff twelvefold. By the end of 1914 it had around 1,200 workers, some salaried and most involved in the International Prisoners of War Agency.[11] This tracing service for POWs was established in Geneva by the ICRC. It was organized into fourteen national sections: one for each country involved in the war plus specialized sections for civilians and medical staff. More than seventy women worked to make lists of prisoners and to create card index files recording them. A total of 4,805,000 files were created, and thousands of letters and parcels were delivered daily.[12]

From September 1914, at the initiative of the Swiss Federal Council (the government), the exchange of interned civilian women, children and elderly internees, who would play no part in the war, was organized. According to the Geneva Convention, severely injured prisoners of war should also be mutually exchanged by the warring parties. A few weeks after fighting started the ICRC and the Federal Council encouraged the governments of France and Germany to ratify and observe these international agreements.

For nine months, from 2 March 1915, the first convoys, involving dozens of hospital trains carrying wounded prisoners of war, simultaneously left Lyon and Constance, crossing Switzerland, to be repatriated to their homelands. Those selected to be exchanged were the most seriously injured, who were unlikely to recover enough to take any further part in the war. As the trains crossed Switzerland, the invalids on board were looked after and cared for by Red Cross volunteer nurses and orderlies. Other Red Cross volunteers met the trains with food and drink as they stopped at stations during the journey. Seeing so many men with amputated limbs, head wounds, breathing difficulties, paralysis, blindness or with mutilated faces through the carriage windows was shocking.[13] These railway convoys carried home some 2,343 Germans and 8,668 French wounded.[14]

Seeing the horrific injuries of these soldiers brought home to the Swiss the reality of the suffering facing warring countries and was also a reminder of those who remained in prison camps. It also showed how they could help ameliorate some of the suffering inflicted in neighbouring countries in a direct fashion by focusing on humanitarian aid while still maintaining their neutrality. Making clothes for soldiers gave many women a sense of national effort through voluntary or charity work.[15]

An agreement for the less seriously wounded to transfer to Switzerland for hospitalization was foreseen from February 1915, although negotiations were slow because the Germans were refusing to return captured medical personnel who should have been regarded as neutral under the Geneva Conventions.[16] This difficulty began in October 1914 when the French government protested against the imprisonment of doctors and nurses. About 2,500 medical staff were held in Germany. From November 1914, several convoys of seriously wounded were repatriated, but this was interrupted by the German authorities in July 1915. From the following September, there was a suspension of all medical convoys until a new agreement was reached in June 1916, thanks to foreign pressure.[17]

The idea of bringing wounded and sick soldiers from warring nations to a neutral state to be interned, based on voluntary agreements, was first brought up in 1906 in the Geneva Convention, Article 2.[18] This was followed in October 1907 by Article 5 of the Annex to the Hague Convention (IV), which allowed for the principle of wartime internment for prisoners of war.[19] In the autumn of 1913, Louis de Tscharner proposed in an article in the newspaper *Berner Tagblatt* that agreements should be made by the Swiss with neighbouring countries.[20] This idea was developed further by Gustave Ador. The Swiss began discussions with the governments involved in the war to allow less seriously injured prisoners to come to Switzerland for medical treatment. This involved negotiating mutual agreements between warring parties, a completely new concept, both diplomatically and logistically.[21] After the personal intervention of Pope Benoit XV in June 1915, they agreed that the most seriously injured prisoners would be exchanged.[22]

> His Holiness in his pastoral solicitude gave great attention to the fate of prisoners of war of the various belligerents who, on account of their numbers, could not obtain the care and assistance demanded by their state of health.
>
> In furtherance of this idea, His Holiness applied to the Swiss Government, whose hospitality and whose concern at the horrors of the present conflict are well known, inviting them to harbour a certain number of wounded and sick French, British and Belgians in some part of Switzerland and a corresponding number of Austrians and Germans in another part until they had recovered their health.[23]

The Swiss president, Guiseppi Motta, approved of the pope's proposal which was agreed by the Federal Council. The plan also established humanitarianism as symbolic of Swiss ideals of neutrality when President Motta, in a speech in September 1915, said that the growing idea of humanity had given neutrality the character of compassion and human tenderness, and without these universal human qualities neutrality would remain without content and lifeless.[24]

Internment of the sick was finally agreed in January 1916 following negotiations between the French and Germans. The transfers began soon afterwards on 26 January with 200 tuberculosis patients (100 French and 100 German) selected to travel to Switzerland.[25] It took longer to negotiate the transfer and internment of British prisoners held in Germany and Germans in Britain. These agreements were not reached and put into practice until the end of May, by which time the internment of French and Germans had extended to wounded as well as to prisoners affected by tuberculosis.

Prisoners eligible to be transferred to Switzerland were identified by camp doctors and then selected from among this group by medical officers who, after giving five days' notice, visited the camps. These delegations comprised two

Swiss military doctors, three from the state of capture and a representative of the Minister of War of that state. It seemed important to the Swiss to send more medical officers to Germany than to France because there were five times as many French prisoners of war in Germany than there were German ones in France. Sometimes the men on the pre-prepared lists were absent, sent out of the camp on work parties.[26] Prisoners were selected for internment who were ill or injured but likely to recover sufficiently to be able to contribute to the war effort if they returned home, if not through further military service then by deployment to other work or releasing an able-bodied person from important work so that they could join up.

The selection criteria for internment were strictly adhered to and fell into a number of categories. The first group were tuberculosis sufferers, particularly those with the pulmonary form of the disease and men with other forms of respiratory illness. Treatment of these conditions had been a specialty in Swiss sanatoria before the war, and so it made sense to transfer sufferers there. Other categories of illness or injury were chronic cardio-vascular diseases, diseases of the sensory, digestive or sexual organs, severe dysfunctions of the nervous system, those who had been blinded or lost an eye, those deafened, amputees, men with rheumatism or arthritis, diseases caused by injuries and wounding or those with conditions that rendered them incapable of military service indefinitely. The men selected for transfer to Switzerland were not wholly incapacitated but in a condition that precluded them from active service.[27] If offered the chance of internment instead of imprisonment, the men had to pledge not to try to escape; otherwise the arrangement would be cancelled and no one else would be allowed to take part in the scheme.

Towards the end of 1915, Swiss professor Edouard Naville visited England to inspect prisoner-of-war camps on behalf of the ICRC. He met with British Member of Parliament Arthur Stanley and Lord Robert Cecil, Under-Secretary of State for Foreign Affairs who also worked for the Red Cross. They supported the proposal to send certain categories of British wounded and tuberculosis-affected prisoners to Switzerland, as the French and German governments were already arranging for their respective prisoners. Mr Dunant, secretary of the Swiss Political Department, had told British ambassador, Sir Evelyn Grant Duff, that German invalid prisoners would be interned in Davos, and French would be sent to Leysin. He also said that if the British government came to a similar arrangement with Germany, then the Swiss would be delighted to assist. Despite Lord Kitchener meeting military attaché Lieutenant Colonel Picot, and both agreeing with the principle of internment, the British government was initially averse, but its views began to change.[28] When serious negotiations began, they were some months behind those of France and Germany.

The Anglican clergyman of the English church in Chateau d'Oex, Reverend Ernest Lampen, wrote to the ambassador championing the benefits of the air and climate of the area, recommending the location as an internment centre. Lampen volunteered to assist in the care of any British prisoners sent there. He assured the ambassador that there was ample room in the hotels for 1,000 officers and men, the community was strongly in favour of the men coming there and the French Swiss would give them a warm welcome.[29] Lampen's letter was forwarded to London where a note regarding a reply from the War Office by Andrew Bonar Law MP, on behalf of the coalition government, gives a clue to the reluctance of the British for the project; the proposal appeared to contemplate the non-internment of the transferred prisoners and was therefore impractical.

> Reply that, in view of the opinion of the military authorities that the transfer of sick and wounded p. of w. to a neutral country is impractical. Mr Lampen should be informed that his proposal cannot be put forward officially, especially as it appears to involve the non-internment of the persons transferred but that his interest in the matter is greatly appreciated.[30]

Non-internment presumably referred to the soldiers transferred being housed in the perceived freedom of hotels, rather than confined in a prison camp, a scheme that would also apply to German prisoners which could cause opposition at home. Once news reached London of the successful transfer of French and German prisoners, the British government's attitudes began to come round to the idea, as seen in a note from Lord Cecil in the Foreign Office to Lord Bertie, British ambassador in Paris, just a few days later on 7 February 1916:

> From various accounts it seems evident that France and Germany have mutually agreed to the transfer to Switzerland of certain classes of invalid prisoners of war.
>
> I should be glad if you would make unofficial enquiries with regard to the scope and general terms of the agreement and let me know the result. It may be that a similar agreement would be practicable in the case of this country and Germany.[31]

Lord Bertie sent a memorandum back to Cecil detailing the agreement between Germany and France. He emphasized that the Germans had fought hard for the principle that equal numbers should be interned but finally gave way, with the result that some 1,600 French prisoners were to be sent to Switzerland from

Germany but only some 500 Germans from France.[32] This was because the French comprised the greatest proportion of prisoners held.

The pope too continued to press for an agreement between the Germans and British as well as another concerning the possibility of Russian officer prisoners going to Sweden that came to nothing, described in a letter to Sir Edward Grey from Henry Howard, dated 15 February which reiterated Britain's inability to accept the proposal:

> I do not understand how it came about that Monsignor Marchetti (of the Vatican) mentioned a possible agreement with England in his telegram, and can only imagine that the Vatican had not informed him of our refusal to accept the Papal proposal on this subject.[33]

Encouragement for Britain to accept the offer of internment and reach an agreement with Germany continued. Ador, the president of the International Red Cross, and his vice-president Naville told British ambassador Grant Duff in Berne that they were both rather surprised that there had been no response to the invitation to take British prisoners of war similarly afflicted to the 1,100 French and 850 Germans transferred to Switzerland in the first round of transfers in January 1916.

> They hoped, both on grounds of humanity and policy, that an affirmative answer to the invitation might soon be received; for they, as well as the chief Doctor in charge of the sanatoria, ... had information from the returned French prisoners that the English whom they had left behind in Germany are suffering terribly.[34]

As Britain had no diplomatic relations with Germany, all communication was done through neutral legations, particularly the US Embassy in Berlin where the ambassador had undertaken a lot of work regarding the treatment of prisoners, including arranging camp inspections. The inspectors assured the British that the prisoners were housed in decent conditions with enough warm clothing, and that thousands of blankets had been sent to them by private charity. Food parcels were sent out from Britain, thanks to the organizations set up under the auspice of the Prisoners of War Help Committee, and bread was delivered from Switzerland.[35] A letter communicating this information to Ian Malcolm MP concluded that 'the question of British wounded being sent to Switzerland is being considered' by the War Office, indicating a shift in the British position over a short period of time. The next day, 7 March, Malcolm asked the prime minister in Parliament whether an invitation had been sent from the Swiss government offering to receive British prisoners and what answer had been sent in reply.

The prime minister, Herbert Asquith, replied that His Majesty's Government had received no official invitation from the Swiss to send wounded prisoners to Switzerland in the event of an agreement with the German government. It was understood, however, that the British government was in favour of the proposal and was taking action in the matter. This exchange, recorded in Hansard, was included in a War Office memorandum noting that it was understood that the transfer of British wounded from Germany to Switzerland was under consideration.[36] A letter illustrating the speed of this change of heart, sent from the War Office to Lord Bertie on 8 March, lists the maladies qualifying a prisoner for internment and states that, subject to the settlement of details with the Swiss government, the British government would be glad if a similar agreement could be arranged with the German government regarding invalid prisoners of war held in the UK and Germany respectively, based on similar principles to that between Germany and France. The letter, signed by assistant under-secretary of state, Sir Bernard Cubitt, concludes that should Secretary Sir Edward Grey see no objection, then the necessary steps could be taken towards reaching an arrangement with the governments of Germany and Switzerland.[37]

The Vatican retained its interest in prisoners of war. On the same day that the War Office wrote to Lord Bertie, Monsignor Marchetti met with Grant Duff in Berne and enquired whether anything had been settled regarding sending British and German invalids to Switzerland. Marchetti understood the difficulties of German prisoners travelling through France to Switzerland and suggested that they could perhaps be sent to Sweden, which the British would not consider, or Norway, which Grant Duff thought they might. Grant Duff still believed the War Office opposed the scheme. He wrote to London on 8 March that the French and German prisoners already interned in Switzerland were doing well, and none had attempted to escape, ending his letter:

> I have the honour to suggest that the matter may be reconsidered as it seems a pity that British tuberculous patients should be allowed to perish when fine air and plenty are so near. However, I confess I know nothing of the arguments against the scheme which may be weighty.[38]

Despite little progress being made due to delays on the part of the British since the scheme was first mooted in October 1915, just five days after sending this letter, Grant Duff telegrammed London, confirming he had asked the Swiss Federal Council whether they would be willing to extend their hospitality to British prisoners released from Germany. A few days later he telegraphed to say that the Swiss would be glad to do so and asked if the wounded prisoners would include officers. The reply confirmed that the proposal would be made to Germany as soon as the French agreed.[39] The decision to go ahead with an exchange of prisoners, however, did cause some ill-feeling with the Vatican. The cardinal who was secretary of state for the Vatican, learnt of the British negotiations with the Swiss from Monsignor Marchetti. From a humanitarian point of view the cardinal was pleased; however, he seemed offended that the pope's proposal for the internment of sick prisoners had been refused by the British government but, when they changed their mind, they addressed the Swiss government rather than the Vatican on the subject.[40] Sir Edward Grey quickly drafted an explanation that the Swiss were approached directly because they needed to reach a settlement as soon as possible and that the British government

> would be deeply concerned if their procedure were interpreted as implying in any degree a lack of cordial appreciation of the friendly and humane interest in the welfare of British prisoners of war, of which the Vatican has given proofs on many occasions and for which they are sincerely grateful.[41]

After the wounded and infirm men began to arrive in Switzerland, Ambassador Grant Duff, was informed that

> His Majesty's Government do not consider that any useful object would now be attained by an attempt to define the relative proportions in which the merit of having initiated the measure in question should accrue to the Pope and the International Committee of the Red Cross respectively.[42]

However, some of the internees who arrived in Switzerland did write letters of thanks to the pope.

A telegram from Grant Duff on 21 March confirmed that the Swiss government would be happy to extend hospitality to wounded British and German prisoners.[43] Throughout the rest of March, April and May, negotiations proceeded with Germany, facilitated by the US Embassy in Berlin which concluded successfully towards the end of May. At the same time, agreements had to be made with countries neighbouring Switzerland. Italy and France had to agree to apprehend and return any prisoners attempting to escape through those countries.[44] French agreement was needed to transport German prisoners by rail across France to Lyon where they would be picked up by the Swiss authorities.[45]

Meanwhile, anxious relatives of British prisoners of war had heard that some French and Germans had already been transferred to Switzerland and were writing to the government urging them to get a move on with their negotiations.

A letter dated 2 April, from Mrs M. E. Toogood of Kings House, Tower of London, the wife of an officer imprisoned in Germany wrote to Lord Cecil:

> I am (amongst many others) so terribly worried about my husband, p/war at Mainz, Germany. I had quite a long letter from him yesterday, in which he says this – 'A good many French Officers have left for Switzerland, and by no means bad cases. Is it not possible for our govt. to arrange the same scheme for us? I am quite alright so don't worry about me, but there are several very bad in which a change to Switzerland seems their only chance. It seems terrible how the French govt have arranged this and nothing is done for us.' On the back of his letter the German censor has written 'Our authorities are quite willing to let English prisoners go, the fault and hindrance to letting them proceed to Switzerland lies entirely with the English Govt.'[46]

A French officer had also written to Mrs Toogood about her husband saying,

> Can't you put the case before some high Govt Official? We have got here, thanks to good arrangements made by our people. This is Heaven from Hell.[47]

Lord Cecil replied the following day, explaining that the military authorities were not in favour of wide exchanges, but that he was glad to say that he thought a plan for interning some British prisoners of war in Switzerland would soon be settled. Cecil reassured Mrs Toogood that there was no reason to suppose that the Germans would not agree to a transfer and arrangements would be made as soon as they did so.[48]

In May British newspaper reports told readers that seven Swiss military doctors led by Lieutenant Colonel Sturzenegger of the Swiss Army Medical Service were in Southampton, with Surgeon General Sir Willian Babtie VC, ready to examine German prisoners who were candidates to be sent to Switzerland for treatment.[49] Those selected from prison camps throughout Britain were concentrated in camps not far from the south coast, in Dartford, Dorchester and Netley. This was to save the Swiss medical officers from having to travel long distances and to simplify the transfer of the men selected for internment to the transport ships at Southampton.[50] A similar medical commission would also visit British soldiers in prison camps in Germany.[51]

A serious accusation made against the German military authorities was that when the Swiss Medical Mission visited the German prison camps to select men for transfer, no 'native' troops, that is, of Indian or African heritage, had been presented for examination, although the medical officers had asked to see them. The Swiss chief medical officer, Colonel Hauser, protested against this breach of faith and insisted on despatching a fresh mission of two doctors being examine these ethnic minority soldiers wherever they were quartered.[52] The British also complained. Sir Edward Grey asked the US ambassador in Berlin to speak to the German government.[53] The result of this intervention was the selection of several Indian and Gurkha troops.

Transport into Switzerland was in military trains, and entry into Swiss territory was under the aegis of Swiss officials and the embassy of the prisoners concerned. In France, once a prisoner was accepted by the medical commissioners, the internment candidate passed easily to Lyon ready for transfer to Switzerland. According to Major Favre, who was Colonel Hauser's deputy, the collaboration between the Lyon commission and the French doctors was excellent. In contrast, for the men coming from Germany entering Switzerland through Constance, control was very strict. Lack of space meant that prisoners waiting to transfer were often detained in camps at Darmstadt, Rastatt and Villingen. Disagreement between various commissions was depressing for the sick and injured men, who arrived full of hope at Constance, only to be refused entry, for a while, into Switzerland.[54] Sometimes this was because of hold ups to convoys of German prisoners leaving Britain or crossing France because of weather conditions on the English Channel, submarines or battle conditions in France. The first convoy of British soldiers arrived in Switzerland on 29/30 May 1916.

Through 1916 and 1917, internment operated on the same basis as initially agreed, but there were attempts to evolve the project to clarify details and to include those who had been imprisoned for over eighteen months. During 1917, France and Germany were working towards an agreement not just for internment but for an international convention on all prisoners of war, including the able-bodied, both civilian and military, who had suffered a long period of captivity. Despite difficulties in these negotiations, which broke down in February 1918 with the German government resuming restrictive measures in the camps, notably of food for French prisoners, meetings recommenced in Berne in March. The first Berne Accord between France and Germany was agreed on 15 March 1918, followed by a second on 25 April, concerned with questions relating to civilian internment and repatriation. The Berne Accords were ratified on 10 May 1918, when arrangements for the transfer of wounded and sick prisoners to Switzerland had already been in place for around two years.[55] The agreement regulated all aspects of internment, such as the precise medical criteria; in addition to existing conditions, officers and men over forty-five years old, fathers over forty with large families and those imprisoned for more than eighteen months were considered for internment in Switzerland.[56]

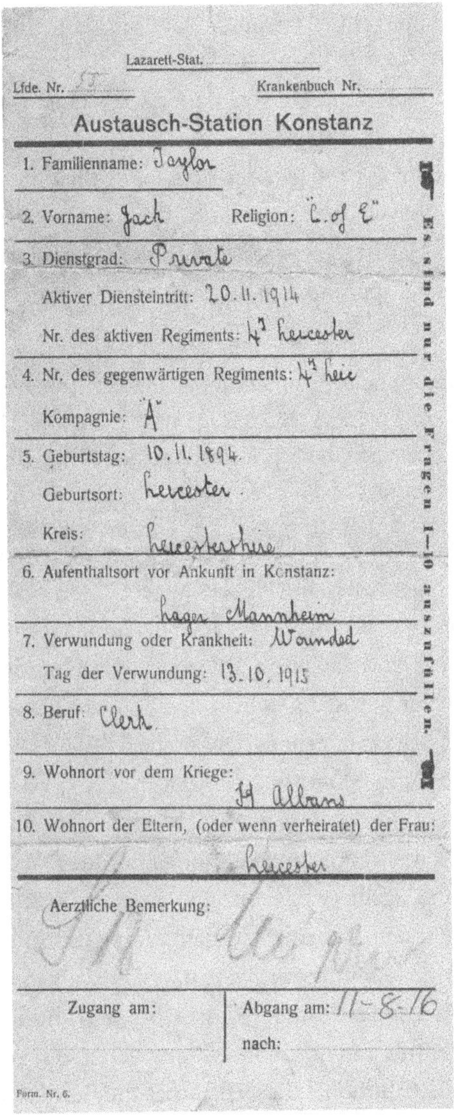

Negotiations and Agreements between the Belligerents and Switzerland 25

Figure 2.1 Exchange document for Private Jack Taylor. Courtesy of Pat and Mark Esling (family collection).

Older men who were already interned could be repatriated home, their places taken by new arrivals. They began to be repatriated under the new terms from 17 June 1918, while officers and those held captive for a long time were to leave their prison camps and travel to Switzerland. The first convoy of French and Belgians under the new conditions of the Berne Accord arrived on 29 March 1918. On 20 April 1918, the United States announced it would seek internment in Switzerland for American POWs, with treatment for the severely wounded, for whom transport back to the States was too difficult. Negotiations began between the United States and Germany on 24 September but didn't conclude until 13 November, two days after the Armistice.

Overall responsibility, management and co-ordination of the internment project was under the charge of Colonel Doctor Carl Hauser, head of the Swiss Army Medical Corps. He was responsible to his government's Political Department and on his appointment made this statement:

> Our country saved, thank God, from the evils of war, has a new and noble task, which is to care for wounded prisoners of war and sick from neighbouring states confined to our care. Warriors who, on the battlefield, have clashed with each other as enemies, now hope to be welcomed on the soil of our peaceful country, to regain strength, courage and health.[57]

Under Hauser's leadership, specially designated internment regions were created by combining towns and villages where internees were billeted into administrative units. Internees were allocated to regions according to nationality in a variety of hotels and sanatoria in around two hundred, mainly alpine towns and villages with existing tourist facilities and infrastructure.[58] Each region could specify which internees they preferred. French and Belgians were accommodated mainly in Montreux, Geneva, Aigle, Leysin, Montana, Valais, Gruyère, the Western Jura Mountains, Schinznach in Aargau, the Bernese Oberland and their surrounding areas although, for the first eighteen months or so, some were sent to Engelberg in Central Switzerland. Germans were interned in Davos, Arosa, Wiesen, Glarus, St Gallen, Appenzell, Ragaz-Pfäfers, Chur and later Engelberg. British internees were based initially in Chateau d'Oex and Leysin for tuberculosis sufferers and then in Mürren. As numbers increased and specialist training centres and hospital facilities were required, or the men were sent to work, their distribution extended across the Bernese Oberland, around Lake Geneva in Montreux, Lausanne and Vevey, in Lucerne and in Fribourg. Soldiers from opposing armies were never housed in the same area. The only region where this happened was in Central Switzerland where German, French, Belgian and English internees were not far away from each other. In Lucerne internees of different nationalities and sides, needing hospital treatment, shared infirmary facilities until a new hospital for Entente internees opened in Fribourg.

The Swiss authorities were urged to prioritize communities that before the war had been tourist resorts. Initially the plan had been to house internees in specially constructed camps, but this changed due to pressure from the tourism lobby.⁵⁹ Instead of military style camps of huts and parade grounds, the men were billeted to mountain resorts where they occupied hotels, starved of their usual guests by the war.

The Swiss tourism industry grew during the last quarter of the nineteenth century, a growth that increased during the first decade of the twentieth century. To meet the demand for hotel and sanatorium spaces, sporting and entertainment facilities, many hotel keepers and sanatorium owners had invested in rebuilding or enlarging their properties and creating luxury establishments. Many of them had borrowed money with mortgages to pay for the construction works. When the war broke out, many hotel guests hurriedly left for home in case they were left stranded and liable to be interned, some leaving bills unpaid. Worse still, hardly any guests arrived for the following and subsequent winter and summer seasons. Many hoteliers were struggling financially, in debt and facing ruin, and so they lobbied their government to send as many internees as possible to their resorts.⁶⁰

The heavy investment of the pre-war tourism boom meant there was an overcapacity of beds which exacerbated competition between individual businesses. In Engelberg in Central Switzerland, for example, accounts for 1912 closed with a deficit of 3,400 Swiss Francs.⁶¹ At the Palace Hotel in St Mortiz, major works financed by third parties had just been completed in 1914.⁶² In Leysin, between 1909 and 1911 a total of forty-three new buildings had been completed compared with ninety-five constructed between 1912 and 1914, with 1914 seeing the most new buildings of the period at thirty-eight.⁶³ With the subsequent lack of visitors, most companies could only pay the interest on their loans so further borrowing was impossible. Hoteliers had no accumulated or liquid reserves and were not in a position to put any money aside for a rainy day. The war was, therefore, catastrophic for the tourism industry as a whole, and many businesses were in debt. Using Engelberg as an example, the number of overnight stays in 1915 was only an eighth of what it had been in 1911. In the alpine resorts many hotels stood empty. Housing internees would provide the hoteliers with income to help the long-term survival of their businesses. The decision to house internees in hotels in tourist areas saved the industry from bankruptcy as the costs of housing and feeding the internees were met by their national governments which brought in a total of 137 million Swiss francs to the industry.⁶⁴ Not as much as would have been received over the same time in revenue from normal tourism but, nevertheless, providing much needed cash flow. However, despite providing some amelioration of their dire circumstances, as the income from internees nowhere near matched that derived from tourists, after the war some hotels changed ownership.⁶⁵

Resorts were selected to become internment 'camps' according to five criteria. The first was they had to have the capacity to house large numbers of internees. Appenzellerland, for example, had around 1,400 vacant beds in February 1916, when enquiries were made about accommodation but was initially disappointed when the first German internees were sent elsewhere.[66] Secondly, they needed the appropriate infrastructure, which included physicians, pharmacies, workplaces and leisure facilities. The third criterion was that the military police had to be confident that the village had administrative structures able to co-ordinate interment. Fourthly, supervision of the internees had to be ensured. The final factor, which would give a community a greater chance of being successful in its desire to house internees, was that it was dependent on tourism.[67]

For the Swiss, welcoming the internees played a functional political role as well as an economic one. Swiss writers acknowledged that there might be a potential threat to their own country due to the population taking sides. This danger did not come from outside but from within, potentially a deep national crisis that threatened the very foundations of the Confederation as it risked undermining cantonal unity, essential to Switzerland's existence. Fortunately, most ordinary Swiss ignored the festering arguments that appeared in the newspaper columns and got behind their country's humanitarian mission.[68] This humanitarianism showed Switzerland as a metaphorical beacon of hope or lighthouse in stormy seas. Externally, internment demonstrated to other nations the value of Switzerland's neutrality. It also helped in its international trade which was under pressure due to the economic warfare and blockades of its warring neighbours. It was able to gain an increase in its import quotas several times, for fertilizers, potatoes and coal, which helped keep transport routes open. In 1917, Germany agreed to supply 74,000 tons (3 per cent of coal imports for 1917) of extra coal for the Swiss.[69] The presence of interned citizens from nations it traded with assisted these negotiations. Internally, internment helped bring together the Swiss of different linguistic backgrounds in a common, noble cause that reinforced national cohesion rather than regional pride and division.[70] Volunteering gave a sense of purpose and fostered humanitarianism as an aspect of Swiss national identity and therefore had a patriotic value, which helped quell some of the partiality displayed to either side.[71]

Initial negotiations regarding where British invalids might be housed emphasized that French-speaking Switzerland was desirable because of an assumption that all German-speaking Switzerland would be pro-German and therefore anti-British. Those resident in Switzerland took a different view; the

British consulate general, Sir Cecil Hertslet, wrote to Sir Edward Grey in the War Office that he hoped that the men would not be sent only to the French-speaking part of the country but that some of them would be distributed among the German-speaking cantons.

> There can be no doubt that they would meet a cordial reception here and their presence would do much to create a good feeling between the two countries. Mr Stronge, His Majesty's Consul at Lucerne, informs me that there is a fervent desire among the population and authorities of that place, that the British prisoners be allowed to proceed to that district.[72]

Lord Newton of the War Office, responsible for prisoners of war, wrote to the British ambassador, Sir Evelyn Grant Duff, in response to Hertslet's suggestion, informing him that His Majesty's Government would object to British prisoners being interned in the German-speaking areas but were content to leave the final decision on localities to the Swiss federal government.[73] The concerns of the War Office were countered by the existing good relations between the Swiss and the British, particularly in the tourist areas. There were suggestions that a second convoy of British internees destined for Switzerland might have to be accommodated in Grindelwald if there was not enough room in Chateau d'Oex. Concerns about a hostile reception were allayed by the knowledge that Grindelwald in the Bernese Oberland, although German-speaking, was so entirely devoted to the tourist traffic in times of peace that political considerations might scarcely have any influence. Hotel keepers, most of whom were Swiss-German, preferred guests who paid their bills promptly to those who do not, irrespective of nationality. Both Chateau d'Oex and Grindelwald, in contiguous regions that would simplify administration, were favourites with British tourists.[74] This was also the argument used when Mürren, where the usual guests were almost exclusively English or American, was chosen as the second British base for interned soldiers.[75]

That the soldiers would bring much needed payment for accommodation and trade for local businesses, deprived of revenue by the war, also influenced resorts to welcome their new guests.[76] The British War Office concluded that it would be a mistake to interfere with the Swiss government in the matter once it had reached such a stage in the arrangements.[77]

Another bonus for Switzerland, whose military age men had been called up to serve in the Swiss Army, was the welcome possibility for some of the internees to take on some of the work their own soldiers had left behind, in industry and in agriculture, at a lower rate of pay.[78]

Once negotiations and preparations for the reception and accommodation of prisoners transferred to Switzerland were concluded to the satisfaction of all sides, train loads of sick and wounded soldiers began to arrive.

Notes

1. Draenert, *Kriegschirurgie und Kriegsorthopädie in der Schweiz zur Zeit des Ersten Weltkrieges*, p. 287.
2. Cotter and Herrmann, 'Quand secourir sert se protéger', p. 241.
3. Charles Borgeaud, 'Switzerland and the War', *The North American Review*, 1914, p. 872.
4. Ibid., p. 872.
5. Ibid.
6. *Appeal to the Swiss People*, 30 October 1914 (quoted by Borgeaud, 'Switzerland and the War', p. 873).
7. Henry Dunant, *A Memory of Solferino*, Geneva, 1862.
8. Daniel Palmieri (ed.), *Minutes from Meetings of the International Prisoner-of-War Agency*, ICRC, p. 3.
9. Ibid., p. 4.
10. Cotter and Herrmann, 'Quand secourir sert se protéger', p. 252.
11. Palmieri (ed.), *Minutes from Meetings of the International Prisoner-of-War Agency*, p. 5.
12. Cotter and Herrmann, 'Quand secourir sert se protéger', p. 249.
13. Bürgisser, 'L'humanité comme raison d'Etat', p. 269.
14. Vuilleumier, 'Dossier', p. 3.
15. Cotter and Herrmann, 'Quand secourir sert se protéger', p. 250.
16. Marianne Walle, 'Les Prisonniers de Guerre Francais Internés en Suisse (1916-1919)', *Guerres mondiales et conflits contemporains*, 2014/1 (No 253), 2014, pp. 57–72, p. 57. DOI: 10.3917/gmcc.253.0057.
17. Ibid., p. 58.
18. Thomas Fuchs, 'Interniert im Appenzellerland', in Heidi Eienhut and Hanspeter Spöri (eds), *Der Erste Weltkrieg und das Appenzellerland*, *Appenzelische Jahrbuch*, Heft 141, Herausgaben von der Appenzellischen Gemeinnützigen Gesellschaft, 2014, p. 54.
19. Convention (IV) respecting the Laws and Customs of War on Land and its Annex: regulations concerning the Laws and Customs of War on Land. The Hague, 18 October 1907. Annex to the Convention: regulations respecting the Laws and Customs of War on Land – Section 1: on belligerents – Chapter II: Prisoners of War – Regulations: Art.5.
20. Fuchs, 'Interniert im Appenzellerland', p. 54.

21 Bürgisser, 'L'humanité comme raison d'Etat', p. 268.
22 *Observatore Romano*, 27 January 1916, TNA 383/215.
23 Ibid.
24 Beni Kühnis, *Deutsche Kriegsinternierte in Davos während des 1. Weltkriegs*, Maturaarbeit SAMD, Davos, 2014, p. 3.
25 Walle, 'Les Prisonniers de Guerre Francais Internés en Suisse (1916-1919)', p. 58.
26 Ibid., p. 60.
27 *Aberdeen Journal*, 23 May 1916.
28 Lieutenant Colonel H. P. Picot, *The British Interned in Switzerland*, London, 1919, p. 26; Sir Evelyn Grant Duff to British Foreign Office, Berne, 30 December 1915, TNA FO 383/215.
29 Revd Ernest Dudley Lampen to His Britannic Majesty's Minister, Berne (Evelyn Grant Duff), 21 January 1916, TNA FO 383/215.
30 Minute from War Office by Mr Bonar Law, dated 31 January 1916, TNA FO 383/215.
31 Robert Cecil to Lord Bertie, Foreign Office, 7 February 1916, TNA FO 383/215.
32 Lord Bertie to Robert Cecil, Paris, 12 February 1916, TNA FO 383/215.
33 Henry Howard to Sir Edward Grey, 15 February 1916, TNA FO 383/215.
34 Ian Malcolm MP to Sir Edward Grey, 23 February 1916, TNA FO 383/215.
35 Lord Newton to Ian Malcolm, Foreign Office, 6 March 1916, TNA FO 383/215.
36 Hansard, 7 March 1916 cutting attached to memo dated 10 March 1916, TNA FO 383/215.
37 Lord Bertie from Sir Bertram Cubitt, Assistant Under-Secretary of State in the War Office, 8 March 1916, TNA FO 383/215.
38 Evelyn Grant Duff to Sir Edward Grey, Berne, 8 March 1916, TNA FO 383/215.
39 War Office to Evelyn Grant Duff, 16 March 1916, TNA FO 383/215.
40 Sir H. Howard (Vatican), 20 March 1916, TNA FO 383/215.
41 Foreign Office to Sir H. Howard (Vatican), 22 March 1916, TNA FO 383/215.
42 To Sir Evelyn Grant Duff, 10 August 1916, TNA, FO 383/217.
43 Grant Duff to Foreign Office, 15 March 1916, TNA FO 383/215.
44 From Lord Acton, Berne, 21 May 1916, TNA FO 383/216.
45 From Lord Bertie, Paris, 24 March 1916; 1 April 1916, TNA FO 383/215.
46 Mrs M. E. Toogood to Lord Robert Cecil, London, 2 April 1916, TNA FO 383/215.
47 Ibid.
48 Lord Cecil to Mrs M. E. Toogood, London, 3 April 1916, TNA FO 383/215.
49 Memorandum to War Office, 23 May 1916, TNA, FO 383/216.
50 Lord Newton, War Office, 18 May 1916, TNA, FO 383/216.
51 *Aberdeen Journal*, 23 May 1916.
52 Picot to War Office, 18 July 1918, TNA FO 383/217.
53 Sir Edward Grey to US ambassador in Berlin, Foreign Office London, 20 July 1916, TNA FO 383/217.

54 Walle, 'Les Prisonniers de Guerre Francais Internés en Suisse (1916-1919)', p. 61.
55 Ibid., p. 69.
56 Cédric Cotter, 'The 1918 Bern Agreements: Repatriating Prisoners in a Total War', *Humanitarian Action*, 29 March 2018.
57 Major Eduard Favre, *L'internement en Suisse*, Premier Rapport, 1917, p. 10.
58 Bürgisser, 'L'humanité comme raison d'Etat', p. 274.
59 Ibid., p. 272.
60 Ibid., p. 284.
61 Julia Durrer, 'Internierte während des Ersten Weltkriegs in Engelberg', *Engelbergerjahrbuch*, 2008, p. 96.
62 Susanna Ruf, *Five Generations of the Badrutt Family, Hotel Pioneers and Founders of the Winter Tourist Season, Pioneers: Swiss Pioneers of Economics and Technology*, Zurich, 2011, p. 66.
63 Liliane Desponds, *Leysin – Histoire et renconversion d'une ville à la montagne*, Bière, 1993, p. 44.
64 Bürgisser, 'L'humanité comme raison d'Etat', p. 279.
65 Durrer, 'Internierte während des Ersten Weltkriegs', p. 103.
66 Fuchs, 'Interniert im Appenzellerland', p. 61.
67 Durrer, 'Internierte während des Ersten Weltkriegs', p. 97.
68 G. Jaccottet, Marcel de Fourmestraux, D. Baud-Bovy, John Locking, *Au Soleil et Sur les Monts, scènes de la vie des soldats alliés internés en Suisse, L'Etape Libératrice*, Geneva, 1918, pp. 6–7.
69 Bürgisser, 'Internees (Switzerland)', p. 8.
70 Cotter and Herrmann, 'Quand secourir sert se protéger', p. 258.
71 Ibid., p. 264.
72 British Consulate General to Sir Edward Grey, Zurich, 5 May 1916, TNA, FO 383/215.
73 Lord Newton to Sir Evelyn Grant Duff, London, 13 May 1916, TNA FO 383/215.
74 Picot to War Office, 21 May 1916, TNA FO 383/216.
75 Picot to Sir Edward Grey, 27 June 1916, TNA FO 383/216.
76 Jaccottet et al., *Au Soleil et Sur les Monts*, p. 26.
77 HR to War Office, 11 May 1916, TNA FO 383/215.
78 Bürgisser, 'L'humanité comme raison d'Etat', p. 279.

3

Arrival and welcome

On New Year's Day 1916, the Davos newspaper, *Davoser Blätter*, told its readers that the humanitarian work for imprisoned sick officers and soldiers from France and Germany was taking shape. Hotels would be made available for a thousand German and French prisoners of war through the mediation of the Swiss *Bundesrat* (federal parliament) with the governments of their countries. Davos was to be allocated a contingent of German prisoners for internment under the leadership of *Herr Oberleutnant* Nieuhaus of the Swiss Army.[1] These first soldiers to be interned in Switzerland were ill with tuberculosis, a disease rife in the unsanitary conditions of the prison camps. German invalids were to be received in Davos, French and Belgian ones in Leysin and Montana. Caring for tuberculosis sufferers seeking a cure for their disease in the high-altitude Alpine air was the specialty of these places where there were sanatoria with existing treatment facilities and medical staff.

The first party of German prisoners arrived in Davos by train at 2.20 pm on 26 January 1916. This group of four officers and ninety-six men came from France where medical inspectors had selected them as they had tuberculosis. When they reached Landquart where they changed trains, they were welcomed by Herr Burchard, the German consul in Davos. As they arrived in Davos, almost all the resident German colony, many of them sanatoria patients, turned out to welcome them. The locals met their arrival with interest, though not always with great joy.[2] The soldiers were taken straight to their quarters in the Hotel Continental and Pension Germania, while the four officers went to the New Sanatorium in Davos Dorf. The press pointed out that a similar number of French invalids were arriving in Western Switzerland.[3] In normal times Davos was home to a large British colony; although depleted since the war began, a group of sixty-two visitors remained who the authorities would not wish to offend.[4] Sixty more German soldiers arrived on 8 February, of whom forty were accommodated in Davos Dorf at the Hotel Mühlehof and twenty-five at the Villa Collina in Davos Platz. This time Herr Burchard welcomed them when they

Figure 3.1 German internees arrive in Davos. Courtesy of Dokumentationsbibliothek Davos.

got off the train at Davos Dorf station. They were joined by another eighty-four men on 2 May: this time the numbers included wounded soldiers as internment was extended to include a wider range of conditions, not just tuberculosis. More arrived and by the end of May 1916, Davos housed 425 *Feldgraue*, a nickname from the colour of their uniforms. A few civilian internees joined them from 4 July 1916.[5] New groups of internees arrived every two weeks during July and August 1916, and by the end of August there were about 650 Germans interned in Davos: some from camps in Britain, others from France. By January 1917, this total had risen to 1,232 internees in the area.[6]

The first German wounded came from France to Eastern Switzerland on 2 May 1916. Departing by train from Lyon, after a nine-hour journey they arrived at St Gallen station where there was a large crowd to greet them. In the decorated hall of the old post office, they were given something to eat and received a welcome from Commandant *Oberst* Nef and *Rektor Doktor* Schulze of the German *Hilfsverein*. From there, the men were allocated their lodgings; seventy went to the Kurhaus Oberwald in St Gallen and fifty-five to nearby Bad Sonder in Teufen.[7] Teufen station was covered with flowers when the invalids arrived there. They were given useful welcoming gifts, and when they reached Bad Sonder they received another warm welcome, thanks to the generosity of local people led by *Frau Minister* Roth, widow of the former Swiss envoy to Berlin, who played an important organizational role, including arranging a supply of new clothing and other essentials.[8] The new arrivals were able to wash and dress in fresh clothes while the uniforms they arrived in were sent to be laundered.

For some internees, the sudden change from imprisonment to being cheered, showered with gifts and adjusting to new circumstances in the relative freedom of Switzerland was overwhelming. After a few days, the local doctor had to be called because of the stress experienced by some of the internees. Rules had to be imposed, not on the internees but on the locals. There were to be no visits without permission, and mass visits were strictly prohibited. Anyone who wanted to show their sympathy for the wounded or sick soldiers was asked not to make gifts to individual soldiers but to donate to the Ladies' Committee which would be grateful for garments, soap, games, writing materials, picture postcards, cigars, tobacco, chocolate, fruit and cash. All gifts were recorded and distributed fairly.[9]

In Leysin where the French and Belgian tuberculosis patients were joined after a few months by British ones suffering from the disease, clinics were transformed into military establishments for several thousand allied soldiers.[10] The sanatoria La Chamossaire, Beau-Site, Les Mélèzes, Sainte-Agnès, Les Sapins, Mont-Fleuri and others became military clinics where heliotherapy pioneer Doctor August Rollier and his colleagues welcomed surgical but mostly pulmonary tuberculosis cases. Officers were lodged in the luxurious Grand Hotel, a name that disguised its function as a sanatorium for the wealthy.[11]

Though not the first French prisoners to arrive in Switzerland, the first Frenchmen in Engelberg appeared on 6 May 1916. They arrived from Germany on the same day as students at the *Kollegium* returned to their studies after the Easter holidays. One of the boys wrote that as their train drew into the station, it felt like their carriage had stopped in the wrong place. French flags fluttered gaily to welcome the first group of French and Belgians. By the autumn of 1917, these French and Belgian internees had all been relocated, to be replaced by Germans in February 1918 after a six-month break.

French gratitude to the Swiss was evident in their magazine, *Journal des Internés Français*, in which it asserted that nothing you will see will be like the tenderness shown to the French arrivals, in their dear sky blue uniforms, and their joy at being greeted on the friendly soil of Switzerland.

A few months later agreement between the British and Germans allowed soldiers and officers from the UK, the British colonies and Empire to come to Switzerland for internment. Prisoners selected from German prison camps by Swiss doctors of the Medical Commission were brought to camps around

Constance ready to be transferred in late May 1916. Some of those selected travelled there only to be disappointed. From the first batch of hopeful prisoners, a hundred men were rejected at Constance and had to return to prison camps. A report claimed these men went away singing, perhaps to keep up their spirits after being devastated to find they had to return to captivity after their hopes had been raised.[12]

The transfer of internees was always done by mutual agreement of the opposing nations, when a group of French or British left Germany a group of German prisoners left Lyon at the same time. This was often the source of delays for the British leaving Constance because of the added complication of a sea voyage across the English Channel and arrangements having to be made with the French government for a convoy of German prisoners to cross France on French trains.[13] Sometimes British prisoners would be held up in Constance for several days, not knowing the delay was caused by bad weather on the Channel, battle conditions or unavailability of railway carriages to carry their German counterparts from Le Havre to Lyon. At Lyon the Germans were transferred onto Swiss rolling stock to complete their journey. When convoys from England and from French prison camps arrived at the same time in Lyon, German men from the different places intermingled, a further source of delays as they had to be reassembled in the correct groups, to ensure numbers of prisoners arriving tallied with the numbers leaving. The first party of Germans from Britain, 16 officers and 215 other ranks, sailed to France on 28 May 1916, ready for transfer to the Swiss frontier via Lyon, with the agreement of the French authorities.[14]

The welcome given to the prisoners on their way out of captivity contrasted with that of their arrival in enemy territory on their way to prison camps. Despite the neutral status conferred on wounded prisoners of war by the Geneva Conventions of 1864 and 1906, captives of all sides reported incidents of ill-treatment during transit through enemy territory from the battlefield to imprisonment. Civilians were often reported as the perpetrators of humiliating, even violent treatment, which included jeering, throwing stones and water and denying prisoners food, drink and medical attention. In 1914, the unanticipated number of prisoners and wounded overwhelmed available resources. Passenger carriages were not always available, and even seriously wounded men were crammed into dirty wagons and cattle trucks. As the trains halted at stations on the journey, the doors were often opened, perhaps to allow ventilation, but perceived by the prisoners as being done to deliberately expose them to the vicious hatred of assembled crowds. This aggression towards helpless prisoners has been identified by Heather Jones as representing a form of bonding on the home front against the external enemy, 'a type of socially constructive aggression' as she termed it in her book *Violence against Prisoners of War*.[15]

A letter home to his family in Ely from Private J. T. Collins of the 1st Suffolk Regiment, dated 2 June 1916, just a couple of days after his arrival in Switzerland, was published in a Cambridge newspaper. Collins had been badly wounded in the left arm by a shell and in the right arm by shrapnel on 8 May 1915. He was in hospital in Duisburg for seventeen weeks, from where he was sent to Munster, to Sennelager and then to Dulman camps. His letter described the grand reception given by the Swiss to the prisoners of war on their arrival. The train he was transported on left Constance on 29 May, Monday, at 9.00 am.

> A railway bridge parts Switzerland from Germany. As soon as we had crossed, where German guards stood with fixed bayonets, the Swiss on the other side gave a hearty cheer and threw flowers at the carriages.[16]

The train slowed down at every station, and gifts were presented to the men who soon became heavily laden. The first stop for the first British convoy was Zurich, where a committee had been preparing to welcome them for days. Thousands turned up at the station, beautifully decorated with flags and flowers. Although admission to the platform was by ticket only, 'the crowd of people wanting passes was so great that the soldiers in charge of the barriers were quite unable to cope with the rush, and consequently, the platform was, at times, impassable'.[17] The train was strewn with flowers, while cigarettes, chocolate, cherries, oranges, cakes, soap, handkerchiefs, eau de cologne, hair cream and wine were distributed. During the half-hour stop in Zurich, each soldier was given a parcel of chocolate and cigarettes purchased by donations made by Swiss residents and businesses: 2,000 francs from Volkart Brothers of Winterthur, 500 francs from an anonymous silk manufacturer, 500 francs plus chocolate and tobacco from Jelmoli general stores, 750 francs in individual gifts between 5 and 25 francs. The Savoy Hotel gave a hamper containing hair brushes, soap, tooth powder and toiletries which was sent to Chateau d'Oex for distribution among the British internees.[18] The British colony in Zurich also gave parcels containing a handkerchief, chocolate, a packet of cigarettes, matches, a postcard and a pencil.[19]

In prison camps and on trains carrying soldiers, strict class divisions were maintained between the middle-class officers and ordinary working-class soldiers or 'Tommies' as they were popularly known. A final insult to the British by their captors was that officers were forced to make the journey to Constance in third-class carriages sitting on wooden seats.[20] In Switzerland, officers had first-class carriages on the trains reserved for them. The class segregation continued when the train carrying the first party of wounded British soldiers arrived in Berne at 12.40 am on 30 May 1916. Carriages containing thirty-two officers pulled up opposite a roped off area where they were met by members of the British Legation, a number of allied diplomats and a reception committee.

> Ropes were stretched across the platform with a small military guard to keep the crowd, numbering at its greatest some 2,000 people, rendering the passage to the restaurant impassable.

Once the officers had been led to the first-class restaurant, the train was moved so that the 272 ordinary soldiers, travelling in the second and third classes, could disembark and be taken to the third-class restaurant in two batches as there were so many of them.[21] Both officers and men were served coffee, rolls and butter. Gifts continued to be showered on them by private individuals, usually fruit, cigarettes, chocolate, postcards and a profusion of flowers. At 3.00 am the soldiers returned to the train, the ropes were removed and the crowd were allowed to circulate freely as they cheered the departing carriages. The second convoy of wounded arrived the next night, but this time there were no officers, only 147 Tommies who benefited from the less-divided attentions of the carers and helpers in the restaurant.[22]

When the British ambassador wrote thanking the different municipalities for arranging such warm welcomes for the British invalids, he had to make an exception in the case of Berne. He had learnt from the British consul there that the municipal authorities had nothing to do with the reception which was a spontaneous outburst of feeling on the part of many of the inhabitants. The citizens of Berne were therefore thanked in the local newspaper.[23]

From Berne the internees travelled to Lausanne where even at 5.00 am, some 10,000 people were at the station. The train stopped for twenty minutes for coffee and milk, and the passengers were presented with 'roses and all kinds of things'. The Red Cross had arranged breakfast at the Grand Hotel in Montreux. By then the soldiers had so many flowers that they couldn't carry them; so they were throwing them over each other, and the road to the hotel was covered with them. 'It was grand!' was Private Collins's verdict. When they set off again for Chateau d'Oex, 'the journey up was lovely, all through the mountains: the hills were covered with narcissi and the scent from them was beautiful'. Hundreds of people were there to greet them, bands played and a choir sang during lunch in the village's *Grande Salle*.

Figure 3.2 Montreux hotel decorated to welcome British internees. Courtesy of Andrew Whitmarsh (www.switzerland1914-18.net).

In the villages and towns expecting internees, reception committees of local people, including hoteliers and business owners, were formed, mostly under the leadership of community leaders and representatives. In Chateau d'Oex, for example, the president of the committee was Monsieur Favrod-Coune who was also leader of the council (*Conseil Communal*). The society's secretary was the village pharmacist, Monsieur Lavanchy; donations towards the cost of welcoming the internees could be left in his shop.[24]

Preparations to receive English soldiers (the term 'British' was rarely used although there were men from each nation of the British Isles as well as from the colonies and Empire among them) were carried out by the reception committee. The whole community was expected to take part and to wear their best clothes. In Chateau d'Oex the arrival date was fixed for 30 May 1916.

A handwritten report by André Paillard, commissioned to chronicle the war years in Chateau d'Oex, gives a lively description of the arrival of internees there, which conveys the sense of excitement.[25] The whole village was decorated; green and white flags of the canton of Vaud fluttered from the church belfry. Every house was said to be hung with flowers; Swiss and British flags and garlands were stretched across the streets. The station had disappeared under garlands and flowers, and, on the terrace, tables were decorated and laid for several hundred people, ready for the arrivals to enjoy some food. The crowd was pressed on the station platform. They came from l'Etivaz, Rougemont (villages in the district) and even Lausanne to help with the reception. The British ambassador was there and also Lieutenant Colonel Picot, the military attaché in Berne. Children stood along the platform: some of them holding flags, all carrying flowers. Girls, dressed in white with scarves in national colours, were lined up in front of the station. The band played 'God Save the King' the moment the train carrying the internees entered the station. Soldiers were at the doors and windows, waving their caps. The people of Chateau d'Oex and beyond threw flowers at them and cheered. Many eyes were wet with tears and hearts sank when they saw all those mutilated young men. Those who were very ill were carried on stretchers, half-smothered in flowers, directly to their accommodation by Red Cross attendants.[26] Nevertheless, the atmosphere was joyful. Everyone was smiling and covered with flowers. The soldiers took their seats at the tables, and the speeches began. Monsieur Favrod-Coune wished them welcome, and the ambassador gave a speech in reply. Then music played, and children sang patriotic choruses. The internees were then allocated to their hotels.[27] Boy Scouts carried the wounded men's luggage. Later the British officers thanked the Scouts with a banquet at the Hotel de l'Ours and General Baden Powell, founder and Chief Scout, sent a letter of thanks.[28]

Ambassador Sir Evelyn Grant Duff, there to welcome the British internees, wrote,

> It is difficult to write calmly of it, for the simple reason that I have never before in my life seen such a welcome accorded to anyone, although for 28 years I have been present at every kind of function in half the capitals of Europe.[29]

The special correspondents of *The Times* and *Daily Mail* had been allowed to travel on the trains all the way to Chateau d'Oex so they could report on the journey in detail. From a propaganda point of view, it was important that the reception, particularly in Swiss-German Zurich, should be publicized in view of the common but mostly erroneous belief in anti-British feeling in

German-speaking Switzerland. At Lausanne and Montreux and on the route to Chateau d'Oex, French officers had turned out to greet them. This was also particularly welcome as stories in the German press had said that relations between the French and the British were not those of friends and allies.[30] In his report to the War Office in London, Ambassador Grant Duff wrote,

> Everywhere the soldiers were pelted with flowers and presents. I called for three cheers for Switzerland. I do not suppose since the beginning of the world cheers were ever given more heartily. Our men were simply astounded at the welcome, many were crying like children, a few fainted with emotion.[31]

As one soldier said to the ambassador, 'God bless you sir, it's like dropping right into 'eaven from 'ell'.[32]

A second convoy of British soldiers arrived in Chateau d'Oex the following day. Rain had set in so the reception was held in the *Grande Salle* with similar ceremonial as had greeted the previous day's arrivals, but with fewer speeches, just a few words of welcome from Grant Duff.[33] For the locals there was a new fascination; among the internees were two Indian soldiers, notable according to Paillard, for their fine, open countenance and teeth of brilliant white. Other individuals, particularly interesting to the Swiss, were Scotsmen wearing kilts, a Gurkha with a turban and an older soldier, sixty-three years old, who had taken part in the Zulu Wars in 1869.[34] Apparently, when two Gurkhas had been seen at Berne station earlier, some Swiss had referred to them as Japanese.[35]

Figure 3.3 British internees welcomed in Chateau d'Oex. Courtesy of Andrew Whitmarsh (www.switzerland1914-18.net).

Although celebrating their deliverance from incarceration in prison camps, the appearance of the wounded soldiers also induced sadness and pity among some witnesses, such as this journalist in Chateau d'Oex:

> I realised that other side and wondered how many shared the sadness that oppressed me. I had watched the train as it drew into the station, the carriage windows lined with smiling faces, and heard the shouts of welcome taken up by our soldiers in loud and ringing cheers, but as one by one they descended from the train and passed down the roped lines to take their places at the breakfast tables and I saw their condition, it required an immense effort of will power to choke back rising tears. For 80 per cent of these men were maimed for life and very ill, the faces all bore marks of great suffering and it was only in the eyes that one realised the spirit that had brought them through everything.
>
> I hoped that Great Britain would remember her duty to these men, I knew how soon the excitement of even such a day is forgotten. I remembered what I had seen in the streets of London and other great English towns in my youth and all that I had read as to what often became of England's soldiers in the past, and again the feeling of sadness dominated me for I thought of the rest of their lives.[36]

News of the warm welcome given to British soldiers was conveyed with gratitude in the newspapers back home. The letter sent by Grant Duff to Ador, of the Red Cross and president of the Swiss National Council, was quoted in the *Sheffield Evening Telegraph*:

> Fribourg, Lausanne and Montreux, as well as other stations and platforms, were covered with hundreds and certainly at Lausanne, thousands of persons, who had hastened to bring to our men their testimony of cordial sympathy. These demonstrations have been greatly appreciated by my compatriots, who were extremely touched by them.[37]

As more British prisoners arrived from Germany, extra accommodation was needed to house them. The Swiss military authorities had in mind the mountain village of Mürren in the Bernese Oberland, where there were 521 beds available, to house a large group of British expected to arrive in July 1916. Although remote, Mürren could be reached from the main railway line at Lauterbrunnen by a funicular and electric railway, which could be kept open in winter so there would be no difficulty in transporting food and coal to heat the hotels in winter, although there was a risk that Germany might cut off fuel supplies.[38]

Sensitivities about Swiss-Germans being associated in the imagination with Germany remained an issue for the British authorities. In August 1916,

Figure 3.4 Mürren welcomes British internees. Courtesy of Chris Twiggs (private collection).

Ambassador Grant Duff proposed to meet a new group of British invalids at Lauterbrunnen. He wrote to the War Office for advice as he thought he might have to make a speech in German, the local language: 'Probably our men would have a good reception, but I am not sure whether His Majesty's Government would approve a speech in German just now.'[39] The response to this in London was quite indignant:

> Mr Grant Duff had better say what he has to say in English – which is understood by many Swiss in that particular part of Switzerland. The British party of invalids, just released from Germany, probably never want to hear German again and would be more than surprised at hearing the British minister making a speech in that language. Tell him to speak in English.

A handwritten annotation on the memorandum commented wryly, 'I wonder that he does not ask us what kind of clothes he ought to wear,' and another from Lord Newton, 'Reply as suggested, but it seems a waste of money'. These remarks imply it should have been obvious to the ambassador that he should make his speech in English.[40] For an ambassador living in Switzerland the association of the German language, as spoken in Switzerland and probably used by him daily, would not necessarily have created a sinister mental link with the German nation. Soon, this would be the case for the British, French and Belgians interned in German-speaking areas where they were mostly met with kindness and sympathy. British soldiers interned in Mürren showed they had no inherent prejudice against the German tongue as a group of them were learning the language in classes, just as others were learning French.[41]

One of the first things the internees did, once they were safely in Switzerland, was to make use of the initially free postal service, to write to family and friends letting them know of their whereabouts and that they were safe. A postcard was the usual first communication home, showing just their hotel address, followed by a letter. Private Collins finished his first letter home on a practical note:

> Will you send me a safety razor? My razor was smashed by shrapnel on 8 May last year. I don't mind at all as it saved me from a nasty wound in the chest. The Germans pinched my wrist watch. Will you please send another along and let me know all the news?[42]

Another important task was to write to thank the prisoners' aid and voluntary committees that had sustained them through their captivity by sending parcels of food. These committees had been established under Article 15 of the Hague Convention of 1907 which stated,

> Relief societies for prisoners of war, which are properly constituted in accordance with the laws of their country and with the object of serving as the channel for charitable effort shall receive from the belligerents, for themselves and their duly accredited agents, every facility for the efficient performance of their humane task within the bounds imposed by military necessities and administrative regulations.[43]

A man writing to the Leicester Committee compared his arrival in Switzerland, which really seemed too good to be true, with the privations of imprisonment in Germany:

> It is with the greatest of pleasure that I am writing these few lines to let you know that I am now interned in Switzerland. I arrived here on 28 November, but it seems too good to be true, to think that I have got my freedom after being so long in captivity. I wish to thank everyone of your splendid committee most heartily for all your kindness during my captivity. ... The food supplied by Fritz is absolutely unfit for human consumption. I can honestly say that in my opinion, no British soldier would ever leave Germany alive if it was not for the food stuffs sent from England.[44]

The Leicestershire and Rutland Prisoners of War Committee, which had, by September 1916, despatched over 21,000 parcels to German camps where local men were imprisoned, was pleased to learn that eleven of their men had been transferred to Switzerland. A number of letters conveyed the appreciation of these men for the kindness shown to them during their imprisonment in Germany, including one from Company Sergeant Major Edward Vines from Sileby serving in the Northumberland Fusiliers, who, although he had been transferred to Switzerland, emphasized the very urgent need for parcels to be sent to men in Germany. He praised the way the parcels from Leicester were packed, despatched and received.[45]

Letters to other aid committees told similar stories of the harshness of captivity in Germany, that only ended once the Swiss border was crossed. Henry Hoggarth of the 4th East Yorkshires, who had been imprisoned at Minden before being transferred to Mürren, wrote to the Hull Voluntary Aid Committee that when they were passed for removal to Switzerland the Germans gave them better food and oil for their boots which made them more comfortable 'as all were cripples'. Hoggarth was told to tell his friends how good the Germans had been to them. Before they were allowed to leave the prison camp, they went one at a time to the office to empty out everything they had in the presence of two German NCOS. Even the soles of their slippers were partly cut off in case letters or coins might be taken out of the country. Balls of wool were pierced with a probe, tooth powder was shaken up and pictures taken from frames.[46] A similar story corroborates these distressing procedures that had to be undergone before being allowed to leave Germany for Switzerland. An interned soldier from Hayle in Cornwall, quartered in the sanatorium Mont Blanc in Leysin, wrote that he left Germany on 28 December 1917. On leaving, all letters and photos were confiscated with the false promise that they would be forwarded later. The dreadful food, cruelty and brutality he had experienced in the camp was all 'past, like a terrible nightmare', since he arrived in Switzerland. In his present camp he had 'a nice room, clean sheets, spring bed, everything for use and civilised people to talk to'.[47] The Mont Blanc, where the Hayle soldier was staying, was a luxury establishment, more like a high-class hotel than a sanatorium specializing in the care of tuberculosis patients.[48] These letters show that the soldiers and officers fortunate to be interned in Switzerland were anxious to use their newly acquired, relative liberty to raise awareness of the conditions endured in the prison camps in Germany and to encourage continued support for those who still remained there. A letter in the *Derby Daily Telegraph*, reprinted from *The Times*, said, 'We were treated worse than cruel. We had to work whether it was snowing or raining.' The Germans took out food and soap from the parcels. 'I never saw such people in the world.'⁴⁹ The soldier from Hayle also emphasized the cruelty he had experienced:

> If the British in Germany were not sent parcels they would have had to live on grass which was sent up last summer for dinner and meat which could be smelt two miles off. Meat was allowed twice a week and it was meat! Even the Russians who received no parcels wouldn't eat it.⁵⁰

Of course, these stories of the barbarity of the enemy not only had propaganda value but could also be used to encourage donations to local prisoners' aid committees.

The French minister of foreign affairs appointed Doctor John de Christmas to conduct an official enquiry among French prisoners brought out of Germany to Switzerland which revealed an overwhelming picture of poor conditions, unhealthiness, abuse and reprisals claimed to be prevalent in German camps. Access to ambassadorial delegations and the Red Cross had sometimes been forbidden in violation of international agreements. Internees reported barbaric punishments, and a typhoid epidemic in eastern German camps in the winter and spring of 1915 due to the systematic mixing of French and Russian carriers and a complete lack of medication. Medical inspectors and neutral observers were never able to penetrate the worst camps in Poland or in Russia. They could only go to 'show camps'.⁵¹

Witnesses reported that there was no comparison between the French captives coming from Germany and the Germans arriving from France. They observed the sombre appearance and ragged clothes of those awaiting transit from Constance to Switzerland. Letters from internees often mentioned the death of comrades shortly after their arrival in Switzerland. The obituaries section in the *Journal des Internés Français* seemed to lengthen week by week.⁵²

Not everyone welcomed the internees to their communities. When a new batch of German invalids arrived at Oberegg on 18 July 1917, the district chief (*Bezirkshauptmann*) refused to officially welcome the new guests, who he described as a 'plague' that haunted the village.⁵³ This was hardly noticeable to the forty-three pale figures in torn uniforms, newly arrived from Lyon. They had already been warmly welcomed by a large crowd when the internees, many of whom had been captured during the Battle of the Marne or at Verdun, arrived at the station of neighbouring village, Heiden, that morning. The welcoming party there had included *Gemeindehauptmann* (mayor) and former member of the *Bundesrat*, Emil Frey. After lunch in the Hotel Paradies they had a bath and new clothes. When they actually reached Oberegg, the men were subdued, probably feeling tired after their journey and the emotional welcome. With more new arrivals in December 1916 and September 1917, there were ninety-two internees in Oberegg. They were under the leadership of *Feldwebels* (sergeant) Johannes Finnern, from Schleswig-Holstein who had been wounded at the Battle of the Marne on 7 September 1914 and taken prisoner by the French. Before coming to Switzerland, he had been imprisoned at Barcelonette, Blaye, La Pallice and La Rochelle. Medical supervision was provided by Doctor Hermann Sonderegger from Heiden.[54] Other places of internment for Germans in the Appenzellerland canton were Trogen and Heiden, where forty-six arrived on 10 May 1916, and Herisau, where there were fifty-two, followed the next month by more from England to Heiden, Walzenhausen and Waldstatt. More arrived in November and December. By the end of 1916 there were around 1,400 German invalid soldiers interned in Appenzellerland.[55]

The arrival of internees and the ceremonial and celebratory atmosphere of their welcome didn't just happen at the beginning of internment in the spring of 1916 but was repeated as new batches of invalid soldiers arrived from captivity. When a group arrived towards the end of 1916, local newspapers throughout Britain reported it. 'About 10,000 British, French and Germans are expected in the next fortnight for internment in Switzerland. The British are to be first, contrary to previous arrangements, and about 1,000 are expected this week. They will be quartered at Mürren, Chateau d'Oex, Leysin and Gstaad,' reported the *Dundee Telegraph*.[56] The news in Manchester was that '18,843 wounded prisoners of war of belligerent countries in Switzerland, are shortly to be increased by several thousands. So far there is no agreement for exchange with Italy and Austria but France and Austria have agreed on the exchange of interned civilians in concentration camps.'[57] A year later, stories of internment were still making news as new invalids arrived, replacing others who had been repatriated. *Sheffield Evening Telegraph* readers learnt in November 1917 that

> a party of British prisoners of war, 81 officers and 3,236 men arrived last night and received a hearty welcome from the British colony. They include a large number of officers of the 10th Army Corps who were captured early in the war. They have spent over three years in Germany. Officers were sent to the district around Montreux, the men divided between Mürren and Chateau Doex [sic]. The party were met at the frontier by Major Wilkinson of the Coldstream Guards, assistant officer in charge of POWs in Switzerland.[58]

Even when the novelty of receiving new arrivals from prison camps had worn off for the locals, existing internees made the effort to welcome additions to their colonies at the railway station. Sometimes the appearance of the new men, 'with white drawn faces and a dazed look',[59] brought back memories of their own imprisonment and how their situation had changed thanks to Swiss hospitality. Perhaps not knowing what else to say, the new arrivals were often asked, 'Are you glad to be here at last?' to which the answer would often come back, 'My word! Not half!'

> The 'old men' seize their feeble kit and carry it for the 'new men'; and if pals meet it's worth being out here to see it. No matter how ill or miserable the 'new men' feel and are, they always find time, and a rag to polish their buttons. ... The 'new men' go slowly to their hotels, because some are on crutches, some very feeble; some dead tired, and some with that nervous cowed manner that makes one's blood boil, as one realises the cause.
>
> They go to their bedrooms, they look at their beds, and think it must be a dream. Beds to sleep on! Most of them have slept on dirty straw for two years, and almost break down at the relief, the weight off their brains when they know they are safe, and can be men again![60]

All these welcoming ceremonies involved financial outlay by the reception committees that were responsible for organizing them. The committees were funded by voluntary contributions. In November 1916, the reception committee in Chateau d'Oex was compelled to write to its supporters asking for donations. Until that time, the letter said, thanks to generous financial support, the committee had been able to cope with the expenses of the welcoming receptions and had not considered it appropriate to resort to the benevolence of those who did not benefit directly from the arrival of internees. In agreement with the Committee of the Society of Hoteliers, the reception committee addressed itself to the owners of hotels, pensions and chalets and the regional negotiators of Pays d'Enhaut, asking them to support a subscription so that it could fulfil its duty of hospitality towards its guests. A new group of internees was expected in a couple of weeks, at the end of November 1916, and so subscriptions needed to be paid promptly so that the committee could organize the planned reception for the internees and the authorities as soon as they arrived.[61] The continuing generosity of many of the Swiss was recognized by the British press; for instance, the *Falkirk Herald* told its readers,

> The threat and rumour of invasion of Switzerland, German spies, hardships and increased expenses of life for the Swiss have not prevented them from showing

kind attentions to invalid prisoners of war, of whom Switzerland is the guardian, with 30,000 internees to look after.[62]

In Britain there was considerable interest in stories of soldiers interned in Switzerland and local newspapers reported news of men from their communities transferred there from Germany, giving their names and regiments. Privates Baker and Boon of the Somerset Light Infantry had arrived in Switzerland reported the *Bath Chronicle and Weekly Gazette* in September 1916.[63] In the *Western Times* there was news of a 'fresh batch of 200 British prisoners of war, including 27 officers', a third of whom were posted to Mürren, who arrived on 29 November 1917.[64] Interest did not seem to wain as such announcements continued, such as in May 1918 the *Yorkshire Post and Leeds Intelligencer* eleven Yorkshiremen arrived and when *The Taunton Courier and Western Advertiser* listed eleven men who had safely arrived there in September 1918.[65] During that same week, the arrival of five Welsh soldiers was reported in the *Western Mail*.[66]

Sometimes letters from internees or repatriated men formed the basis of newspaper stories about the experiences of individuals at the front. For instance, Bombardier Eales of Long Buckby in Northamptonshire was wounded at le Cateau, where shrapnel hit him in his right thigh and in the face. All went blank until he woke to find himself a prisoner in hospital in Potsdam. He was in hospital for three months where he underwent two operations before being sent for convalescence to Döberitz Camp. He recounted how discipline was strict, and the guards were quick to use their rifles. 'It was horrible', he said, 'the beds were verminous, prisoners went unwashed as soap was unprocurable, the food wasn't fit for pigs and no tobacco was seen. English soldiers were seen smoking the bark of trees and leaves.' Bombardier Eales was then sent to Dyvotz Camp where he was one of several eye cases treated by Swiss doctors. From there he was transferred to Mannheim Lager where again the beds were filthy, huts worse than pigsties, bread horrible and soup like water. Luckily he was only there a fortnight as the terrible conditions made him ill. He was transferred to Berne and then onwards to Mürren where he was chosen as postman for the British officers. Sent to Lausanne, Eales managed to see some English newspapers which gave him news of the state of affairs regarding the war. This, he said, was the happiest time of his detention.[67]

Stories about internment in Switzerland also appeared in the United States, as after the Americans entered the war, negotiations to offer a similar opportunity to their captured, wounded men were underway. Also there were some Americans among the British interned, who had joined up by posing as Canadians.

Internment in Switzerland was soon judged a success. Of the British, the chief officer in charge, Lieutenant Colonel Picot, was able to report in July 1916 that

> all ranks had made a good impression in Switzerland and are rapidly establishing friendly relations with their hosts at Chateau d'Oex. Their dignified bearing is continually spoken of, and I have heard many flattering remarks from Colonel Hauser and the officers in charge during their journey regarding their cleanliness and soldierly attitude.[68]

Notes

1. *Davoser Blätter*, 1 January 1916.
2. *Davoser Zeitung*, 26 January 1916.
3. Kühnis, *Deutsche Kriegsinternierte in Davos*, p. 6.
4. *Davoser Blätter*, 13 May 1916.
5. Kühnis, *Deutsche Kriegsinternierte in Davos*, p. 7.
6. *Davoser Blätter*, 27 January 1917.
7. Fuchs, 'Interniert im Appenzellerland', p. 50.
8. Ibid., p. 63.
9. Ibid., p. 51.
10. Desponds, *Leysin*, p. 28.
11. Maurice André, *Leysin – Station medicale*, Pully, 2002, p. 29.
12. Report by Mr Goodhart of H. M. Legation at Berne, in *The Reception of Wounded Prisoner Soldiers of Great Britain in Switzerland*, despatch from the British minister in Berne, Evelyn Grant Duff, British ambassador to Switzerland, 2 June 1916, p. 7.
13. Lord Newton, War Office, 18 May 1916, TNA FO 383/216.
14. Cubitt, War Office, 28 May 1916, TNA FO 383/216.
15. Jones, *Violence against Prisoners of War in the First World War*, p. 39.
16. *Cambridge Independent Press*, 16 June 1916.
17. Picot to Sir Edward Grey, 6 June 1916, TNA FO 383/216.
18. Ibid.
19. Ibid.
20. Goodhart, *Reception of Wounded Prisoner Soldiers of Great Britain in Switzerland*, p. 7.
21. Ibid., p. 6.
22. Ibid., p. 7.
23. Grant Duff, Sir Evelyn, to War Office, 5 June 1916, TNA FO 383/216.

24 *Comité de Réception des Internés Anglais*, Chateaux d'Oex, 16 November 1916.
25 André Paillard, *Notes sur les événements politiques de 1914 à 1919, à Chateau d'Oex*, 1919, p. 44.
26 Evelyn Grant Duff, *The Reception of Wounded Prisoner Soldiers of Great Britain in Switzerland*, despatch from the British minister in Berne, 2 June 1916.
27 Paillard, *Notes sur les événements politiques de 1914 à 1919*, p. 44.
28 Ibid., p. 46.
29 Grant Duff, *The Reception of Wounded Prisoner Soldiers of Great Britain in Switzerland*, p. 1.
30 Picot to Sir Edward Grey, 6 June 1916, TNA FO 383/216.
31 Grant Duff, *The Reception of Wounded Prisoner Soldiers of Great Britain in Switzerland*, p. 4.
32 Ibid.
33 Ibid., p. 4.
34 Paillard, *Notes sur les événements politiques de 1914 à 1919*, p. 46.
35 Goodhart, *Reception of Wounded Prisoner Soldiers of Great Britain in Switzerland*, p. 7.
36 Jaccottet et al., *Au Soleil et Sur les Monts*, p. 269.
37 *Sheffield Evening Telegraph*, 18 September 1917.
38 Picot to War Office, 27 June 1916, TNA FO 383/216.
39 Grant Duff to War Office, 6 August 1916, TNA FO 383/217.
40 War Office Memorandum, 7 August 1916, TNA FO 383/217.
41 Report from Mürren, November 1916, NA FO 383/219.
42 *Cambridge Independent Press*, 16 June 1916.
43 Convention (IV) respecting the Laws and Customs of War on Land and its Annex: regulations concerning the Laws and Customs of War on Land. The Hague, 18 October 1907. Annex to the Convention: regulations respecting the Laws and Customs of War on Land – Section 1: on belligerents – Chapter II: Prisoners of War – Regulations: Art.15.
44 Leicester, Leicestershire and Rutland Prisoners of War Committee 1914–1918 (LLRPOWC), Report, Records Office Leicester, Leicestershire and Rutland, (ROLLR) 14D35/24, p. 21.
45 Meeting of the Executive Committee of LLRPOWC and Finance Joint Committee minutes, 10 December 1917, ROLLR 14D35/24.
46 *Yorkshire Post and Leeds Intelligencer*, 4 September 1916.
47 *The Cornishman*, 28 February 1918.
48 Barton, *Healthy Living in the Alps*, p. 79.
49 *Derby Daily Telegraph*, 25 May 1918.
50 *The Cornishman*, 28 February 1918.
51 Walle, 'Les Prisonniers de Guerre Francais Internés en Suisse (1916-1919)', p. 60.
52 Ibid., p. 59.

53 Fuchs, 'Interniert im Appenzellerland', p. 54.
54 Ibid., p. 60.
55 Ibid., p. 62.
56 *Dundee Evening Telegraph*, 22 November 1916.
57 *Manchester Evening News*, 25 November 1916.
58 *Sheffield Evening Telegraph*, 29 November 1917.
59 *British Interned Magazine (BIM)*, Vol. 2, No. 13, August 1918.
60 Ibid., n.p.
61 *Comité de Réception des Internés Anglais*, Chateaux d'Oex, 16 November 1916.
62 *Falkirk Herald*, 24 January 1917.
63 *Bath Chronicle and Weekly Gazette*, 14 September 1916.
64 *Western Times*, 30 November 1917.
65 *Yorkshire Post and Leeds Intelligencer*, 29 May 1918, *Taunton Courier and Western Advertiser*, 18 September 1918.
66 *Western Mail*, 17 September 1917.
67 *Northampton Mercury*, 21 September 1917.
68 Picot to War Office, July 1916, TNA FO 383/329.

4

Conditions of internment

At the mainline railway stations such as Zurich, Berne and Lausanne, prisoners were divided into smaller groups and transferred onto regional trains to travel to their centres of internment. Specially designated internment regions were created by joining host towns and villages into administrative units, with internees placed into regions according to nationality. French and Belgian prisoners were scattered over a wide area, often in small communities, mostly in French-speaking Switzerland, such as Montreux, Leysin, Valais, Gruyère, Jura, Fribourg, Bex, Villars, Central Switzerland and the Bernese Oberland. Germans were interned in the Swiss-German regions, in the Central Swiss cantons, Glaris, St Gallen, Ragatz and places in Appenzellerland, in Chur, Arosa, in and around Davos and other locations in Graubunden in Eastern Switzerland. By the time the British prisoners of war began to arrive, from 30 May 1916, it had become apparent that having internees spread over nineteen areas of internment in relatively small groups, as the French and Belgians were, was not the best way of organizing from a logistical point of view nor in terms of discipline or providing employment. Colonel Hauser, the chief medical officer of the Swiss Army, at the top of the command structure and in overall charge of internment, therefore decided that the British should be concentrated in larger groups in just a few regions, preferably in contiguous areas. Each region was under the command of a Swiss medical officer, directly accountable to Colonel Hauser. It was soon found that it was easier to manage British soldiers in collaboration with their own officers, who organized the internal life of the internment centres, under the supervision of a senior British officer with authority delegated through the ranks of junior officers and NCOs. This system also reaffirmed the authority of British NCOS, which had been undermined in German prisons.[1]

When the first group of British arrived they were all allocated to Chateau d'Oex and its vicinity in the canton of Vaud, a favourable arrangement for the British government as it was a French-speaking area where it was assumed there would be support for allied soldiers. When accommodation there began to be full, from July 1916 parties were sent to Mürren in the neighbouring Bernese Oberland, an announcement that caused some concern over fears that the German-speaking inhabitants might favour the Germans, as discussed in Chapter 2. The Canton of Berne established five regions for internment. The 'Bernese Oberland Region C' or 'English Region Mürren' was under the authority of its Swiss commandant Captain Doctor Llopart who was also a medical officer and village doctor. Other centres of British internment were opened in response to the education, training or medical needs of the internees in Montreux, Vevey, Meiringen, Brienz, Seeburg near Lucerne, Leysin, Bex and Villars. The aim was that soldiers from opposing sides in the conflict should not come into contact with each other although the French were the first to break this rule when some internees were sent to the area around Lake Lucerne causing fears that embarrassing situations might occur if there were encounters between Germans and French on lake steamers or elsewhere as 'in the heat of summer, soldiers are not always masters of their feelings'.[2] The Lucerne area was the only place where German, French, Belgian and British were near each other. 'Lucerne is a decent place but surprised to see so many square heads about,' wrote Private R. Timms using an uncomplimentary term for Germans on a postcard from Lucerne to his friend Private Alf Gibbs.[3] When internees of opposing sides did meet, the encounters were reported as polite and amicable; for example, in Berne station French and Germans exchanged such greetings as 'The war is over or us' and 'Let's be friends'.[4] Internees were not allowed to leave their region of internment except for work or medical reasons, although a special pass could be obtained to travel further afield. Leave Passes were issued by the medical officer and had to be presented at the destination's police station. Internees carried an identity card to be shown on police request. Monthly roll calls checked everyone was present who ought to be.

These were tourist areas, and hence whatever their native language was hotel owners and local people were used to catering for English-speaking visitors and so bore them no animosity. In fact the Swiss doctors who visited the prison camps in Germany, to inspect and select cases suitable for internment, were sometimes accused of making decisions based not on health but on the potential profit for Swiss hoteliers by making enquiries about the financial situation of prisoners and whether their family was likely to come to live with them in Switzerland, a circumstance that would mean extra income from those in the tourism industry.[5] This was alleged to have happened in the case of prisoners in Soltau Camp, but the accusation was never substantiated. However, the Swiss hotel industry did lobby its government to allow them to accommodate

Figure 4.1 British internees at the Hotel Edelweiss, Mürren. Courtesy of Pat and Mark Esling (family collection).

internees at a time when few other tourists were coming to the resorts. Another accusation made about hoteliers was that a few of them made petty claims for damage to hotel property by dirty hands, the sticks and canes of amputees or for excessive use of beds by bedridden patients.[6] The arrival of the internees, though seen as a work of humanitarianism, could also be advantageous. Here and there, an individual may have speculated under cover of charity. The immense majority of hotel owners offered their rooms and services without a thought of profit or speculation, in a simple act of solidarity, claimed a souvenir book for French internees.[7] In Engelberg, where first French and Belgian and then Germans were interned, Herr Cattani, a hotel owner and local politician, not only provided accommodation but organized amusements for the internees. In Mürren, teenagers Walter and Max Amstutz of the Hotel Alpina, who ran its gift and photographic shop, were happy to work with British internees.[8] If any lobbying by individual hotel owners took place, it was just as likely to have come from British businesses, such as the Polytechnic Touring Association, who wrote to the British War Office offering the use of its chalets at Seeburg as accommodation and Sir Henry Lunn's company who ran the Palace Hotel and Hotel des Alpes in Mürren who offered to take in internees, provided there was a minimum of 200 of them. Before an agreement regarding internment between the British, Germans and Swiss had been reached, the War Office stated that there should be no involvement whatsoever by the Polytechnic, Lunn or Thomas Cook and Son due to the experiences gone through with Lunn and Cook in the summer of 1914 in connection with the repatriation of British subjects stranded in Switzerland on the outbreak of war, although no detail is given as to what these negative experiences were.[9] However, the facilities of Lunn in Mürren and the Polytechnic chalets and staff at Seeburg were all made use of.

Swiss hotels and sanatoria were particularly suitable for lodging injured and sick soldiers. The most modern had lifts, essential for those recovering from serious leg wounds, wide doors and balconies large enough to wheel a bed or chair through so the bedridden or wheelchair users could enjoy fresh air, an architectural feature of the health tourism Switzerland was famous for. They had large public rooms where men could assemble for celebrations, entertainment, meetings and education or receive visitors. Despite being in mountainous locations, some of the larger hotels had a flat space outside that could be used for exercise, sport or skating in winter. Snow and ice on the paths and roads could curtail outdoor activities for the seriously injured with mobility problems if they were unable to make use of the winter sports facilities.

In the hotels and pensions where they were billeted, internees were normally in shared rooms with two, three or four beds, with single rooms for officers. Accommodation was allocated according to rank. In Mürren, for instance, although British officers and lower ranks might share hotels, in the Hotel des Alpes the officers had the best rooms with mountain views to themselves while the Tommies shared rooms with two or three beds at the back.[10] Accommodation costs were paid to the hotels by the Swiss government and reimbursed by the internees' home nations. Many officers chose to lodge privately with local families, paying for this themselves, although some stayed in hotels to supervise the lower ranks.[11] Internees were issued with booklets explaining the *General Regulations for British Prisoners of War Interned in Switzerland*, outlining the conditions of their internment, which contained the following sections:

A Object of Internment
B Discipline
C Senior British Officer
D Group Officers
E Orderly Officers
F Local Orders
G Leave and Travelling

H Complaints
I Work [sic]
K Miscellaneous Orders.[12]

All internees, of whatever nationality, were interned under identical conditions and paid an allowance, as agreed between their governments. Rates of pay were set at 7 Swiss francs a month for private soldiers and corporals, 15 francs for sergeants and higher NCOs, 20 francs for warrant officers, 72 francs for officers below the rank of captain and 120 francs for captains and officers of higher rank, a huge differential. Payments were made to the internees by the Swiss government and reimbursed by the individual national governments.[13] They were also allowed to access their own money and could earn a small amount from any work undertaken. Officers were exempt from having to work.

The soldiers were in a bedraggled state when they arrived, wearing old and sometimes ragged clothing. The Red Cross, organized into twelve local committees in Switzerland, helped supply hospital clothing and underwear as soon as they were installed in their various new homes.[14] Lack of clothing was a serious difficulty for the French when they arrived from Germany.[15] French internees were supplied with replacement sky blue uniforms, plus chevrons for officers and NCOs, and sets of work outfits – three smocks and trousers.[16] National governments were responsible for supplying uniforms and stores opened in the main centres of internment to meet this need. For centres with less than 100 internees, a hotel room was used but in the larger regions internees would be employed and paid to run shops.[17] An estimated 1,200 British soldiers were expected to be in the first contingent from Germany in May 1916. The British embassy in Berne recommended that 600 sets of khaki, complete with puttees and caps, be despatched from England and also, if possible, 1,200 hairbrushes.[18] Boots could be procured at more reasonable rates from the Swiss Military Department than from England.

Once installed the internees began a life of routine and recuperation from their injuries. A daily schedule for a German soldier shows how the men occupied their time. At 6.30 am they woke up. Between 7.00 and 8.00 am there were medical rounds; at 8.30 am there was the first breakfast with coffee; between 9.00 and 10.00 am the men were cleaning indoors; 10.00 am until 12 noon was spent in their various work or training roles. Officers, who did not have to work, could go out if they chose. Midday was lunch time. Afternoons were free for outings, occupations, games or sport until 9.00 pm. Lights out was at 10.30 pm. Similar routines were followed by French, Belgian and British internees according to their state health which determined whether and how long they could work.

Figure 4.2 British internees in Mürren. Courtesy of Chris Twiggs (private collection).

Food for the interned was supplied according to a fixed weekly diet which included 350 to 400 grams of bread, 750 grams of milk, 175 grams of meat without bones, 500 grams of potatoes and a similar amount of rice, macaroni, noodles, beans or peas, vegetables to the value of 10 centimes, 50 grams of cheese or 40 grams of bacon or sausage, 16 grams of coffee, 20 grams of cocoa, 20 grams of sugar, 10 to 20 grams of butter and 20 grams of fruit or preserves. This menu would not have given the hotel keepers much profit out of the 6 francs a day paid for officers and 4 francs for ordinary soldiers. For tuberculosis patients, for whom more food was prescribed, the ration was a little higher as was the amount paid to the hotels of 8 francs per officer and 5 francs for soldiers.[19]

What internees could expect to be fed was the subject of international agreements and a list of rations to be provided to each internee was published. The Berne Accords between France and Germany agreed in 1918, stated in Article 26 that 2,000 calories should be allowed for non-working prisoners of war, 2,500 for ordinary workers and 2,850 calories for those undertaking heavy work, although for some this was a reduction.[20]

There were complaints about the food served, some of it perhaps related to cultural differences but perhaps also reflecting scarcity and the need to prevent waste. Examples of complaints were as follows: From the Palace Hotel at Montana, 'Everything they make they put in some cheese which does not smell of roses. One is very badly fed; I had a slice of white meat that the dog didn't want. The eggs are rotten'; at the Hotel de Couronne in Interlaken, 'The salad is without oil, nothing but vinegar! The meat was gone off' and from the Hotel Union in Leukerbad, 'Everything has water, without oil or fat, the food disgusts me and we freeze cold in our rooms.'[21]

In Leysin where there were French, Belgian and British internees, a Board or *Commission pour la Nouriture* was established, composed of an officer, an NCO and private of the different nationalities there, plus a Swiss civilian member. The board dealt with a complaint about food at the Hotel Beau Site in November 1916, which improved and became more varied as a consequence.[22] Nevertheless, most were satisfied with their situation and praised the food they received acknowledging that they had a good life in Switzerland where for some French internees it felt like being in France, with the food good and accommodation being more than comfortable. This would depend on their background, for many poorer soldiers conditions were better than at home.

As the war progressed, supplies in Switzerland became scarcer and rationing was introduced, the population was issued with ration cards for bread and fat. Coal was also rationed as supplies from Germany dwindled. Despite agreement with Germany which the Swiss had hoped would secure a supply of coal, some for the comfort of German soldiers, as the war dragged on, fuel became scarce. Fuel shortages affected rail transport and heating for hotels with modern heating systems, such as the Palace in Mürren which had to close for the winter of 1917 to 1918. Internees complained that the hotels were cold; Major Ernest Collins wrote to his father that the heating in all these places was indifferent owing to restrictions on fuel.[23] By the end of 1917, according to Major Collins, only a few hotels remained open with just a third of rooms allowed to be heated, but only up to 54 degrees Fahrenheit.[24] Transport problems also affected the delivery of food supplies. In late 1917 Colonel Hauser issued guidance restricting travel to save coal. Journeys purely for pleasure or on Sundays or holidays were only authorized in exceptional cases.[25] Major Collins wrote home,

> All of you in England have no idea of the effect of the war, your lives at home are almost normal, but here on the Continent and especially in this country and France, everything is different to what you entertained.[26]

The price of bread rose rapidly from 34 centimes a kilogram before the war to 46 centimes by December 1914, to 70 centimes in 1917 and 75 centimes in mid-1918.[27] Rising food prices caused problems for the hotels, as the total cost of internment required another 1.5 million francs and increased monthly running costs by about a quarter of a million francs.[28] As costs increased the hotel proprietors called for an increase in the payment they received for the internees' board and lodging of 50 centimes a day.[29] *Deutsche Internierten Zeitung* assured German internees that their government would not fail to ensure they would be adequately catered for, even taking into account that men, working hard in workshops and on the land, needed plenty of energy giving food.[30] As their own living conditions worsened, attitudes hardened among some of the Swiss towards their foreign war guests. Internees, their families and visitors, were increasingly perceived as a burden, consuming food and fuel that might otherwise have been available to the Swiss.[31] There was also the anxiety that should Switzerland be drawn into the war, there would already be enemy soldiers installed in the country. Due to problems getting coal and food and perhaps in response to these political pressures, Switzerland began to limit the number of internees that could be taken in to 30,000 at a time. The most serious cases that showed no improvement were repatriated during 1917 to be replaced by new invalids.[32]

Following their arrival, internees soon made themselves at home in their mountain refuges. In Mürren the streets were renamed ironically after familiar names in London, such as Bakerloo, Billingsgate, Old Kent Road and Westbourne Grove where a shop was situated, given the name Whiteley's after the well-known London department store.[33] This practice was common in the trenches and continued into the Second World War when underground tunnels in military air raid shelters were also named after prominent streets.[34]

Medical care was usually delivered in the place of internment. In each station, the sick were concentrated in a single building with special facilities for treatment and care. In Chateau d'Oex hospital facilities were in the Soldanelle sanatorium. In Mürren sick men stayed in a couple of rooms set aside in the Hotel Regina, under the care of a trained nurse and a residential orderly. In the basement of the Regina, in what was the skittle alley, a mechano-therapeutic room was set up with a large variety of apparatus for exercising stiff joints, including an electric vibrator for massage purchased with money donated by a visitor. In this facility Captain Doctor Llopart treated up to 200 war injuries a month.[35] There were two women trained in massage and a dressing room for outpatients provided other treatments.[36] There was also a dispensary. When an operation or specialist treatment was needed, patients were sent to an allocated hospital. For internees needing orthopaedic treatment, facilities and specialists, like Doctor Müller who treated the Germans, were available. As well as physiotherapy, orthopaedic boots and apparatus, including prostheses, were provided.[37] There were specialist workshops in Stans and later in Lucerne and Engelberg where prostheses were made.[38] Amputations were common during the First World War but, without the benefit of antibiotics, infections were also common and wounds could take a long time to heal. A badly set broken leg would mean a permanent limp.[39]

During the summer of 1916 a military hospital, the *Armeesanitätsanstalt* or ASA was founded in Lucerne in the Swiss Accident Insurance (SUVA) hospital led by Hans Brun, where French, Belgian, British and German internees were treated.[40] Only cases for surgery or requiring treatment not available elsewhere in Switzerland were sent to Lucerne. Patients had their operations in the ASA before being transferred elsewhere for convalescence, massage or other therapies. The treatment at the ASA was excellent with only one or two failures in difficult procedures such as leg stretching.[41] Often patients needed surgery to correct injuries treated inadequately when they were captured or during captivity, for example, to improve the position of limbs, the movement of joints or removal of bone. Common conditions treated were skull and brain injuries, injuries to the extremities, fractures that had not healed properly, pseudo-arthrosis and damage to the central nervous system.[42] It gave the Swiss medics the opportunity to develop skills in complex orthopaedic and neurological surgeries, a field that their country's neutrality and consequent lack of involvement in wars had given them little occasion to practice.[43] If treatments were successful, patients joined their compatriots in the hotels, for convalescence and follow-up examinations under the care of the local doctor.

For convalescence British patients were transferred to the nearby chalets owned by the Polytechnic Touring Association at Seeburg, where they were cared for by Polytechnic staff who normally looked after holidaymakers. The chalets were said to be ideal as they were in the countryside with grounds and woods for walking and the lake for boating and fishing. The Bezirks Hospital at Interlaken also performed surgery, and there was a British convalescent facility at Manor Farm by Lake Thun run by Miss Simpkin. Normally she took in tourists but did a good job looking after internees. As well as men recovering from operations, Manor Farm was home to internees, mostly heart cases, relocated from Mürren which was unsuitable for them because of its high altitude. There were four officers and thirty men at Manor Farm in June 1917.[44]

In December 1916, Lieutenant Colonel Jones of the Royal Army Medical Corps visited Switzerland to look at arrangements made by the Swiss military authorities for the medical and surgical care of the British interned. Jones looked at the possibility of additional hospital accommodation should further British contingents arrive. Colonel Hauser suggested a new hospital at Fribourg, built before the war but which remained unopened owing to lack of funds. The civil authorities in Fribourg would place it at the disposal of the military authorities

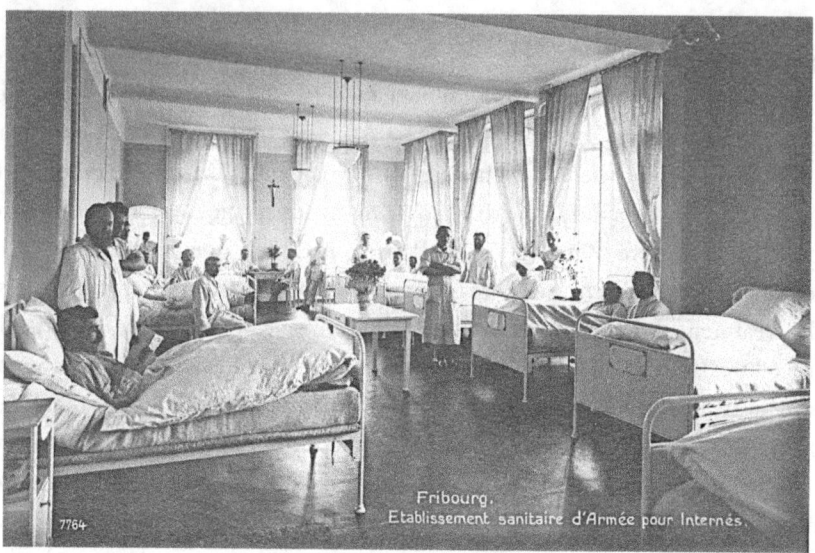

Figure 4.3 A ward in Fribourg Allies Hospital. Courtesy of Pat and Mark Esling (family collection) and Chris Twiggs (private collection).

for use by 120 British, French and Belgians if they supplied the 100,000 Swiss francs needed to equip it. The Swiss would pay running costs and provide staff, including resident surgeon Doctor Clement, formerly at ASA Lucerne, provided the hospital was handed over, fully equipped, at the end of the war.[45] Negotiating for the Fribourg authorities, Madame de Zurich said that the French Red Cross had set aside between 60,000 and 65,000 francs for equipment. She hoped the British Red Cross would contribute 25,000 to 30,000 francs to supplement the French grant. The facility would be better than having internees needing hospital care distributed to several different centres. Postcards showing Fribourg's operating theatre were sold, including one sent by a patient to a comrade saying, 'I haven't had my operation yet as the shrapnel keep moving about.'[46] Once the Fribourg hospital opened, the ASA in Lucerne was dissolved and replaced by another there solely for German internees. For officers there were additional facilities for consulting specialists and several were examined by Doctor Roux, a celebrated surgeon in Lausanne and other physicians. They were able to choose their own physicians and surgeons if they did not wish to avail themselves of the facilities provided.[47]

A Liverpool dental surgeon, Joseph A. Woods, went out to Switzerland to treat the internees. This was a necessary service for out of 301 dental examinations, carried out in October 1916 in Chateau d'Oex, there were only 10 men who did not require treatment. In Leysin only 11 out of 159 cases examined needed no

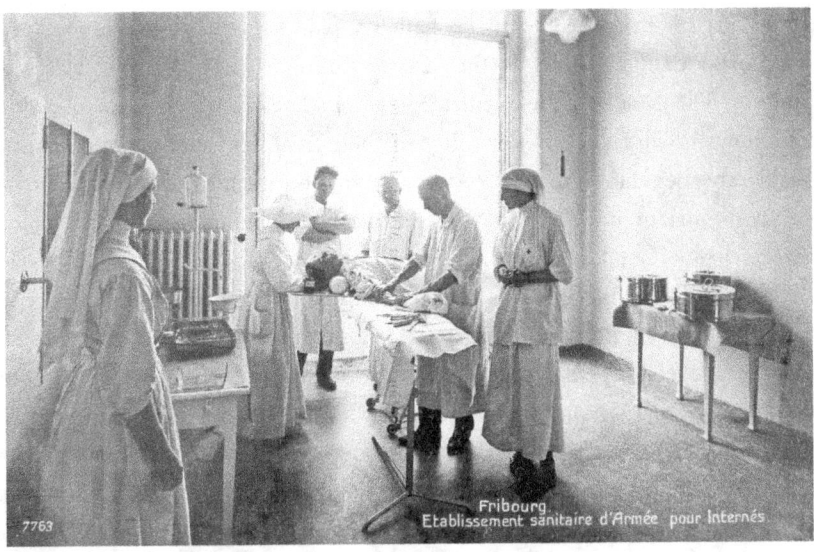

Figure 4.4 Operating theatre in Fribourg Allies Hospital. Courtesy of Pat and Mark Esling (family collection) and Chris Twiggs (private collection).

dental treatment.[48] Dentistry became important during the First World War as many volunteers for military service were rejected on account of defective teeth. It was estimated that 70 per cent of British recruits and men at home needed dental treatment. The British and Scottish Dental Associations and individual dentists offered to treat some of the men rejected free of charge which acted as an aid to recruitment. Facial injuries among the wounded were common, and dentistry expanded its role into facial reconstruction of broken jaws where dental technique and plastic surgery combined to minimize disfigurement.[49] 'If parts of the bone structure had been destroyed, plastic and dental surgery came to the rescue with transplants or artificial substitutes, not only to prevent disfigurement but also to make mastication possible.'[50] Abscesses related to poor dental health could cause inflammation of tissues and general infection elsewhere, which emphasized the need for dental care among the wounded and tuberculosis sufferers. Germany too developed its dental surgery to play a role in the healing of the wounded and facial reconstruction. In Germany at the beginning of the war, dentistry was less developed and the condition of the nation's teeth was even worse than in Britain. It was calculated that only 2 per cent of German school children had strong teeth, and the figures were probably similar for soldiers; at recruitment men could be recommended for service or dental treatment.[51]

Allied internees with tuberculosis were sent to the sanatoria at Leysin or Montana where they benefited from specialist treatments and a trained nurse sent to care for British tuberculosis patients, paid for by the government with board and lodgings funded by the Swiss.[52] Red Cross funds gave at least two grants of 500 francs to the medical officer in Leysin, which were useful as they allowed Swiss doctors flexibility in their treatment recommendations, a considerable benefit to the men.[53] At Leysin, the routine included weekly weigh-ins, an important indicator in the condition of tuberculosis patients and a characteristic of sanatorium life before and after the war.[54]

Although the Swiss provided excellent surgeons and physicians, sometimes of international standing, the same could not be said of nursing care where it was often alleged they were quite backward. Sometimes doctors could not get on with nursing staff. Nursing was said to show a carelessness approaching neglect by British standards. The Insel Hospital in Berne had a surgeon of the highest world-wide standard in Professor Kocher, but 'once off the operating table the care given to the patient is poor from our standpoint, the food is indifferent, and it cannot be denied that there is room for adverse criticism'.[55] A Swiss nursing sister was sent to Mürren to help out during the influenza outbreak, paid for by the Red Cross, but she could not work in harmony with the medical officers.[56] There were problems at the Soldanelle in Chateau d'Oex too where the medical officer in charge, Captain Ricklin, refused to allow nurses to help care for the patients. Nurses were regarded with suspicion and even accused of being spies. When the senior British officer at the time, Colonel Earle, sent officers to visit the men they too were accused of being '*espions*', going into the hospital without Captain Ricklin's knowledge. Captain Ricklin's accusation was seen as not only unjustified but also offensive. Lieutenant Colonel Picot complained about it to Colonel Hauser. Picot wrote of the incident in his report to London, claiming he had experience of the mentality of Swiss medical officers on the subject of spying.

> I have had occasion in the past, more especially in connection with the Soldanelle, to urge upon the authorities the advisability of having nurses, British or Swiss, attached to this and other hospitals. I explained that whatever the custom might be in Swiss hospitals, our men would never be satisfied with their treatment until nurses were appointed. I invariably found that my views on the subject were antipathetic to the medical officers. They were of the opinion that the presence of nurses would render the work of the doctors more difficult, and that the advantage of their presence would not compensate for the disadvantages. On asking where the disadvantage lay, I was informed that nurses were invariably spies and inclined to disregard orders; further that British nurses in a Swiss hospital would certainly be impossible. The prejudice against British nurses seems to be general. I have heard medical officers say that they would resign rather than consent for one minute to the presence of British nurses.[57]

Ricklin and Earle did not got on, and Colonel Earle was replaced as senior officer by someone inferior in rank, after Ricklin alleged he was suffering from 'neurasthenia', something Earle and his supporters denied. After a long and uphill fight, Picot succeeded in obtaining consent for Swiss nurses, mostly from religious foundations being appointed in hospitals in Leysin, Chateau d'Oex and Mürren. Captain Ricklin was replaced in 1918 at Soldanelle by a new medical officer and commandant, Carl Jung, the well-known psychologist.[58]

Sometimes, despite all efforts, deaths could not be avoided. When an internee died they had a funeral with a procession of comrades, a band playing a funeral march, local people and Swiss military following the coffin. At the graveside, a rifle volley was fired in salute by Swiss soldiers as internees could not carry weapons. This form of funeral, with military honours, was allowed for all nationalities of deceased soldiers. Some deaths were accidental, or possibly unrecorded suicides of traumatized men. One such may have been Private N. Chapman of the Royal Irish Rifles, for whom a verdict of misadventure was recorded after he fell from the path between Lauterbrunnen and Mürren. Fifty officers, NCOS and men from Mürren with wreaths, led by Major Barton, and forty French internees from Lauterbrunnen attended his funeral on 13 May 1918. Three volleys were fired by the Swiss Army.[59] A French officer, Captain Abeille, was killed by a train in Interlaken station as he was travelling to Berne to consult a specialist about his wounds, an incident recorded as an accident.[60]

Descriptions of funerals appeared regularly in English, French and German internee journals and in the Swiss press. The death rate from wounds was highest in the early months of internment as those in the first contingents tended to be the worst cases. Three French soldiers died at Leysin in February 1916, within weeks of their arrival. Their funeral services were held in a Catholic chapel decorated with flags and the French colours of red, white and blue. Most of the internees attended the funeral, and the Swiss military doctors wore their uniforms. The honour of a rifle volley was given by Swiss soldiers garrisoned at St Maurice.[61] Funerals were evidence of amicable relations with locals who voluntarily attended.[62] Relations between German internees and locals in Davos were strengthened further when they worked to dig a train out of the snow after it was derailed and buried by an avalanche on 29 April 1917 which helped them gain acceptance as part of the community.[63]

The influenza epidemic, or Spanish Flu, was another cause of death, especially tragic as it killed a number of young men who had survived battle, serious wounds and imprisonment with just months to go until the end of the war. Some of the women who had volunteered to help care for them also died. At Chateau

Figure 4.5 German internees involved in rescue work after an avalanche derails a train near Davos. Courtesy of Dokumentationsbibliothek Davos.

d'Oex six men died between 2 and 7 July, and at Vevey, twenty-five men were hospitalized by early July 1918.[64] By September at Vevey, four out of five men had flu or '*Grippe*' as it was known by its German name, and Corporal D. Ross and Private Martin Corrigan died there. The sufferers were nursed by Sister Boloney and Madame Kaylensky. Seeburg was affected by thirty-three cases of influenza by September.[65] At Couvet Miss Dubied died after nursing sick soldiers.[66] She was one of sixty-nine nurses and carers in Switzerland who died during the epidemic. New arrivals in Switzerland and those who moved around had to be quarantined and all gatherings were cancelled.

All internees were under military discipline, following the same rules as applied to Swiss soldiers, with the Swiss military authorities having overall control, although for the British their own officers played a role in supervision. The weakened state of the first prisoners to arrive meant it was hard to imagine that there would be any need for serious sanctions for misbehaviour other than being confined to bed, but as many of the sick and convalescents began to regain strength, they felt a need for movement and activity. After months of captivity and pain, they craved independence and freedom which led to acts of indiscipline for which the modest bed arrests were inadequate penalties.[67] Punishments for soldiers and officers were announced in a decree of the Swiss Federal Council of 14 October 1916. An internee could be confined to their quarters to do chores, forbidden to go to inns where alcohol was consumed, put under arrest in a police station or transferred to a disciplinary establishment for a fixed period. Officers could be more severely punished as they were expected to set a good example to the men. An officer who committed an offence could be confined to their quarters for up to thirty days, or confined to their internment area for up to three months. More severe cases could be imprisoned in the cells for up to thirty days or, most severely, returned to captivity in a prisoner-of-war camp. Offences were recorded in military reports as 'crimes': the most common were alcohol related, insubordination (disrespecting a superior or failing to carry out an order) or absence, usually being away from their quarters outside designated hours and curfew times. Most of the cases were of men being found in cafes by the Swiss police, which carried a standing punishment of four days imprisonment.[68] A fight in a Herisau dance hall in October 1917 between German internees and locals made the headlines, and sometimes there were cases of lawbreaking such as theft and even rape, as recounted in Chapter 7, but the crime rate of internees generally was not above that of the Swiss.[69] Sometimes, internees could be the victims of crime; for example, the German Lieutenant Bulle interned in Teufen near St Gallen was involved in an unpleasant incident with two drunk Swiss soldiers who he passed on the road. One of the Swiss insulted him, calling him a '*sauchoge Schwab*' (a filthy Schwabian pig), shouting after him that they would teach him to salute. The Swiss ran after Bulle and attacked him, grabbing his overcoat, pinning him to the ground and threatening him with their fists. Bulle managed to escape to a restaurant and called the police. The two Swiss were sentenced to three months and three weeks in prison.[70]

Drunkenness was a serious problem among the internees: in Central Valais 30 per cent of all punishments were due to drunkenness. In the area where French and Belgians were interned, 80 per cent of disciplinary cases were due to alcohol consumption.[71] By the end of 1916 there had been 8,032 punishments of soldiers and NCOs. Of these offenders 4,618 (57.5 per cent) were French, 1,905 (23.7 per cent) were German, 791 (9.85 per cent) were Belgian and 718 (8.44 per cent) were British. The most punished seem to have been French NCOs. The threat to return a prisoner to enemy military captivity was carried out in severe cases, and fourteen French and eight Germans met with this punishment.[72]

Sometimes both internees and locals seemed to forget that the soldiers were prisoners and they would enjoy a drink together. Reports noted that breaches of discipline were caused mainly by 'alcohol and sexual immorality'.[73] These problems or pleasures, depending on one's point of view, were often linked as both could be associated with inns and cafes. For local cafe and innkeepers this was good for business. Measures were taken, and rules were introduced to restrict access to alcohol and visits to inns and promote alternative amusements. Alcohol was prohibited during the day except with the midday meal, two decilitres of wine or half a bottle of beer, with the authorization of the physician.[74] Ordinary soldiers were allowed out until 9.30 pm while officers above the rank of sergeant could stay out until 10.00 pm. This did not necessarily solve the problem. To make up for less drinking time, shots of absinthe could provide the desired effect in the shorter time they were allowed out. Despite the risk of antisocial behaviour, many Swiss cafe owners, who were finding the sale of alcohol to internees profitable, opposed these restrictions, and when soldiers were barred from entering drinking establishments, they collaborated with them to break the rules. In Leysin the local authorities did not wish to take any steps to keep interned men out of cafes as it was a good source of income

Figure 4.6 German internees visit the Weber Bakery, Davos, 1917. Courtesy of Dokumentationsbibliothek Davos.

to small businesses. In the Teufen area, instructions to close the offending establishments were sent by army physicians to innkeepers who were known to provide an excessive supply of alcoholic drinks to internees.[75] Sometimes internees were so desperate to get to an inn; they climbed out of windows or burst out en masse.[76] It wasn't just alcohol that caused discipline problems, women too were often seen as being a dangerous influence on men deprived of female company for so long. It was always the same story, said one monthly report from Central Switzerland, 'Wine, women and song, and song is the least harmful.'[77]

British soldiers interned in Mürren allegedly had too much money to spend: 8,000 francs poured into the camp in just two days on 20 and 21 September 1916. As a consequence there were sixty-five punishments for alcohol-related incidents compared with only six between 12 and 31 August despite a ban on drinking liquor and the closure of cafes. In Diablerets 270 men received 23,000 francs in two months, and there was disorder there too. In a postcard sent to a fellow internee, a British soldier wrote, 'Am getting Fr 20-80 per week all clear on my job. I am on the drink.'[78] Internees were allowed to receive money of their own or sent by their families using money orders. To get their cash they needed to get a signed certificate from a commanding officer where they were interned authorizing such a remittance and this certificate presented at a post office.[79] Steps were taken to restrict the amount of cash available to internees so as to reduce the temptation to spend it all on alcohol. Interned soldier, Arthur March, writing home to Canada in December 1917, told his family,

> It seems that it is difficult to get money here, a great many of the old soldiers had a weakness for 'booze' and a poor sense of responsibility. They failed to remember that they were guests of one of the greatest little countries on the earth, so the British government, ashamed of their conduct, not only punished them but also took steps that would prevent them having too much money.[80]

After their traumatic experiences, alcohol was used as a form of self-medication for some of the psychological problems experienced. Measures to prevent drunkenness and antisocial behaviour were introduced along with punishments. Leisure facilities were created. Huts provided by the YMCA offered meals, companionship, games and pastimes. In Chateau d'Oex, there was the Grey Hut for the men interned there, offering food, whist and social activities. After two months of the Grey Hut opening crime was down 90 per cent, and drunkenness was almost nil. Among the British, during October 1916 there had been nine cases of drunkenness in Mürren, eleven in Chateau d'Oex and twenty-three in Leysin, worrying as it was a much smaller group of invalids.[81] The number of cases of drunkenness began to fall once men were given more to occupy them and the amount of money they could receive at once was controlled.

These measures were not effective in cases of dependency, so alcoholics were confined to special, segregated camps with heavier restrictions. Banned from cafes, alcoholics were often sold drink by local people, bought with money sent to friends and passed to them.[82]

Problems relating to alcohol consumption were a recurring theme in documents and letters discussing and advocating occupation, sport, work, foyers and visits from relatives. As Miss Bates, who worked in the foyer for English prisoners at Rougemont near Chateau d'Oex, wrote in a letter advocating that mothers as well as wives be allowed to visit internees:

> There has been trouble about drink and severe punishments which of course one does not question, but the men are not normal, and it would make your heart ache to see how their nerves are raw, and yet how happy and cheery and bright they are.[83]

Offences related to alcohol consumption were common across all nationalities of internee. In Chateau d'Oex there were a few cases of drunkenness within the first few weeks of the British arriving. This was put down to the friendliness of the local population, who would insist on treating them. When the drunkenness could be traced to its source, to restaurants and cabarets, the owners were heavily fined.[84] Among the British, Leysin seems to have had more cases of drunkenness than other places. Drinking was commented on at Lucerne too, where the internees went for surgery then convalescence at Seeburg. In one night in Lucerne where there were six cases of drunkenness and an absence, a report admitted,

> It is difficult to get control of these hospital cases especially as most of them are too ill to be imprisoned and more especially as I can find no way of getting them any occupation. The 'drunks' are either committed or instigated by a few Irishmen in hospital and the rest of the men in hospital were being inconvenienced by them as the Swiss were anxious to punish them all alike. It was the Irish question in miniature.[85]

The senior British officer dealt with it by advising the Swiss to send the offenders to an inebriates camp as soon as they were well enough to be moved. Three men in hospital were awaiting trial by Swiss court martial on a charge of selling government boots, probably in a desperate attempt to raise money to buy drink.

Despite the trouble caused and his apparent hostility to the Irish in particular, the senior British officer showed some sympathy and understanding for the men.

> Owing to the rather abnormal conditions here, I believe the drinking was appreciable. There is not much that the men can do here in the way of work and most of them could not do so owing to their state of health. They have a very natural feeling of wanting to have a 'Bust' after being cooped up in hospital for weeks or months, in some cases on their backs.[86]

The French soldier, Marius Bertrand, was sentenced to thirty days of imprisonment in July 1917. On 1 July, a policeman, Chevally, in his report said he came across an aggressive Bertrand, drunk at 11.30 pm in the street of Les Planches at Montreux, a time he should have been in his lodgings. Bertrand was with his wife, Marguerite, and a group of other French internees and women, all drunk, outside a cafe. They were noisy and became threatening when asked to be quiet. One of them punched the policeman in the neck and kicked his legs, causing him to fall over. Bertrand was sent to the central military prison in Berne for his rowdy behaviour and scandalous conduct to which he willingly exposed his wife.

The case of a drunk British soldier led to a charge of insubordination against Corporal D. Marshall of the Royal Irish rifles. Company Sergeant Major Birtles of the Cheshire Regiment passed a group of men on a hotel landing in Mürren when he heard a scuffle. He turned back and ordered the men to their rooms but the drunken Marshall confronted him with the words 'What the fucking hell do you want?' Other men in the group swore that they did not hear Marshall use bad language, but he was found guilty and punished.[87]

The British army recognized alcoholism as a serious condition that needed treatment and established a special camp for inebriates at the Hotel Signal du Bougy above Rolle, with views across Lake Geneva. The camp had room for 50 men with a Swiss officer in charge, whose duties also covered Gimel where there was a large establishment for up to 150 French and Belgian alcoholic internees.[88] This was seen as a last resort, after punishments had failed, as in the opinion of the Army Council the internment of a man in a special camp for inebriates was a very serious matter, which, should it become known, could hamper his chances of employment in civilian life. The council had no objection to disciplinary action taken against a man who misconducts himself, but he should not, in their opinion, 'bear such a lasting stigma as internment in a camp reserved for inebriates'.[89] However, twenty-three men were sent to Bougy from

Leysin, where there were particular concerns over alcohol abuse: 'they were all men who had been a constant nuisance in their hotels. The general discipline at Leysin ought to improve now that these men have gone' was the view of Swiss Medical Officer Captain Faljambe.[90] A report from Bougy said that things there were generally satisfactory and the men found plenty of work in the fields and orchards surrounding it to keep them occupied. An alcoholic officer sent there, Captain George, was said to be greatly improved in health and was content to remain there.[91]

The experience of prisoner-of-war camps, where enemy guards had more power than their own officers, tended to have an undermining effect on military hierarchy. For the French, internment in German camps had a very negative effect on the spirit of the prisoners, obliged to servitude and reprimanded if they refused, they had, according to reports, acquired a certain repugnance to recognize authority.[92]

For more serious crimes, offenders could be sentenced to a term of imprisonment at the penitentiary at Witzwil. There were some complaints that the law and punishment were not administered in an even-handed way, with discrimination shown by the authorities to one side or the other. In the Swiss-German areas some internees felt that Germans seemed more favourably treated than the French. A report based on the content of letters read by the military postal commission during January 1917 claimed that in a locality reserved for French internees, some German ones were able to go to an inn without being disturbed by the police, but three French found in a concert hall after curfew were dragged off and arrested. Another letter writer claimed that in Brienz, where there were many French and Belgians, the pastor prayed every Sunday for his brave German brothers.[93]

The ultimate punishment could be being shot, as a poster on the use of arms displayed in internment locations warned. Offenders could be shot for resistance, if a man under arrest or a prisoner or internee under guard failed to obey an order to stop after the challenge *Garde à vous!* had been issued three times. If there was an immediate or serious danger a shot could be fired without warning.[94]

Of course, far from being out drinking, many internees were in such a poor state of health they needed to be treated in hospital or sanatoria, but for those who were well enough, distractions were clearly needed to occupy their minds and help them readjust to life outside the prison camps, ready to return to a normal home life after the war.

Notes

1. Picot to War Office, 7 July 1916, TNA FO 383/217.
2. Foreign Office Memorandum, 21 May 1916, TNA FO 383/216.
3. R. Timms to Private Alfred Gibbs, 4th Leicester Regiment, 7 December 1917.
4. Franco Arnold, *'Unsere Kriegsgäste' oder 'Verräter ihres Landes?' Die Wahrnehmung der ausländischen Bevölkerung durch die Einheimischen im Oberwallis während des Ersten Westkriegs*, Masterarbeit eingereicht bei der Philosophischen Fakultät der Universität Freiberg, 2011, p. 78.
5. *Quartier-Général to Chefs d'établissements par la voie hiérarchique*, 20 September 1916, Archives de Vieux Montreux, Musée de Montreux.
6. Bürgisser, 'L'humanité comme raison d'Etat', p. 284.
7. Jaccottet et al., *Au Soleil et sur les Monts*, p. 26.
8. Max D. Amstutz, *Die Anfänge des alpinen Skirennsports/The Golden Age of Alpine Skiing*, Zurich, 2010, pp. 56–7.
9. Foreign Office Memorandum, 21 May 1916, TNA FO 383/216.
10. *The New York Times*, 31 August 1917.
11. Durrer, 'Internierte während des Ersten Weltkriegs', p. 99.
12. *General Regulations for British Prisoners of War Interned in Switzerland*, Papers of Corp H. D. Munyard, IWM Documents 10733.
13. Notice – Requests and Complaints, 7 March 1918, Archives de Vieux Montreux, Musée de Montreux.
14. Grant Duff to War Office, 14 April 1916, TNA FO 383/215.
15. Grant Duff to War Office, 10 April 1916, TNA FO 383/215.
16. *JIF*, A2, No. 23, 7 April 1918.
17. *JIF*, A2, No. 16, 17 February 1918.
18. Lord Acton to War Office, Berne, 19 May 1916, TNA FO 383/216.
19. Samuel McCune Lindsay (ed.), *Bulletin of Social Legislation on the Henry Bergh Foundation for the Promotion of Humane Education*, No 5, New York, 1917, pp. 22–3.
20. Jones, *Violence against Prisoners of War in the First World War*, p. 241.
21. Walle, 'Les Prisonniers de Guerre Francais Internés en Suisse (1916-1919)', p. 63.
22. Capt C. W. S. Faljambe, senior medical officer, Leysin, December 1916, TNA FO 383/219.
23. Major E. R. Collins to mother, 19 December 1917, IWM Documents 15679.
24. Ibid.
25. *JIF*, A2, No. 5, 2 December 1917.
26. Major Collins to mother, 19 December 1917, IWM Documents 15679.
27. Martina Walser, 'In selbsloser Hingabe und Vaterländische Treue – Marta Pfenniger als Soldatenmutter im Grenzdienst', *Der Erste Weltkrig in das Appenzellerland*, pp. 66–78.

28 *Deutsche Internierten Zeitung (DIZ)*, Heft Nr. 46, 5 August 1917.
29 Picot, Berne, 23 March 1917, TNA FO 383/329.
30 *DIZ*, Heft Nr. 46, 5 August 1917.
31 Anja Huber, *Fremdsein im Krieg – die Schweiz als Ausgangs und Zielort von Migration 1914-1918 (Die Schweiz im Ersten Weltkrieg)*, Zurich, 1918.
32 *Derby Daily Telegraph*, 16 May 1917.
33 *BIM*, No. 4, 1916.
34 Air raid shelter tunnels beneath a Leicester park with names such as Piccadilly, Granby Street and High Street were seen by the author in 2011.
35 *Mürren Mini Museum* booklet, 2014.
36 Report on British Soldiers Interned at Mürren, Switzerland, June 1917, TNA FO 383/329.
37 *DIZ*, Heft Nr. 40, 24 Juni 1917.
38 Draenert, *Kriegschirurgie und Kriegsorthopädie in der Schweiz zur Zeit des Ersten Weltkrieges*, p. 293.
39 Julie Anderson, *The Soul of a Nation: A Social History of Disabled People, Physical Therapy, Rehabilitation and Sport in Britain, 1918-1970* (PhD Thesis, De Montfort University, 2001), p. 33.
40 Bürgisser, 'L'humanité comme raison d'Etat', p. 275; Draenert, *Kriegschirurgie und Kriegsorthopädie in der Schweiz zur Zeit des Ersten Weltkrieges*, p. 293.
41 Report on British Soldiers Interned at Lucerne, Switzerland, June 1917, TNA FO 383/329.
42 Bürgisser, 'L'humanité comme raison d'Etat', p. 275.
43 Ibid., p. 275; Vuilleumier, 'Dossier', p. 8.
44 Report on British Soldiers Interned at Interlaken, Switzerland, June 1917, TNA FO 383/329.
45 Picot to War Office, Berne, 2 February 1917, TNA FO 383/329.
46 Post Card to Private Alf Gibbs from patient in Fribourg hospital, 19 October 1918.
47 Picot to War Office, 2 July 1916, TNA FO 383/217.
48 Picot to the War Office, 30 November 1916.
49 Major-General MacPherson, 'The Dental Health of British Recruits', *History of the Great War*, Volume 1, Medical Services, pp. 134–8.
50 John R. McDill, *Lessons from the Enemy – How Germany Cares for Her War Disabled*, Philadelphia, 1918, p. 137.
51 Ibid., p. 135.
52 Picot to War Office, 7 July 1916, TNA FO 383/217.
53 Monthly report from SBO Leysin, 29 June 1917, TNA FO 383/329.
54 *BIM*, Vol. 2, No. 4, April 1918.
55 Picot, Report 22 June 1917, TNA FO 383/329.
56 Monthly report from Mürren by Col Neish, March 1917, TNA FO383/329.

57 Picot, Report, 20 June 1917, TNA FO 383/329.
58 Aniela Jaffé, *From the Life and Work of C G Jung*, Einsiedeln, 1989, p. 170.
59 *BIM*, Vol. 2, No. 5, June 1918.
60 *JIF*, A2, No. 12, 20 January 1918.
61 *Tribune de Lausanne*, 25 February 1916.
62 Arnold, '*Unsere Kriegsgäste*' *oder* '*Verräter ihres Landes?*', p. 80.
63 Photograph, Zugsunglück, 29 April 1917, Dokumentationsbibliothek Davos, Nr. 133/26.
64 *BIM*, Vol. 2, No. 6, July 1918. The men who died were Private W. Garden of the Gordon Highlanders; Private T. Lane, Royal Munster Fusiliers; C. Martin, AB, RNVR; Private J. Terrio, Canadians; Sergeant T. Fisher, Suffolk Regt; Lieutenant Colonel E. Bunn, New Zealand Forces.
65 *BIM*, Vol. 2, No. 9, 15 October 1918.
66 *BIM*, Vol. 2, No. 7, 15 September 1918.
67 Jaccottet et al., *Au Soleil et sur les Monts*, p. 71.
68 Captain E. W. S. Faljambe, SMO Leysin, Report, December 1916, TNA FO 383/219.
69 Fuchs, 'Interniert im Appenzellerland', p. 65.
70 Ibid., p. 52.
71 Walle, 'Les Prisonniers de Guerre Francais Internés en Suisse (1916-1919)', p. 65.
72 Bürgisser, 'L'humanité comme raison d'Etat', p. 274.
73 Lindsay (ed.), *Bulletin of Social Legislation*, p. 29.
74 Ibid., p. 30.
75 Fuchs, 'Interniert im Appenzellerland', p. 51.
76 Ibid., p. 61.
77 Lindsay (ed.), *Bulletin of Social Legislation*, p. 31.
78 Private Cavner to Private Alf Gibbs of the Leicestershire Regiment, 15 October 1917.
79 *Daily Gazette for Middlesborough*, 2 February 1917.
80 Arthur Cyril March, *Letters Home from the Front*, 30 December 1917, South Shore Genealogical Society.
81 Picot, Report 30 November 1916.
82 Bürgisser, 'L'humanité comme raison d'Etat', p. 274.
83 Miss Bates to Mrs Crozier, 10 August 1916, TNA FO 383/218.
84 Picot to War Office, 7 July 1916, TNA FO 383/217.
85 Report from Lucerne, SBO, 1917.
86 Report on British Soldiers Interned at Lucerne, Switzerland, June 1917, TNA FO 383/329.
87 Summary of evidence against Corporal D. Marshall, RIF, by CSM Birtles, Cheshire Regt, July 1917, TNA FO 383/217.
88 Picot to Department for Prisoners of War, 11 December 1916, TNA FO 383/219.

89 Picot to War Office, 7 July 1916, TNA FO 383/217.
90 Faljambe, SMO Leysin, Report, December 1916, TNA FO 383/219.
91 Major Alexander, 2/3 Gurkha Rifles, Report July 1917, TNA FO 383/330.
92 Albert Antouard, *L'assistance aux prisonniers de guerre*, p. 20, quoted by Walle, 'Les Prisonniers de Guerre Francais Internés en Suisse (1916-1919)', p. 65.
93 Walle, 'Les Prisonniers de Guerre Francais Internés en Suisse (1916-1919)', p. 63.
94 Use of Arms, poster issued by the Swiss Federal Council, 22 February 1918, Musé de Vieux Montreux.

5

Work, education and training

Prisoners of war undertaking some form of work during their captivity was not a new phenomenon in the First World War, although for the first time there were attempts to regulate it through the Hague and Geneva Conventions. During the American and Napoleonic Wars, prisoners crafted decorative boxes, toys, models, automata and other items out of bone, straw and paper which they were able to sell.[1] At Norman Cross Prison near Peterborough, sales of prisoners' work were held twice a week at the local market or daily at the prison gate. Illiterate French prisoners were given the chance to learn to read and write in French and English. Construction of the Church of St Michael and All Angels near the prison on Dartmoor was begun by French prisoners of war, and, when they left in 1814, it was completed by Americans captured during the War of 1812.[2] Prisoners of the French were also required to work. Austrian prisoners were sent to Corsica, between 1800 and 1801, to build roads on Napoleon's home island.[3]

During the Boer War, in which prisoners of the British were transported around the world to camps far away from South Africa, such as in Bermuda, St Helena and India, captives worked during their confinement. They carved souvenirs, including boxes, pipes and pen holders which they made using improvised tools, such as saws converted from table knives, umbrella wires turned into frets and stones made into hammers. Skilled workers were allowed to get jobs outside the camps, their employers taking responsibility for them. Trusted prisoners had permission to find their own lodgings, subject to a curfew.[4]

The Hague Convention of 1907, Chapter 2, Article 6, building on the Geneva Convention, clarified the position regarding the work of prisoners within a framework agreed internationally.

> The State may utilize the labour of prisoners of war according to their rank and aptitude, officers excepted. The tasks shall not be excessive and shall have no connection with the operations of war. ... Wages of prisoners shall go towards

improving their position and the balance shall be paid to them on their release, after deducting the cost of their maintenance.⁵

The British, Belgian, French and German military prisoners of war, transferred to Switzerland for internment, were employed under the terms of this section of the Hague Convention.

Civilian internees were exempt from work although many chose employment for themselves, both to pass the time, maintain their skills or out of financial necessity. They could become involved in camp administration, like the men who became police officers at Ruhleben camp that housed interned British civilians in Berlin.⁶ Others were able to continue their pre-war trades, such as tailors, cobblers and barbers. J. Davidson Ketchum, in his account of Ruhleben camp life, identified how earning pennies for their keep through businesses as shoe blacks, barbers, launderers and stewards was an important means of survival for penniless internees.⁷ Trading goods and services was a feature of internment camp life and important both financially and as a means to obtain items to be used in other activities, such as books, paper, sports equipment, additional food and clothing.⁸ Panikos Panayi in *Prisoners of Britain* also identifies the importance of work and education to internees and shows how vital it was for keeping depression and barbed-wire disease at bay.⁹ Some camps developed employment schemes, including Douglas, Knockaloe, Hackney Wick and Islington but in others the majority of prisoners found little useful work, which meant that they had to find different ways of keeping occupied.¹⁰

Education was one way of passing the time while simultaneously preparing for a return to life outside the camp after the war was over. At Ruhleben, some of the internees formed the Arts and Science Union, a camp school that organized lecture courses for the British interned there. Among the men interned, up to perhaps 7,000 of them at some points, were businessmen, professors and teachers of English, students at German universities, technical schools and musical academies, musicians, engineers in electrical, dying and mining industries, skilled workers and apprentices in many trades, along with professional football players, jockeys and trainers, entertainers, hairdressers and others.¹¹ Among these men who happened to be living and working, studying, performing or just on holiday in Germany when war broke out in August 1914 were at least 200 professors and teachers. These academics and other skilled and educated men were able to offer a programme beginning with twenty open-air lecture courses. This programme offered a broad curriculum that included calculus, psychology, music, chemistry, physics, literature and languages.¹² Organizing and teaching on the education programme involved a lot of voluntary work and time, something the internees had plenty of: enlisting teachers, enrolling pupils, securing space, arranging timetables and keeping records of attendance, progress and expenses.[13]

For German citizens interned in Britain educational activities were also an important part of camp life. Panayi illustrates how 'some educational events took the form of formal lectures, all types of schools and even universities emerged on a sophisticated and significant scale, especially in the large and long-lasting camps on the Isle of Man, as well as in predominantly bourgeois Lofthouse Park'.[14] German military prisoners too were engaged in educational pursuits. Swiss Embassy officials in London contacted the Prussian Ministry of Education via the German Foreign Office in order to determine the curriculum for military prisoners and to formalize the issue of certificates for those who successfully completed courses to use as qualifications after the war.[15]

Once the military prisoners of war were settled into their new lives interned in neutral Switzerland and the novelty or shock of the sudden contrast with the prison camps and the enthusiasm of the welcome had worn off, new problems began to surface. Just what were these groups of young men to do with their time? Many were ill or injured, some with life-changing conditions. As well as the injuries, there was the trauma associated with the circumstances of how they came to be injured and adjustment to a new kind of life. The horrific scenes they had witnessed resulted in shell shock for some, and there was the likelihood of further psychological problems due to having been incarcerated for a long time, suffering the privation of life in prison camps, without knowing when they might return home, which led to a condition that became referred to as barbed-wire disease.[16] All the soldiers were fit, young men when they left home for the front, some only teenagers looking forward to beginning adult life, others had wives and young families to provide for. Many had left school in adolescence, hoping for secure work in manual trades, a prospect that disability seemed to have snatched away. Lacking in basic education, clerical work might not have seemed a viable prospect for some of them. Other young men had been studying towards qualifications and university degrees, but their student life had been cut short.

Most of the internees had been in captivity for at least eighteen months before being transferred to Switzerland. Their injuries or illnesses meant that many of them had been in hospital during this time. In Switzerland, many were bored and had little to occupy them. It's not surprising that some of this distress sometimes manifested itself in inappropriate behaviour and alcohol abuse.

Although they were paid a small allowance for their work, a proportion of it was retained to pay for their keep. This was an important means of ensuring that the men did not have too much cash available that they might spend on drink. Something structured was needed to occupy the men, to provide distraction and to help them return to normal life and prepare them for future employment, reconstructing their masculine role as provider.[17]

As well as physical health, the Swiss authorities focused on the internees' 'moral regeneration'. They were eager that the men should return home as useful members of society, in countries damaged by war that would have to be rebuilt. Discipline, work and education were seen as the way to achieve this. This would go a long way towards relieving the boredom and sense of uselessness that drove some towards alcohol induced antisocial behaviour. The *Coventry Evening Telegraph*, when writing in support of a training school for mechanics set up for internees, commented on the

> necessity to think of mental fitness and the future of those interned in neutral areas, when the novelty has worn off, they are faced with boredom arising from forced idleness. This is a danger as it leads to deterioration of character and brain power.[18]

An article in *Journal des Internés Français* said of the French internees in Beatenburg in the Bernese Oberland that sometimes the beauty of the mountains was impregnated with an infinite sadness where sounds took on a strange significance. Internees become bored, although the countryside was adorable, the village was morose and the inn the only distraction.[19] Some form of occupation, appropriate to individual strengths, capacities and abilities, was not only desirable but when available became compulsory. Even those in hospital were expected to perform some light work or take part in education. Discipline and willingness to learn were an important ethic. Everyone should return home, when the time came, with valuable skills. For the Germans it was emphasized that even if they could not be warriors, they could be defenders of national values and in this way prepare for the future in the interest of their country. For the Swiss the work of the internees was evidence of a peaceful, useful life in a neutral country.[20]

As the fate of the internees would be of interest and concern for family and friends back home, local newspapers, such as the *Birmingham Daily Post*, published details of the arrangements for internees' employment and how they were assessed into six categories according to rank, position, aptitude and health: Category One: incapable of work; Category Two: partially capable of light work inside camp; Category Three: partially capable of part-time work outside camp; Category Four: capable of any work; Category Five: apprentices, the incapacitated learning new skills; Category Six: students.[21] Readers were reassured that no Swiss labour would be supplanted or undercut by the employment of internees and that civilians, officers and NCOs from sergeants upwards would be exempt from compulsory work. In Switzerland, opposition by labour unions and socialists, who feared interference in their own fields of work, led to the inclusion of equal proportions of employers and labour representatives on Regional and Central Commissions for the employment of internees.[22] By July 1916 there were 8,947 French, 2,667 German, 1,095 Belgians and, as yet, only 452 British ready and capable of work, although the number quickly increased.[23] Regulations concerning employment were published and distributed to internees and supervising Swiss.[24]

Many of those injured would be unable to return to their previous occupations after the war or had no qualifications or experience. These men needed some form of rehabilitation to help them find employment. For medical historian, Suzannah Biernoff,

> The Victorian work ethic was central to the concept of rehabilitation, particularly the powerful association between working-class masculinity and skilled labour. Financial independence was a precondition for their return to domestic masculinity.[25]

After months or years of forced idleness, the men needed to relearn the work ethic, self-discipline and routine. The British government sent out trainers and teachers to run training centres and workshops in Switzerland where internees could learn new skills. Courses were available in motor mechanics, driving, accountancy, bookkeeping, leather work, printing, bookbinding, foreign languages (particularly French), basic literacy and numeracy. Initial funding to start up these training establishments, which also functioned as small enterprises providing useful services, was loaned by the British Red Cross.[26] Experience could be gained in Swiss businesses or in enterprises that served the internee community. In Mürren there was a watch repairer, a carpenter, a printing office that produced the monthly newspaper and a tailor's shop under Lieutenant Russell, where it was claimed that no work was too difficult to be handled. There was a boot shop supervised by Lieutenant Shillington, who could do any kind of first-class boot-making and who made special boots for the internees. Bookkeeping, shorthand, telegraphy and blacksmithing were all successfully carried on alongside gardening squads led by Lieutenant Eric Smith of the Canadian regiment, Strathcona's Horse, a scheme that employed thirty-three men in market gardening by June 1917.[27] All employed internees and were soon making small profits.[28]

British Interned Mürren, told its readers that all workshops, including the tailors', shoemakers' and carpenters', were in a sound position, as the accounts had been regularly audited since September 1916. Charges were kept to a minimum as all capital expenditures, lent by the Red Cross, had been refunded.[29] The NCOs in charge of the shops and officers who superintended them were credited with this satisfactory state of affairs. Sometimes internees were able to visit their allies to share skills. A Frenchman came to Mürren for ten days to teach British internees how to make bead chains which were then in fashion. Strings of beads made by the class were sent to London to be sold; by November 1917 ten had been despatched and another fourteen were ready. Two chains of beads had been sold even before they were finished, and four orders had been received.[30] By purchasing products made by internees, people at home were able to give support and demonstrate to the makers that their work was useful and valued.

For those without physical injuries or whose wounds had healed, there was an immediate need for agricultural labour, particularly at haymaking and harvest time, to make up for the absence of Swiss men who had been mobilized. Alpine farming wasn't suitable for everyone; according to André Paillard's report on Chateau d'Oex, British men were not really suited to this kind of work.[31] They lacked the necessary experience as most were from urban, industrial communities, had difficulties understanding the language and were generally unhappy. Another problem, according to Paillard, was that enforced idleness in captivity and hospital meant that many had lost the inclination to work, even if they had the capacity. French internees, many from rural backgrounds, adapted much better to this kind of work. They would also have been able to understand and follow instructions in French-speaking Switzerland. Interned in Swiss-German areas, German internees were equipped to work alongside local people, most of whom would be able to speak High German as well as local dialects.

Being part of a work party, sent to other regions, gave some internees the opportunity to see more of Switzerland than the villages where they were interned. In June 1916, a delegation of German internees from Teufen in Appenzellerland visited Brunnen for an introductory course in making slippers. Once trained they passed on what they had learnt to others. By the end of February 1917, around 800 pairs of slippers had been made by 14 men in Teufen.[32] Germans in Oberegg also tried slipper-making, along with woodwork and agricultural labour.³³ Soon about 400 pairs of slippers a month were being made. At Beiden, also in Appenzellerland, Germans could work on two vegetable gardens growing potatoes and flowers.³⁴ There too they could help on farms, work in trade or work in their own small-scale industries, such as insurance, wood and bone carving, marquetry and cobbling. By the end of January 1917, their handiwork had raised about 12,000 francs in sales. Useful work carried out in Beiden was the manufacture of orthopaedic apparatus for physiotherapy to be used in the local hospital.³⁵ Much of the work was seasonal. As well as making slippers, internees in Teufen helped on farms and worked with residents to plant an orchard. From late autumn until the following summer, there was basket weaving. Some of them did mental work, studying for their future professions through the winter of 1917 and 1918, with support from the Central Library in Berne. Courses offered were German, English, stenography and civics.³⁶

A subsection of the Red Cross in Switzerland, *Pro Captivis*, was formed in Berne in 1915 to assist prisoners of war.³⁷ Once internees arrived in Switzerland it began to work to raise the morale of internees who had been unable to find suitable employment. There were both protestant and Catholic groups that took on the task of finding or providing work for some of the internees. *Pro Captivis* managed its own workshops and factories located close to where internees were staying and provided apprenticeships in nine employment sectors for British and German internees.³⁸ There were workshops for carpentry, shoemaking, toy-making, wickerwork, making cutlery, office work, business, aviculture, agriculture, languages, drawing and mechanics. As well as work these facilities offered training, particularly important for men whose injuries meant they could no longer go back to their previous trades because of physical incapacity. For some of those injured, these activities could serve as occupational therapy. Chateau d'Oex internees had much better results in carpentry and bookbinding workshops, where they worked and learnt under the direction of tradesmen, than they had in farming.³⁹ Others in Chateau d'Oex learnt to work as woodcutters.

In Engelberg, French internees produced goods for sale, toys, clocks, carpentry work and tailoring. Some of them were imaginative and worked on their own ideas. One man collected snail shells to paint and sell. Another got bones from the butcher and made napkin holders from them.⁴⁰ Examples of this work survive in the *Talmuseum* in Engelberg, where there are many brightly painted, two-dimensional, wooden models of soldiers in a variety of situations. There is a soldier sitting smoking a pipe on a milestone pointing to Verdun, a Senegalese soldier cooking his meal on a camp fire, a couple ice-skating, a comic pair on a sledge, a chef and several figures mounted on horses. The mounted figures and their horses perhaps represent a higher level of skill or experience as they incorporated a spring to give a galloping movement and were on wheels. Some of them were made of several parts. Another item in the collection is a wooden inkwell and pen stand with a carved helmet with an edelweiss flower on top which lifts to reveal a glass inkwell. It is engraved with the words '*Engelberg 1916-1917. Hommage à la Suisse*' on the rear and on the front '*A Le Franc*' [sic]. The idea for making the toys seems to have come from Captain Galet-Lalande, who thought the products could be sold to raise funds and the skills developed prove useful for an occupation after the war. Funds for the initiative were donated by the chocolate company Peter, Cailler and Kohler at Vevey, and the charity *Travail Internés Militaires*. After a while, experience showed that demand for toys was limited in times of war and that it would be better for the internees to make useful objects needed in France.[41]

The severity of an internee's injury would determine the hours of work expected of him. Most worked for around four or five hours a day and were paid 20 cents an hour, up to a maximum of one franc a day. The worker was allowed to keep 40 per cent of his pay, 30 per cent went to the Swiss government towards his keep with the remainder for expenses.[42]

The French and Swiss governments worked together to create a labour office for French internees in Switzerland (*l'Office du Travail des Internés Français en Suisse*), following a decree on 11 December 1916.[43] This created a network of French National Workshops (*Les Ateliers Nationaux*) which were overseen by the French ambassador in Berne. From modest beginnings without any machines, the workshops made up for the lack of means through the good will of those working within them. The workshops expanded quite quickly and soon woodwork machinery was installed. In the workshop for the Gruyères region, an area with good communications and accessible wood for materials, a carpentry workshop was installed at Châtel-St-Denis. Here the internees made tables, stools, drawing boards and other small items of furniture. Once the machinery was installed, the work was almost exclusively making doors and windows for temporary shelters to house people displaced from the areas of France invaded by Germany. Some of the workshop's products were displayed at the Exhibition of Work of Internees in April 1917. Profits from the sale of the work went to procure the wood and to hire a saw mill. Initially the saw mill was water powered, but this proved inadequate, so two electric motors were added. The work at the mill occupied twenty internees and provided a good return on the initial investment. All the products of the saw mill and the joinery and carpentry workshop were sent to France to be used in the creation of pre-fabricated dwellings and barracks for the reconstruction of areas devastated by war. During the first month of operation only five of these barracks were made by the inexperienced workers. In the second month thirteen were completed, but after that, once they improved, production was a steady sixteen to eighteen structures a month.[44] An astonishing 1,000 pre-fabricated wooden houses, 10,000 doors and 2,000 beds were produced.[45]

A similar operation was set up at Beatenburg, where Lieutenant Fournier created a series of workshops. Fournier discovered a dilapidated, water-powered saw mill. When brought back into operation by French internees, the saw made light work of pine trees brought down from the mountain. The planks it made were transformed in the carpenters' workshop into pre-fabricated houses and shelters. The work was described as joyful in the *Journal des Internés Français*; the tasks gave new energy to the weak, as evidenced by the contented expressions on the faces of the workers. Working for France, rebuilding the homes of the destitute, allegedly put pride in the internees' hearts.[46] The Beatenburg National Workshops made use of some of the traditional skills of men from Brittany who were proud to be able to produce clogs. As well as clogs they were able to use their skills to make waterproof shoes and boots with soles of wood and tops of canvas which were light, solid and cheap.[47] The canvas came from inside of old tyres, and the rubber from which it was separated was recycled to make rings to seal bottles and preserve jars. Another workshop used a small oven to prepare wood to make buckets, devised by Lieutenant de St Germain, a technician working for *l'Office de Travail*. At Chexbres was a carpentry school, initiated by a British man, Benjamin Greene, who died shortly after the school opened in 1916. Greene left provision for the school to continue after his death.[48]

At Diablerets there were two workshops set up by the *Ateliers Nationaux*. In one of them things were made of wicker and raffia, light work which needed no great effort, suitable for convalescents and those regaining their strength.[49] Men recovering from wounds and sickness could work for a few hours as part of their moral and physical re-education. In the second workshop the work was more demanding. It contained wheelwrights' and carpenters' workshops where wheelbarrows were manufactured as well as the ubiquitous pre-fabs or temporary shelters. The wheelbarrow workshop, employing twenty-five men, was on the ground floor of Pension du Moulin, where the Diablerets ice rink was located. For materials, an officer of the *Ateliers Nationaux* bought wood, sometimes in the form of logs which were sent to a saw mill to be cut into planks or blocks, before being taken to the workshops. As snow comes early in high-lying Diablerets, the workshops were unusable much of the time, so then the men worked under cover, concentrating on doors and windows for shelters.

The people of Lausanne donated and helped to organize workshops for the soldiers in Leysin. Thanks to the items and tools received, internees there were able to make children's toys in the woodwork shop. The tailors of Leysin needed a sewing machine, also suitable for use by shoemakers, raffia was also required for basketwork and appeals for these items appeared in the *Journal des Internés Français*.[50]

Items made by French internees were mostly sold through an office in Paris. Not all the products of the French workshops were intended to be sold; a request by the *Union Chrétiennes de Jeunes Gens* (YMCA) was sent out to the workshops to make some 2,000 domino sets, harmonicas and puzzles to be sent as gifts to Russian prisoners held in camps.[51]

There were only a few purely Belgian workshops. In Interlaken there were Belgian workshops for training and woodwork that opened in March 1917, where window frames, doors, toys, tables and other furniture was produced for refugees.[52]

Some Germans developed skills in carpentry and joinery. An elaborate model of an Appenzeller house built in the German internees' joinery workshop was sent to a sales exhibition in Frankfurt in March 1917. The elaborate and intricate scale model was said to be a symbol of friendship between the internees and local residents. Another exhibition and sale of work in the Casino in Berne in April 1917 showcased the work of Allied internees. The British section included examples of bookbinding, wood carving, basket work and needlework, with carpets a special feature.[53] Orders for articles were welcomed from England via the Red Cross.

Some men with particular trades or skills were placed to work in existing businesses, something which was viewed with mistrust by Swiss trade unions who feared wages would be undercut by internees who were paid less than Swiss workers. However, due to their injuries or being out of the habit of working, internees were likely to be less productive than the Swiss. As there was no local labour market due to conscription of Swiss men, the internees were a useful resource for businesses with the added bonus that they were relatively cheap to employ. Trade unionists and socialists demanded that internees were not used purely as cheap labour to the detriment of local workers. Criticism was countered by the argument that the use of internees was for therapeutic goals and to provide discipline and a moral influence, so that they could return home as useful members of their communities.

Work, Education and Training

Figure 5.1 German internee's carpentry workshop. Courtesy of Andrew Whitmarsh (www.switzerland1914-18.net).

To encourage gardening by British internees, the Red Cross promoted a vegetable show in Berne on 13 September 1917. There were six events at the show, attracting seventy-eight entries from Interlaken, Chateau d'Oex and Seeburg. A competition for the best six potatoes, with a donated prize of 100 francs, attracted the most interest. There were nineteen exhibits warmly admired by both judges and visitors. The winner was Private Smith of Manor Farm, Interlaken, who had grown six magnificent specimens. Private Smith also did well with his fine examples of carrots and onions. Sergeant Field of Chateau d'Oex was successful with his first-class cauliflowers and cabbages. He was also judged to have the best collection of assorted vegetables. Captain Watson of Seeburg exhibited a collection which included a group of fifteen potatoes all grown from one root.[54] The YMCA often provided land for gardening behind their huts during the summer months, such as in Interlaken and in Mürren which had sixty men cultivating foodstuffs for the community on their plot.[55]

Learning new skills was an important feature of internment for all nationalities. Vocational training centres were set up to teach them so they could find work when they returned home. In Mürren, Vevey and Meiringen there were training centres where British internees could learn to drive, become mechanics, accountants, carpenters, watch and boot makers or learn a foreign language. The Technical College at Meiringen included a tailor's shop, boot shop and printing office which, in November 1917, were in a sound financial position despite other shops suffering due to the number of men repatriated while replacements were awaited from Germany.[56] Similar vocational training took place in Chateau d'Oex where two school masters who came out from England ran classes for British internees in the chalet home of local judge, Monsieur Chablez. Local residents volunteered to teach the men French with varying results. For some the subtleties of French grammar were difficult, but others were good scholars who applied themselves to their studies. As well as coming from Britain, teachers and instructors were recruited from appropriately skilled internees. Some of the training was funded by the Joint War Committee of the British Red Cross Society and Order of St John which allocated £2,600 for training projects and invited Lord Sandwich to draw up a scheme to train internees in Switzerland with a view to them getting employment after the war.[57]

A motor school was set up in Mürren by Captain Wallis. It was the horror of the long, weary hours of idleness during his captivity that Wallis claimed gave him the first incentive for the scheme, generously supported by the Red Cross. After a year the motor school moved to larger premises in Vevey; then *Autocar* magazine stepped in and volunteered to take responsibility for raising the funds to support the school until the end of the war.[58] Julian Orde, secretary of the Royal Automobile Society, inspected the motor school while he was visiting his interned son. The premises comprised a fully equipped machine shop, a fitting shop, a running shop with accommodation for two cars, a lecture room, an electrical room with lighting and starting installations, a vulcanizing shop, drawing office, store room, an office and a viewing room. The workshop was rigged up with the latest equipment, its main charms being a good-sized drilling machine, a splendid sawing machine, a water grindstone, a carborundum wheel and two lathes – all power driven by a generator devised on the premises which supplied light and could recharge accumulators. The workshop was set up at a cost of 20,000 francs.[59] Courses extended over five months, with training for six hours a day, six days a week and accommodated forty pupils and five assistant instructors teaching motor mechanics. A hundred men could be trained in a year. The instructors were all British officers and NCOs. The cost of training was £8 15 shillings a term for one man or 1 shilling and 4 pence a day. At the end of their training, men would be fully trained as motor mechanics and taught to drive, fitting them for their return to civilian life with a means of gaining a livelihood. British magazines other than *Autocar* became interested in supporting the project, and there were plans to extend teaching to include motor traction farming.

The British were not the only group of internees to have the opportunity to learn in a specialist motor school. The French had their own *Apprentissage de*

Motoculture pour les Internés Français (AMIF) at Clarens, close to Vevey. This was apparently the inspiration of two internees, Captain Jarsaillon of the 4th Battalion, *Territorial de Chausseurs Alpin* and Sergeant Dumond of the 99th Infantry, previously a car maker in Lyon, who became director of the school. According to the *Journal des Internés Français*, Jarsaillon and Dumond had the idea of a mechanics' school but lacked the funds and authorization to make it a reality.[60] These they obtained from *le Service de l'internement* and the French ambassador while the commandant of the Montreux region gave encouragement and advice. Money arrived for the project after letters were sent to Swiss firms. Piccard-Pictet of Geneva sent a car, vices and other tools. When Jarsaillon was repatriated, he was replaced by an airman, Captain Godet. Like the British motor school, the French one had a machine room with lifting towers, milling machines and a drill, all worked by electric motors. There was a vast room with bays, a forge and a large garage where advanced pupils took apart and reassembled cars. Lessons in mechanics, electricity, arithmetic, geometry and industrial design were taught in a classroom. Galvanization and welding training were also provided. After four months, the pupils were placed in different Swiss factories to perfect their skills. Preference for training was given to wounded men unable to pursue their old professions, internees with no trade and also farmers as the agriculture of the future would become mechanized.

Other training camps were set up at the Polytechnic Chalets at Seeburg for crafts using machinery, a busy work centre where fifty British internees developed skills working in carpentry, electrical work and where leather bag-making and watch-repairing classes, plus fine arts, were added to the curriculum.[61] In Meiringen, large rooms in hotels were put to use as workrooms for trades not requiring machinery. Teachers went out to start classes in joinery, acetylene welding, electric wiring, tailoring and watch repairing. English piano-building firms and businesses in the leather trade offered training with the prospect of employment in Britain.

As well as vocational training courses, internees whose education had been interrupted were able to continue their studies. In the Appenzellerland village of Beiden the inhabitants set up a schoolroom for use by the German internees based there. Here courses were offered in German, French, English, stenography, accounts, bookkeeping, business and drawing.[62] There were correspondence courses for the French military schools at Saint Maixent and Samaur. Business School courses were available to both French and Belgians.

Germans in Davos were able to study at the *Fridericianum*, an established *Gymnasium*, on courses that were certified and recognized in Germany. The

Fridericianum, named after Archduke Friedrich 1 of Baden, opened in 1878 as a school for young Germans with respiratory illnesses. As many classrooms were used and subjects taught as were possible but as demand was high, there was a shortage of places and teachers. Another problem was that the learners had to walk there from all around the Davos area, quite a long way for some of them. Ideally, no one should have been expected to walk for more than half an hour to their classes. To overcome these problems, education was arranged on three sites: at the *Fridericianum* in Davos Platz, at the Casino in Davos Dorf and at the *Pauluskirche* community building, also in Davos Dorf.[63] There was still a shortage of teachers, but some volunteered for very low payment. More than half of the internees joined in education during their stay in Davos, or as Hugo Bach put it, German soldiers seized the opportunity to improve their own future.[64] In addition to vocational courses, there was a General Education department to improve soldiers' basic level of education, which offered teaching in literacy, writing, arithmetic, accounting, citizenship and languages (French, Spanish, English, Italian and Turkish).[65] Classes were relatively small, with around twenty pupils. As well as General Education there was a department of Business Education where accounting, stenography, bookkeeping, typing and geography were taught. Metalwork, woodwork classes, basic practical courses and skilled level or *Meister* tests were delivered in the handicrafts section. Preparation for the advanced level qualifications, *Abiturientenexamen* and *Primärereife,* was offered in the *Gymnasium.* Prior knowledge was required for these higher level courses which included German, maths, algebra, geometry, French, English, history, physics, geography, Greek and Latin.[66] Internees were allowed to join the normal classes of the *Fridericianum* to study for these, although few of them did so. In addition to these education programmes, there were specialist courses for lawyers, technicians, business professions, theology, economics and artistic drawing.

When the number of internees in Davos rose to more than 1,300, the education system expanded to meet demand. No fewer than 800 men sought places, a weekly total of 280 hours of teaching.[67] Another feature of the education offered to German internees in Davos was a special school for Germans from the colonies. Here learners received training to prepare them for life overseas. Courses offered were colonial law, agriculture, African geography, tropical hygiene, British colonial experiences and native religions.[68] This establishment was led by Lieutenant Doctor Eifler, formerly based in Cameroon and under the medical supervision of Doctor Möri. The lecturers came from Togo, Cameroon, German East Africa and also Nigeria, Rhodesia and British East Africa.

Figure 5.2 German internees in an art class, Davos, 1918. Courtesy of Dokumentationsbibliothek Davos.

The colonial Germans lived in the Seehof Sanitorium, a German establishment where there were 120 beds, a classroom, reading room and library.[69] The colonial school was visited by Doctor Dolf, secretary of state in the Imperial Colonial Office (*Reichskolonialamt*) in April 1918. Doctor Dolf commended the internees' bravery when faced with 'an earthquake of enemies', and their quiet preparation for future colonial operations. He believed Germans interested in colonial work would have a secure future.[70]

Education wasn't just for practical or basic skills and vocational training; higher education was offered to anyone qualified. Swiss universities and the Zurich Technical School admitted students with an academic background, and access was given to their libraries. All courses were free. By January 1917 there were 749 French students, 407 German, 195 Belgian and 13 British.[71] The *Ouvre Universitaire Suisse des Etudiants Prisonniers de Guerre* (the Swiss Open University for Prisoners of War) was established to organize this. According to need there were elementary classes, secondary and university teaching. The Swiss universities were each assigned to different internment regions. Participating educational institutions were the universities of Berne, Fribourg, Geneva, Lausanne, Neuchatel, the Federal Polytechnic of Zurich and a number of secondary and professional schools where courses in commerce and other specialisms, such as dentistry and Belgian law at the J. J. Rousseau School of Science and Art, were open to internees. In Berne and Zurich, civilian dress was required by internee students, who normally wore their military uniform. There was a shortage of lecturers, however, a problem solved by recruiting graduates and men with PhDs from within the ranks of the internees. Instructions on how to apply were published and interned lecturers and teachers were invited to teach their comrades. The *Journal des Internés Français* appealed for a graduate or doctor of science to run a course in chemistry and physics in the faculty at Neuchatel for the special military school there.[72] There were also periodic appeals for teachers of accounts, commercial maths, law and French, English and German.[73] A welcoming address to French-interned students, made by Professor Gariel of the University of Fribourg, appeared in the *Journal des Internés Français*.[74] For the French and Belgian Walloons there would have been no language barriers to participation in the institutions in their internment sectors, such as Geneva, Lausanne, Fribourg and Neuchatel. Likewise, German speakers could attend classes provided by Berne University and the Polytechnic at Zurich. For British internees, however, few had the language fluency to join existing university courses and so only thirteen of them were able to take advantage of the opportunities for formal higher education. Flemish Belgians, unless bilingual, might also have found difficulties in taking up the educational opportunities offered.

In Walzenhausen, a branch of the Zurich Technical School opened, which had the only Department of Gas and Heating in Switzerland. It ran a three-month course teaching the basic operation of a gas works. The practical part of the course was done at the gas works in St Margrethen. The first lecturer on this course was *Leutnant der Reserve* Hofbauer, previously an engineer at the Munich city gas works. He was followed in March 1918 by engineer *Leutnant* Ernst Axer and civilian internee, *Herr* Sauter. A five-month course in construction was also offered leading to the same exams as taken in Prussia.[75] In Walzenhausen, the German internees benefited their Swiss hosts when they built a footpath and a park for the local tourist office.

Due to the 'glorious deaths' in battle of many notaries, there were now opportunities for war invalids, proclaimed an advertisement in the *Journal des Internés Français*. Training for notaries was organized by Professor Maillard, president of the *Bureau Central de l'Ouvre Universitaire Suisse*. The school was open to notary clerks and solicitors' clerks who hoped to become registered on their return home. These courses were especially for the wounded who could not do more active work. The notary school was installed in the Hotel-Pension du Village Suisse, overlooking Lake Geneva near Lausanne, where it offered theoretical and practical training in civil, commercial and financial law and insurance.[76]

Work was reserved for the lower ranks. Officers were exempt from having to undertake work other than supervising their men. However, some French and Belgian officers assisted the Engelberg community in planning road building. They worked on the Gerschni and Schwandstrasse. A reforestation scheme in Horbis was another project. In Chateau d'Oex, it had been hoped that British internees might help with a long-projected road building scheme, but this was never implemented. Paillard's report blamed the internees for this as he claimed that a number of soldiers had lost the taste for work following their long idling in German prison camps.[77]

The *British Interned Mürren* magazine explained the need for training and retraining to its readers:

> Out of over 600 here, a very large percentage will, after the war be confined, according to the nature of his disabilities, to some special kind of work: and it has been the aim of the Senior British Officer, Lieutenant-Colonel F Neish of the Gordon Highlanders, that every man who has no trade, or is incapacitated from his original calling, be trained as far as possible in some line of work, which will fit him to preserve the same independence after the war that he had before enlisting.[78]

Neish was repatriated by September 1917.[79] Major H. Charley of the Irish Rifles was then in charge of the arrangements and did a good deal to help a large percentage of the men.

Major Charley, the officer in charge of Technical Education for the British Interned, escorted Mr Davis and Mr Ryan who had been active in forming technical classes for disabled soldiers back in Britain, on a visit to Mürren on 9 February 1918. They explained to a meeting of internees that they were going to introduce similar classes in Switzerland. Seeburg was to be the location of these classes led by Davis. Mr Ryan would take charge of the tailoring class at Meiringen. Major Charley said that men were wanted for watch-repairing, painting and drawing classes. Mr Davis encouraged men to take up leather work as the fancy leather goods trade had been doing well before and during the war. Before the war he had employed fifteen workers who turned out goods to the value of £5,000 a year. He was now employing ninety to a hundred workers turning out goods worth £25,000 a year. In order to keep this trade in British hands after the war, an output of at least £3,000,000 a year would be necessary, claimed Davis. To find enough workers, Davis had turned to disabled soldiers and came to the internees with a message from the Fancy Leather Goods Manufacturers' Association which had said to him, 'Go out to Switzerland and do the work. We will support you.'[80] He claimed there were openings for at least 3,000 men. He made the internees a business offer; many of them would have around £25 or £30 saved up by the time they returned home. He proposed they invest this money by joining him in business. He assured them there was no catch in this and described the wages that a leather worker might earn, £2 a week once he was experienced, an amount that would be boosted by payments from the War Pensions Scheme.

Under the War Pensions Scheme, a British soldier returning home, would be shown a list of trades and the period of training required for each. In the fancy goods trade a man would receive 27 shillings and 6 pence a week during the training period of six months. His wife or mother would receive an allowance of 13 shillings and 4 pence a week while children would be supported with a sliding scale of 5 shillings a week upwards. Once training was completed a bonus of 5 shillings a week and a set of tools, worth up to £5, would be received. A Trades Exhibition in March 1918 displayed goods made by disabled service men worth £700. Mr Ryan told the internees that the trade unions would welcome men who had undergone training in Switzerland, even though they had not done the traditional apprenticeship. In tailoring, modern methods of production and the division of labour system were taking the place of apprenticeships as men learnt to make single pieces of a garment rather than the whole thing. Ryan claimed he would like to employ 200 to 300 men to start a factory making uniforms. Pay would depend on the results, but a good worker could make £2 to £3 and 10 shillings a week while pressers could make £2 to £3 a week. Even after the war there would be a demand for uniforms from the police, municipalities and foreign armies.

Providing work and training to rehabilitate men with life-changing injuries into employment was also a priority for the French authorities. These jobs were more numerous than one would think, according to an article in the *Journal des Internés Français*, especially for those who had lost legs, but for those who had lost arms the choice was more restricted. With modification of technique many jobs could be adapted to a number of disabilities. Although many men would want to work in administration, the places given to mutilated men were almost all inferior to the lowest professional situations, and the numbers seeking them were more than would be needed. Other sedentary careers could be as cashiers or in shops. A person without a right hand could learn to write perfectly well with his left. The journal claimed that it was quite easy to write using the stump of a forearm after an amputation of the hand, with the aid of a brace.

Other suitable jobs might be tailoring, basket making, wicker work, leather work, saddlery or furriery.[81]

Although the work done by internees in neutral Switzerland was not allowed to be militaristic or have value for the war effort, it was frequently described in patriotic terms as having a national value. For instance, Hugo Bach, writing about the educational institutions for Germans interned in Davos, said that the future of our internees is the future of our Fatherland.[82] Likewise, of the French workshops, it was emphasized in the *Journal des Internés Français* that, through their work, internees were contributing towards reconstruction; they were proving their value to the nation through their work which was allowing them to regain their strength, lost in the service of France.[83] This may have been important to the morale of the internees, some of whom felt a sense of guilt at having been captured and spending much of the war in safety when others had been killed or were still suffering in the trenches or prison camps.

Refusal to work was considered a serious breach of discipline and an offence under military law. British internee Bombadier P. Plunkett of 123rd Battery RFA was accused of being one of the ringleaders in an organized attempt at refusing to work at Rossinières, near Chateau d'Oex in July 1917. Plunkett was punished by the Swiss military authorities by being sent to the penitentiary at Witzwil for an indefinite period. Major Simpson, one of the senior British officers considered his conduct in inciting other men to disobey orders made Plunkett

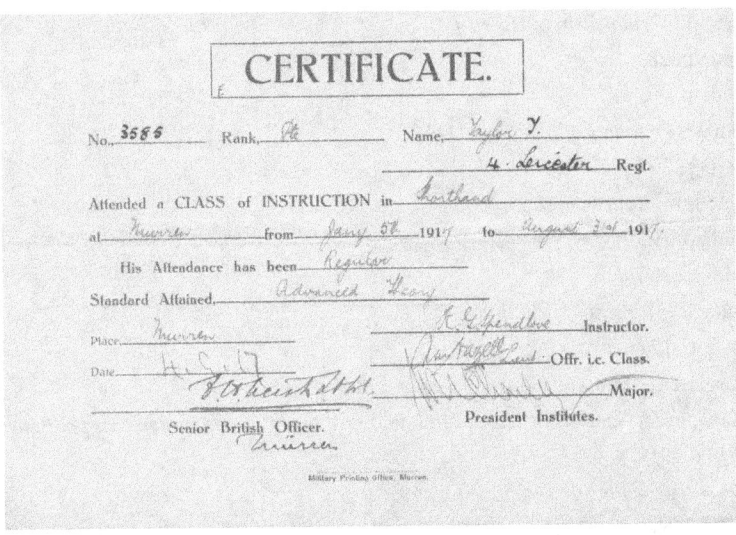

Figure 5.3 Certificate awarded to Private Jack Taylor. Courtesy of Pat and Mark Esling (family collection).

totally unfit to be an NCO and recommended his demotion. The rest of the men were punished with at least a month's imprisonment. 'This is the first sign of organised insubordination that I have had and I feel very strongly that it must be suppressed and very severely punished,' was his verdict.[84]

Work experience, vocational skills or educational qualifications were important factors in whether a former soldier might find work on his return home in a labour market where thousands of demobilized men would be looking for jobs simultaneously. The training given in Switzerland would help those disabled or physically impaired to compete more effectively with able-bodied men in the search for gainful employment, supplemented by a war pension, important to the social construction of masculinity of men as providers.

Notes

1 Clive Lloyd, *The Arts and Crafts of Napoleonic and American Prisoners of War, 1756-1816*, Woodbridge, 2007.
2 Trevor James, *Prisoners of War at Dartmoor: American and French Soldiers and Sailors in an English Prison during the Napoleonic Wars*, Jefferson, 2013, p. 201.
3 Michael S. Neiburg, *Soldiers' Lives through History*, Westport, 2006, p. 89.
4 *Boer Prisoners on St Helena*, St Helena National Trust Education Packs, 4.3 Island Prisoners – Boers 1900-1902.
5 Hague Convention, Chapter 2, Article 6, 1907.
6 Ketchum, *Ruhleben*, p. 26.
7 Ibid., p. 28.
8 Ibid., p. 30.
9 Panayi, *Prisoners of Britain*, p. 224.
10 Ibid., p. 167.
11 Ketchum, *Ruhleben*, p. 5.
12 Ibid., p. 195.
13 Ibid., p. 200.
14 Panayi, *Prisoners of Britain*, p. 176.
15 Ibid., p. 177.
16 Bürgisser, 'L'humanité comme raison d'Etat', p. 268.
17 Makepeace, *Captives of War*, p. 153; Paillard, *Notes sur les événements politiques de 1914 à 1919*, p. 48.
18 *Coventry Evening Telegraph*, 4 July 1918.
19 *JIF*, A2, No. 16, 17 February 1918.
20 Fuchs, 'Interniert im Appenzellerland', p. 63.

21 *Birmingham Daily Post*, 21 September 1916.
22 Picot to War Office, 14 July 1916, TNA, FO 383/217.
23 Ibid.
24 *Organisation des occupations des interné*, Etat-major de l'Armée, Berne 8 July 1916; *Organisation des Ateliers de travail sous une direction suisse*, Etat-major de l'Armée, 12 December 1916, Musé de Vieux Montreux.
25 Suzannah Biernoff, 'The Rhetoric of Disfigurement in First World War Britain', *Social History of Medicine*, 24:3, 1 December 2011, p. 676.
26 *BIM*, No. 2, August 1917.
27 *BIM*, No. 1, July 1917.
28 *The New York Times*, 31 August 1917.
29 *BIM*, No. 6, September 1917.
30 *BIM*, No. 9, November 1917.
31 Paillard, *Notes sur les événements politiques de 1914 à 1919*, p. 48.
32 Fuchs, 'Interniert im Appenzellerland', p. 51.
33 Ibid., p. 61.
34 Ibid., p. 63.
35 Ibid.
36 Ibid., p. 51.
37 Cotter and Herrmann, 'Quand secourir sert se protéger', p. 254.
38 Bürgisser, 'L'humanité comme raison d'Etat', p. 279; Walle, 'Les Prisonniers de Guerre Francais Internés en Suisse (1916-1919)', p. 66.
39 Paillard, *Notes sur les événements politiques de 1914 à 1919*, p. 48.
40 Durrer, 'Internierte während des Ersten Weltkriegs', p. 100.
41 Jaccottet et al., *Au Soleil et Sur les Monts*, p. 100.
42 Walle, 'Les Prisonniers de Guerre Francais Internés en Suisse (1916-1919)', p. 67; Durrer, 'Internierte während des Ersten Weltkriegs', p. 101.
43 Walle, 'Les Prisonniers de Guerre Francais Internés en Suisse (1916-1919)', p. 67.
44 *JIF*, A2, No. 23, 7 April 1918.
45 Walle, 'Les Prisonniers de Guerre Francais Internés en Suisse (1916-1919)', p. 68.
46 *JIF*, A2, No. 23, 7 April 1918.
47 Ibid.
48 Ibid.
49 *JIF*, A2, No. 9, 30 December 1917.
50 *La Revue, Lausanne*, 3 March 1916.
51 *JIF*, A2, No. 5, 2 December 1917.
52 Draenert, *Kriegschirurgie und Kriegsorthopädie in der Schweiz zur Zeit des Ersten Weltkrieges*, p. 149.
53 *Manchester Evening News*, 16 April 1917.
54 *BIM*, No. 8, October 1917.

55 *BIM*, Vol. 2 No. 3, March 1918.
56 *BIM*, No. 9, November 1917.
57 *Newcastle Journal*, 10 August 1917.
58 *Aberdeen Weekly Journal*, 26 July 1918.
59 *BIM*, Vol. 2 1918.
60 *JIF*, A2, No. 16, 17 February 1918.
61 *BIM*, No. 4, 1917.
62 Fuchs, 'Interniert im Appenzellerland', p. 64.
63 Hugo Bach, *Der Ausbildung der deutschen Internierten in der Region Davos*, 1917, p. 7.
64 Ibid., p. 1.
65 Kühnis, *Deutsche Kriegsinternierte in Davos während des 1*, p. 15.
66 Bach, *Der Ausbildung der deutschen Internierten in der Region Davos*, p. 11.
67 Ibid., p. 1.
68 Walter K. Hoffman, 'Die Lehranstalt für internierte Kolonialdeutsche in Davos, Spätformen Kolonialer Ausbildung', *Neue Zürcher Zeitung*, 13/14 August 1977.
69 Ibid.
70 Doctor Dolf (Secretary of State in Imperial German Colonial Office), letter 1918.
71 Walle, 'Les Prisonniers de Guerre Francais Internés en Suisse (1916-1919)', p. 67.
72 *JIF*, A2, No. 5, 2 December 1917.
73 *JIF*, No. 38, 14 July 1917.
74 *JIF*, No. 2, 2 November 1916.
75 Fuchs, 'Interniert im Appenzellerland', p. 65.
76 *JIF*, No. 38, 14 July 1917.
77 Paillard, *Notes sur les événements politiques de 1914 à 1919*, p. 49.
78 *BIM*, No. 1, July 1917.
79 *BIM*, No. 7, September 1917.
80 *BIM*, Vol. 2, No. 3, March 1918.
81 *JIF*, No. 23, 7 July 1917.
82 Bach, *Der Ausbildung der deutschen Internierten in der Region Davos*, p. 1.
83 *JIF*, A2, No. 23, 7 April 1918.
84 Major C. J. Simpson to officer in charge, British Interned in Switzerland, 9 July 1917, TNA FO 383/329.

6

Sport and internment

Summer, field and indoor sports

As seen in the previous chapter, work, vocational training and education were important in the rehabilitation of men who had suffered long periods of incarceration, physical and emotional deprivation, injury and pain. These occupations helped internees adjust to the routines of normal life and prepared them to return to employment after the war was over, with the hope of a future livelihood and the restoration of their masculine role of provider. Work though is not all there is to life, and it only occupied a fraction of the internees' time. Outside working hours there was still plenty of time to fill. During the Edwardian years, when many of the enlisted men had grown up, sport was an integral component of life for many of them. For many working-class men and boys, association football filled an important role in their weekly routines, either through taking part or as spectators. Professional football was, by the end of the nineteenth century, an established form of mass-market, commercial entertainment, and most British communities had a team to collectively support.[1] The sport had become part of a national culture, 'one that resonated with the realities of working-class life, a collective struggle of a team against a hostile world'.[2] Football, or 'footer' as some of the men called it, was already being recognized outside Britain as the national game which was being played in other countries. In a letter to Private James Gray, a prisoner of war in Germany, later interned in Switzerland, a Swiss friend, Madame von Duton, wrote, 'I wish your son a lot of success in your national game, football. My grandchildren are all very fond of that game which they play at school.'[3] Football was played in Switzerland, thanks to the presence there of British professionals and students in boarding schools who formed teams and invited Swiss to join in. In the 1870s there were teams in Geneva, Châtelaine, Vevey and Montreux. Many Swiss gymnastic teachers, attracted to British sports, introduced football into many schools in the 1880s and 1890s.[4] The Swiss liberal constitution put no restrictions on freedom of assembly or association, and so sports clubs were able to thrive. By 1914 there were 115 football clubs in the Swiss Football Association.[5] By the time war broke out, football was becoming popular among the Belgians, Germans and Swiss, for whom it was a sport of boarding and business schools, technical colleges and polytechnics.[6]

Football spread into the urban industrial towns and cities of Germany, where it was less of a working-class game as it was imported via British tradesmen, businessmen, engineers and sales representatives from the textile factories of Northern England.[7] Sports historian Tony Collins, in *Sport in Capitalist Society*, identifies that young men who took up the game outside Britain were largely drawn from the middle-class technical and managerial classes. Football was played by German soldiers during the war both as a diversion and to strengthen morale. According to Christian Koller and Fabian Brände in their cultural history of the game, *Goal!*, football allowed high-ranking officers to use sport to gain social recognition for themselves among the other ranks, thereby providing a stabilizing influence. This association of football with the military led to a Germanization of the sport where 'determination, bravery, fortitude and discipline were attached to the existing British values'.[8]

For the French, pre-war sport played a less important social role. Gymnastics, akin to drill, was the only exercise practised in most schools. After the defeat of 1871, Frenchmen turned towards manners and dandyism for self-expression, leading to what Arnaud Waquet defines as a crisis of masculinity.[9] No official provision for sport was made by the French military until, after a mutiny in 1917, measures were taken to improve the well-being of soldiers, including recreational activities. Before this, *Poilus*, who had seen their British allies playing football began to play too.[10] *Poilu*, meaning hairy one, was the nickname given to French soldiers, the equivalent of the British Tommy. In prison camps French POWs had no hesitation about joining in the games of their British and Belgian fellow prisoners.[11] Waquet identifies playing football in prison camps as a contribution to football's diffusion throughout Germany.[12] Belgian soldiers had been encouraged to play football by King Albert I who arranged for thousands of balls and hundreds of boots to be delivered to all regiments.[13]

Sport offered a way for athletically gifted working-class males 'to gain respect in their community and a potential route out of manual labour'.[14] Cricket and rugby were popular sports among the British that had more of a cross-class appeal, but for the middle and upper classes, professionalism was shunned, and an amateur ethos prevailed during the early twentieth century. Boxing was a sport embedded among the different nationalities of armies involved in the war. Individual sports, such as boxing and athletics, provided not only personal advancement for the athletes but also entertainment and involvement for spectators through betting. Games were rarely played between the social classes.

Sport was one of the early factors in stabilizing the mental state of the British male civilians interned in the Ruhleben camp. Beginning with casual kickabouts, teams were soon formed, and fixtures were organized as part of a league system, along with the acquisition of balls and team uniforms. Ketchum recalled that each of the men involved 'knew what barrack teams would play today, tomorrow and for weeks ahead: he was living in a better organized world, and was therefore less governed by impulse and suggestion'.[15] Sport therefore played a functional role in establishing not only a form of control but also a means of planning ahead and looking to a future in circumstances where those interned had no way of knowing how long they would be detained or what might happen to them, depending on the war's outcome. Sport played an important role in developing a sense of identification. Men used the term 'we' to describe their own barrack's team and had a set of shared goals whether they were players or not.[16] Sport in Ruhleben gave participants with talent higher prestige than any other activity: 'There is no surer passport to being influential and respected in Ruhleben Camp than proficiency in sports'.[17] Sport introduced into the camp familiar formalities from pre-war life: uniforms, team colours, numbers on shirts, score boards, mascots and cheering. There was even a *Handbook of the Ruhleben Football Association* produced in September 1915.[18] The internees' journal *In Ruhleben Camp* published from 5 June 1915 featured news of teams and competition results for prizes of cups and medals supplied from Berlin that re-echoed the interests of the men which provided circular reinforcement of their sporting interests through feedback.[19] Top football officials were mainly ex-professional players, who had had the misfortune to be in Germany when the war began. They were generally admired throughout the camp. Programmes were produced for football, rugby and cricket matches. There were tennis tournaments, a golf club with membership cards for an improvised course, lists of local rules that took into account camp conditions, score cards and officially headed team and club notepaper. Men who had been snatched out of one social world succeeded, under difficult conditions in building another.[20] For Ketchum, the ritual and ceremony associated with sport, though unnecessary to physical survival, were of deep psychological importance; 'By dramatizing man's petty activities they rescue them from insignificance and endow them with dignity and value'.[21] More than this, historian Panikos Panayi in *Prisoners of Britain* claimed that sport in the all-male environment of both civilian internment camps and prisoner-of-war camps could be a substitute for previous lives.[22] Sporting events, festivals and training or playing for amusement were attempts to carry on with the normalities of life. Sport 'relieved boredom and created a sense of camaraderie or positive mental unity'.[23] Panayi collates information to demonstrate that in Britain most camps, for both civilian internees and military prisoners of war, had sports facilities provided by the authorities.

Sport developed more sophisticated structures in the civilian camps where men were interned for a long period of time, allowing a settled infrastructure, leagues and routines to develop, such as at Douglas on the Isle of Man, where German civilians were interned for the duration of the war, which had two playing fields with five tennis courts, a football pitch and running track. In one week in April 1916 there was a 'football world championship' on Wednesday and on Thursday it was training day for the sports club.[24] There was a tennis tournament there in July 1915. Civilians at Wakefield camp had similar facilities, several sports fields, tennis and a gymnasium, while Stobs Camp in the Scottish Borders held a sporting festival.[25] For military prisoners too, camps provided sporting facilities: for example, at Rosyth POWs had access to a sports field and a bowling alley, at Leigh there were three recreation grounds, in Jersey there was an exercise field and sea bathing and at Colsterdale there were facilities for football, handball, rounders and gymnastics.[26] Naval prisoners at Oswestry found talking about football with their British guards acted as an icebreaker in communicating as well as helping them improve their English.[27]

British prisoners of war held in some German camps had similar access to sporting activities. Officer prisoners at Gütersloh played hockey, tennis, fives, football and cricket. Being officers, they were trusted on their word of honour to leave the camp on parole to enjoy country walks in the surrounding area.[28] At Holzminden, a camp with high security for prisoners who had a history of escape attempts, there was a *Spielplatz* with areas for football, hockey, tennis courts, parallel bars and baseball for Canadians. There was even a mock race meeting with betting in the camp, where the prisoners acted as horses. Games were important for fitness and morale but were withdrawn by the German authorities after an arc light was broken, even though the prisoners paid for the damage, showing that sport could be used as a form of discipline, a privilege or reward for good behaviour that could be withheld as an instrument of control.[29] This and the diversion and preoccupation it provided prisoners longing for home or escape could assist in the management of the men and helped the smooth operation of the camps by acting as an outlet for aggression. While most of the ordinary soldiers had work to occupy them for much of the day, sometimes outside the walls of the camps, the officers who did not have to work had more time to devote to sport. It was not only imprisoned men for whom sport was used as a disciplinary tool. Particularly after the Armistice in 1918, sport was used to occupy the troops and maintain control as they awaited demobilization.[30]

For men of the internees' generation, physical activity would have been integrated into their education. The public schools and grammar schools attended by British officers were renowned for their playing fields and sports, but since the Boer War, from around 1904, Swedish drill as practised by the military was incorporated into the curriculum in elementary schools. From 1906 games such as cricket, football and hockey, although supplementary to drill, were accepted as part of the curriculum for all boys, regardless of class.[31] Nevertheless, for many children lack of a playing field or adequate outdoor space restricted access to organized games. In France, pre-war physical education was confined to the rather static gymnastics.[32]

Within the British army, sport had become an officially sanctioned and established part of military life by the First World War. In *Sport and the Military* Tony Mason and Eliza Riedi illustrate how sport was valued not just as a leisure activity but had other benefits for the army. These benefits included increasing fitness, discouraging drunkenness, enhancing relations between officers and men, helping build a regimental identity and improving morale.[33] Other benefits important within the context of internment were that sport could help prevent boredom and provide interest and also develop physical confidence and rebuild strength and stamina for men who had perhaps been immobile for months previously.[34]

Sport, as an important part of civilian life, could provide a vital link with normality and home and played a role in rehabilitation and convalescence of the injured in neutral Switzerland. Sport was therefore promoted among the internees and those who were able participated enthusiastically. Before their capture, the men would have joined in with the exercises and games of the Army Gymnastic Staff behind the lines. Not only were games popular but, according to George Newman, the chief medical officer responsible for physical training in schools, by 1917 the experience of games behind the front lines had changed the attitude of soldiers to physical activities. 'These men had been spectators, rather than players of games, but the enthusiasm of the Army Gymnastic Staff led soldiers to resent the professionalism of games back in England, to wish to continue playing games when the war was over, and to express a desire to inculcate a love of games in their children as well' was the verdict of historian

Joanna Bourke in *Dismembering the Male: Men's Bodies, Britain and the Great War*.[35] This probably overstates the case as sport was already an important part of working-class popular culture by the late nineteenth century. Football in particularly was popular as an informal game played on urban streets, with organized works, church and community clubs and also as a professional game for spectators to support and watch and that boys could aspire to play for. The physical culture surrounding masculinity in which Bourke identified the influence of sport and physical training on the preparation of young men for military service and also noted the concerns derived from the rise of sport as a form of entertainment, a passive rather than active interest. 'Britain was "a land of sportsmen" – so read the legend. In practice, it was increasingly admitted that men talked sport, read sport, looked on life through sport spectacles … but practised no form of sport themselves.'[36] Sport was, therefore, something that internees of whatever background would have been familiar with and understood, although for many it would have been as spectators rather than as players, a role that played an important part in the experience of internee sport. The conditions of modern warfare forced soldiers to develop new skills and gave birth to what Waquet defines as 'a more manly model of masculinity, that of the soldier-sportsman'.[37]

For the wounded, physical activity was important in regaining strength and body confidence as part of a holistic healing process as well as being a means to promote morale, combat homesickness and depression and provide an interest. British and Canadians with facial, chest and arm injuries played football during their convalescence, and sport was introduced into French rehabilitation centres to enable the body to recover its mobility.[38]

As the internees arrived in Switzerland, they soon realized that they were in the midst of a sporting community where football, lawn tennis, boxing, skating, skiing and ice hockey were freely indulged in, according to the season.[39] Hotel facilities and resort infrastructure, such as tennis courts, ice skating rinks, playing fields and mountain railways made a wide variety of sports available. In the first page of the first article in the first edition of the internees' magazine *British Interned Mürren*, in an essay entitled 'Life in Mürren', there is a paragraph that emphasizes the importance of sport in the daily life and routines of internees. 'For sports, we have the Grand Hotel des Alpes oval, which is used exclusively for men's games, and is the real centre of interest for most of the men.'[40] This emphasis never abated, as a later edition of the magazine, renamed *British Interned Magazine* in January 1918 and distributed across the region of British internment, shows that the chief vice of the Interned Prisoner of War is playing football, cricket, hockey etc. They are so depraved that at times they will indulge in those vices in the pouring rain. The only way they can be tempted to desist is by the offer of a meal.[41]

During the warmer months, the British in Mürren had almost constant use of the Hotel des Alpes ground for cricket, football and baseball. Inter-hotel cricket and football tournaments took place and daily matches provided recreation for the men. Officers, who were able, joined in these matches and also supported them financially.

> The officers have paid the management of Hotel des Alpes Frs 200.00 for damages to tennis courts, owing to football and further paid the management of the Grand Hotel Kurhaus, Frs 15.00 for each player on these tennis courts. It is estimated that this will cost Frs 450.00 thus approximately the officers will have spent Frs 650.00 in order to give the men the whole use of the Hotel des Alpes ground. This sum will be defrayed out of the Officers' Sports Fund, to which at present the weekly contribution is Frs 2.00 per week from resident officers. The Swiss Authorities allow some outside football matches to be played.[42]

As well as the sports ground of the Hotel des Alpes, thanks to the support of activities organizer Arnold Lunn, the internees had free use of the tennis courts at the Palace Hotel, as football and cricket grounds. The men felt especially fortunate in obtaining this concession as flatland for football pitches was difficult to obtain in some parts of Switzerland.[43]

Although football matches had been organized at Chateau d'Oex by a group that called itself the 'Merton Club',[44] the internees there had no proper 'footer field' until the spring of 1918, when one was hired at great expense.[45] It was put to use immediately and on Easter Sunday a team of officers was beaten 3–0 by a team of sergeants. That this took place on Easter Sunday shows a change in attitude and a promotion in the importance of sport, as in 1916, the Montreux Football Club had asked to play against Chateau d'Oex internees on a Sunday, their only free day, but the Senior British Officer Colonel Earle had to forbid it, against his own wishes, in deference to the clergy.[46] The next day, on Easter Monday, there were trial games, preliminaries for a big match, Chateau d'Oex against Rougemont, in which the home team was beaten 3–0 by the smaller, neighbouring community. On the same day, there was a 'Marathon Race' which attracted eleven runners. Although it was called a marathon, the distance of the route was only about six miles, run from Rougemont and finishing on the 'footer field'. The race was won in less than thirty-five minutes by Private

Grogan, with Captain Harrington coming in second. After an exhibition football match, presumably to show off their pride in the newly acquired pitch, prizes were awarded by Major P. J. Bailey to all who had completed the course.

Football was organized across the British and French internment regions. The *British Interned Magazine* and the *Journal des Internés Français* both give frequent and regular accounts of football matches. Competitions were organized between hotels, resorts and sometimes internationally between internees of different nationalities and Swiss teams. The importance of sport was officially recognized by the British and details of activities were sent to London in the monthly reports despatched by Lieutenant Colonel Picot. This report from the autumn of 1916 shows that sport was important enough to be of interest to the War Office in London:

> Football – matches have been played at Chateau d'Oex against British Internees and at Interlaken against Swiss. A match is being arranged to be played at Berne against a Swiss football club. No football, tennis and hockey possible at Mürren since 16 October.[47]

Outdoor sports were confined to the summer and early autumn as at other times the ground was covered with snow. The British later had a Football Challenge Cup to compete for, a silver one, scarcely over a foot high but which 'symbolised the British pride in lusty strength and healthful sports and the visible sign of our vaunted prowess'.[48] The Sports Committee intended to send the trophy to the proposed War Museum in London as an exhibit after the war was over, demonstrating how important the sport had become as signifier of national identity, worthy of memorialization. As in Ruhleben civilian camp, sporting skill was a means by which men could gain recognition from their peers; for example, 'no member of the football team was more admired for clean play, pluck and general sportsmanship than "young Harris" and probably no player in Mürren has so captivated the hearts of the crowd'.[49]

British internees developed a league system with matches played by teams representing the different hotels in the villages, which developed a sense of rivalry between hotels within the internment communities. In Mürren, the Palace Hotel football team claimed it was going strong in 1917, having won 7 out of 8 points. Although only winning by small margins, they claimed to have shown a remarked superiority with some good goals from Thacker against the Jungfrau and from 'Curly' Hunter and Walker against the Edelweiss.[50] Even so, the Palace's rivals from the Hotel Eiger also celebrated a particularly strong team that dominated the local league. The long awaited match-of-the-season on 13 July 1917, top of the league Eiger against the second position Palace Hotel, turned out to be a disappointment as it was so one sided. The Palace team was completely outclassed; the first goal was scored against them in just three minutes, with the Eiger forwards demonstrating 'the sort of football spectators love to watch'.[51] Palace played poorly in comparison, the final score being 3–0 to Eiger. Perhaps a hint at the physical condition of the convalescent internees, a player referred to as 'poor old Buck' was compared to a wounded war horse in the second half of the game. The Eiger bookmaker was disappointed too, the result giving little profit from gambling. In another match on 9 July, the Eiger team met the Hotel Regina squad. The Regina managed to score first but 'Newman equalised and from then on the Regina gave way to the far-superior team of the Eiger'.[52] Regina were bottom of the league with just 3 points, but there was a good reason for this poor performance. Although the Regina was one of the larger hotels, 75 per cent of the men there were more seriously injured. The team 'consisting as it does of "cripples", has put up some stiff fights against overwhelming odds. Much credit is due to their sportsmanship in turning out'.[53] Other hotel teams in the Mürren league were the Jungfrau, Edelweiss, Alpenruh and Bellevue.

Sport provided the means for mixing not just between social classes but also between different nationalities. In front of a large group of spectators, on 26 November 1916, the Swiss first team of FC Berne played a match against a team of British from the Bernese Oberland, managed by Mr Buxton, previously a player at Bristol City FC. The match ended with the Berne side winning 9–3. After the game, the internees were presented to the British ambassador, and there were speeches, cheers and applause. This match was reported within days for French readers in the *Journal des Internés Français*.[54] Ten months later, the Berne team, Young Boys, came out to Mürren to play against a team of British internees and were due to play a return match in Berne although there were difficulties getting permission for the trip.[55] This was probably due to transport restrictions caused by fuel shortages. Later, the Chateau d'Oex team played against La Servette of Geneva in September 1918.[56]

Belgians and French too, enjoyed football, a game encountered for the first time by many *Poilus* when they saw their allies playing. Plans to create a football society in Berne by French internees with the title *Poilu FC*, affiliated to FC Berne, were announced in January 1917. FC Berne offered to contribute to the new sports club and put their training ground at the disposal of the French internees.[57] The team played its first official match the following spring, when Poilu FC Berne played against a team of French and Belgian students studying in Neuchatel at FC Berne's ground. The players had the ardour of a trooper coming out of his trench to mount an assault on the position of his enemy, who must be removed at all costs, was how the *Journal des Internés Français* described this game of the *beau sport*.[58]

In Spiez a sports club, *Centre Sportif des Internés de Spiez*, was formed by Lieutenant Martin for the French internees there. Its professed goal was to distract internees and to allow them to recover their weakened health. Plans were made for friendly matches with neighbouring French, English, Belgian or mixed teams. Monsieur Legrand at the Hotel Lötschberg was responsible for membership.[59] In a match with a British team interned in Gunten, the first team of the *Centre Sportif de Spiez* lost by 7-0 with Sergeant Wilson's performance reported as particularly remarkable. The French report of the same match noted that the English team were better trained but were far from always dominating.[60] In a game between the second teams, the British were again victorious, this time beating the French 5-0.

The *Sporting Club Franco-Belge des Internés d'Engelberg* was organized by French and Belgian officers with Swiss *Commandant de Place*, Major Gros and Monsieur d'Ivry as honorary club presidents. There were two sections, one for football and the other for physical culture and athletic sports, demonstrating how popular football had become among the French soldiers, even before sport was officially sanctioned by their military authorities. The acting president was Sub Lieutenant Podevin, a well-known French sportsman, who by the spring of 1917 was studying in the Olympic Institute at Lausanne where courses were offered that combined sport with traditional subjects. The *Sporting Club Franco-Belge* had seventy members and, weather permitting, trained daily in the *Salle de Culture Physique*. The team wore blue shirts bought with the society's funds and white shorts, donated by a Lucerne ladies' committee.[61] In a friendly international match on 1 November 1916, a team of Belgians were beaten by the French, 11-3.[62] The Belgians improved and in a follow-up friendly game less than a couple of weeks later, although still easily beaten, lost by the much smaller margin of 5-1.[63] A combined team of Allies, Belgian and French, from Engelberg descended on Lucerne to meet the second team of FC Lucerne which beat them 2-0. Completing the international theme of the match, the referee was an Englishman named Flynn.[64] The Engelberg team played again against FC Lucerne at Lucerne on Sunday 10 June 1917. Lucerne were beating the Engelberg team, handicapped by the repatriation of its best players, 3-1 at half-time, but a violent storm caused the match to be abandoned.[65] It is interesting that those referred to as the best players had been repatriated as that indicates that they were the most seriously injured, with little chance of recovery, despite their participation in sport. Presumably their injuries were of the upper body. Another game by a team of French and Belgian Allies took place in Neuchatel on 16 December 1917 when the *Association Franco-Belge* played on the ground of Cantonal FC against a team of internees from Geneva, Neuchatel were leading 3–0 at half-time, eventually winning 5–2. Members of the public attended as spectators, showing wider interest in the games than just that of the players.[66] In the same region, at Peseux near Neuchatel, the *Association Franco-Belge* met FC Comète, losing 7–0. Again the internees were said to be missing their repatriated team members.[67]

Another international match took place in Fribourg when a British team from Chateau d'Oex met Stella FC de Fribourg in March 1917. International sporting events often had a ceremonial aspect with music, songs and speeches common; for example, the British entertained the Fribourg team with a serenade of bagpipes before some speeches after the game organized by *La Société Française et les Internés Franco-Belges de Fribourg*.[68] As in civilian Ruhleben camp, associated ritual and ceremony were used to endow the sporting event with dignity and value.[69]

German internees played football too; although reports of matches in their internee magazine are few there is plenty of photographic and other evidence. A team interned in Appenzellerland, with a league player from Cologne in goal, played against FC Au in St Galler-Rheintal in the late autumn of 1916. The Germans lost by 4–2, but according to FC Au's report, they were an example of the endurance of wounded German soldiers.[70]

Cricket was played enthusiastically during the summer months by the British internees. The various hotels had their own teams, as they had for football. Because the sports pitches were covered by snow in winter, the football and cricket seasons were concurrent. As well as good football players, the Eiger Hotel housed some strong cricketers. Indeed, the Eiger men seemed to be victorious in every sport in which they took part. In July 1917, every man in the Eiger contributed his winnings to help celebrate the seven firsts, seven seconds, six thirds, an individual championship, a second runner-up, the football championship, runners-up in the tug of war and the hotel championship which were all won by representatives of the Hotel Eiger.[71] Perhaps to encourage a more competitive approach from men interned in the Hotel Alpenruh, Corporal H. D. 'Bert' Munyard presented an engraved silver medal to be won by the best all-round sportsman in that hotel. Munyard himself was a keen sportsman, having played football in his prison camp in Germany and for the Chateau d'Oex team, as well as being involved in boxing, which explains the remark 'Luckily for the remainder of us, he is barring himself'.[72]

These sporting activities were organized by committees of internees and were not provided for them by the authorities. This was also how activities had been organized by guests in the alpine resorts before the war who formed their own amusement committees, tobogganing and skating clubs.[73] People with an interest in a particular sport or pastime clubbed together to organize facilities and events in individual hotels and across resorts as a whole.

An inspection of the internment 'camps' at both Mürren and Chateau d'Oex in the autumn of 1916, by W. E. Hume-Williams for the Red Cross, noted that the men were excellently fed and were so rapidly recovering under the influence of good food and good air that they already played football and were looking forward to skating and winter sports generally in December.[74] The report from Chateau d'Oex, appended to Picot's monthly report for November 1917 when arrangements were in hand for the winter, questions how these activities were to be paid for and shows that sports there were run by a committee led by Major Jones, the officer in charge of sports and games:

> You told me you would fix a compulsory subscription for the men for recreations. I should be glad if you could name me the sum. I think, more than ever, that the men ought to subscribe, and I think there ought to be a fixed rate for all the British soldiers in Switzerland.[75]

Another report from Chateau d'Oex shows that Colonel Earle arranged to collect old newspapers and sold them in Vevey, the proceeds going to a fund for sports and recreations.[76] The problem of how sporting activities should be funded in Mürren was solved, with costs met by officers and civilians, in return for the unpaid labour of the ordinary soldiers, thereby reinforcing class differences and discipline through patronage as well as fostering good relations between officers and other ranks. The scheme continued all year round to include winter as well as summer sports:

> All arrangements for the ice-rink at Hotel des Alpes are completed, the whole finance being borne by Officers and Civilians. The men will have free access to the rink, and in return will assist the Swiss ice-men to sweep and prepare the ice in the evenings.[77]

Although officers with their higher incomes paid for the hire of pitches and rinks, ordinary soldiers contributed to running costs. In Mürren, the Eiger men led the way, by pledging to contribute 40 centimes each pay day towards sport, and the hotel's sports committee paid 50 centimes each month to a central committee.[78] For football and cricket, 10 centimes were given each pay day from all ranks whether they played or not. All might benefit as if they didn't take part they could watch. There are 'few pleasanter pastimes than sitting on slopes in the sun, and watching a really keen game of cricket or football' *British Interned Magazine* told its readers.[79] The running costs were high with a good football costing at least 30 francs but lasting only for about four matches. Extra expenses were needed for travel to away matches. The Mürren Boxing Club had its own system for financing its activities. Captain Lister was the club president and Corporal Williams the honorary secretary. Each hotel had its own representative on the committee: Private McCuire for the Alpenruh, Private Buchanan for the Bellevue, Edelweiss and Alpina, Private Jones for the Eiger and Seaman Chandler for the Jungfrau. One franc was collected monthly on the second pay day, presumably because other subscriptions were due on the first. It was not necessary to be a boxer to join the club as membership covered admission costs to watch the contests organized. Private Buchanan and Corporal Buckley acted as instructors free of charge on Monday, Wednesday and Saturdays evenings. The boxing club hoped that many men would join and support 'this healthy and manly sport'.

On 28 April 1918, fighters came from across the internment zones to Interlaken to take part in an event promoted by Fighting Jack Georgy which was well patronized by British officers, NCOs and men. There were five bouts at different weights. Fighting Jack himself beat middleweight Dejoice of Geneva with a knockout. Private Franklin of the Queen's Regiment interned in Chateau d'Oex beat Belgian internee Désiré Depieter and Ted Simeth of Geneva knocked out Private Vaughan of Meiringen and Private Wilkins of the Norfolk Regiment beat Private Starr of the 4th Dragoon Guards, both interned in Interlaken, again by a knockout. In Chateau d'Oex on 25 January 1918, a four-round novice competition in the *Grand Salle* was promoted by Captain Chapman. There were eight fights with a 50 franc prize for the winner of each. One of the fighters, Lieutenant Corporal Egan, who not only conceded much weight but also had only one eye, put up a plucky fight but was counted out in the second round.[80] Several boxing matches between Swiss and English champions were held in Chateau d'Oex. These spectacles were without precedent in the valley and attracted not only internees but also members of the public, male and female, as spectators. Paillard, the Chateau d'Oex chronicler, recognized that despite objections that could be made, the sport developed energy, courage and endurance.[81]

Further evidence of the popularity of boxing was discovered among the private papers of former internees. Private James Gray, originally from West Ham in London, owned a photograph of a group of men in front of Chateau d'Oex station with 'departure of three champion Swiss boxers from Chateau d'Oex' written on it with the date 17 March 1917.[82] Among the papers of regular soldier, Lance Corporal Munyard, is a reference to his involvement in army boxing in 1912. During his captivity in Döberitz military prison camp, he wrote an article about boxing for the *Gazette de Döberitz*, a journal produced in both French and English, describing a boxing club formed in the POW camp with two punch balls sent by friends in England. While the members were learning boxing, 'they were at the same time improving their health, for there is perhaps no sport which makes a man more quick and nimble, while at the same time exercising every muscle in the body'.[83] The article said the club was particularly fortunate in having such capable 'professors' as 'Bert' Munyard and a couple of others, as instructors. Among Munyard's personal papers was a large collection of photographs from his time as an internee, many of them not only of boxers but also of other sports, such as tennis, gymnastics, bob sleighing, skiing, football teams and of individual internees, often sent by his comrades as souvenirs.[84]

In Engelberg French and Belgians, and Germans, interned at different times, made use of the sporting facilities of the Kurhaus, where they boxed in the main hall.[85] A big difference between French, Belgians and Germans in sport was that the more egalitarian French and Belgian officers took part in the sports with their men. There were also bouts between boxers of different ethnicities, a photograph shows an African, Senegalese fighter in the ring with a white opponent surrounded by a crowd of spectators, including children.[86] A three-round boxing match, sandwiched between songs and a piano concert, was an unusual part of the entertainment for French internees on Christmas Eve 1917 in the *Salle des Fêtes* at Leukerbad. The fight was between 'our friend Decourcelle', champion of Amiens, and Haid Ourbil, the 'negro champion' who had come over from America specially 'to raise the glove'.

Boxing wasn't the only individual combat sport available. There was a fencing room for French internees at *Le Foyer de Soldat* in the Hotel Eiger on Belpstrasse in Berne.[87] Belgian and French soldiers in particular, some of whom had been fencing 'professors' before the war, excelled with the foil and sabre; in a military tournament at Neuchatel, in which officers of the Swiss Army and Allies competed, they held their own against the Swiss exponents of fencing.[88] For the British, success was limited to the bayonet competition, where they beat all comers in the team matches and took the first and many other prizes for individual fighting.

Gymnastics was another sport popular among internees, both as individuals or in teams. At Salvan, one of the smaller internment centres for French and Belgian

Sport and Internment 113

Figure 6.1 Boxing match between French internees. Courtesy of Privatbesitz Rita Eller-Banz, Engelberg.

internees, roads were rare and footpaths rocky so it was judged that it would be best to have gymnastic exercise on a miniscule piece of flatland that transformed into an ice rink in winter.[89] Athletics too enabled men to not only regain and improve fitness, but a competitive element gave added interest and an incentive to train. Two months after their arrival, interned officers in Chateau d'Oex organized a sports day for Swiss National Day on 1 August 1916.[90] There were jumping competitions, athletics events and sack races plus other amusing races for the local children, while a festive atmosphere was provided by the internees' orchestra. At an athletics event held at Chateau d'Oex in September 1918, teams from Mürren, Seeburg and Interlaken joined men interned locally in competition. There were the usual athletics events plus a three-legged race and pillow fighting perched on a bar. Distances were in yards and miles for the British competitors but in metres for the French and Belgian internees and Swiss civilians taking part. The event attracted nearly 500 spectators. A later sports day, held in Interlaken, drew 120 spectators from Mürren as well as local inhabitants. The Mürren team won most of the open events, including the mile, the relay race and tug of war. Apparently the Belgians 'put up a good fight but lacked science'.[91] French internees in Bagnes celebrated Bastille Day 1917 with two days of festivities that included a day of games on the Sunday: a sack race, cock fight and various other contests, which the local Swiss helped organize.[92] A photograph from Engelberg shows the start of a running race with French and Belgian internees in a variety of athletics costumes.

Swimming galas were also held occasionally, with outdoor swimming in the lakes, such as those in Lake Lucerne at Seeburg in the early and late summer of 1918 and the Water Carnival at Gunten on Lake Thun in September.[93] Watersports were available in Lausanne, where men could bathe in Lake Geneva and play water polo.[94] At Engelberg, there was a swimming pool used by French and later by German internees.[95]

Most resorts and some hotels had tennis courts. Tennis, a middle-class sport in Britain, was played by both officers and men. A tournament for officers, which included a ladies' singles competition for their wives and daughters, was organized in Interlaken in September 1918 but had to be abandoned because of rain. Prizes were therefore awarded to those with the highest percentage of wins over the season.[96] Another week-long tennis tournament in Montana, due to take place in August 1918, had faced a similar fate because of heavy rain.[97]

Sport was available at the convalescent centre at Seeburg, which opened in July 1917 with thirty NCOs and men accompanied by three officers, while twenty-two NCOs and men were in hospital in nearby Lucerne. A Seeburg football team organized a game with *Sporting Club des Internés d'Engelberg* to be played on FC Lucerne's Tribschen ground.[98] The two teams met on 22 April 1917, with the Seeburg team reinforced by players from Chateau d'Oex. On a rainy day, there were few spectators watching Engelberg defeat the British team 5–0.[99] As well as football there were other sporting activities: tennis, billiards, fishing, swimming, walks and rowing. A monthly report from the officer in charge at Lucerne and Seeburg showed

Figure 6.2 French and Belgian internees line up to start a race, Engelberg, 1916. Courtesy of Talmuseum Engelberg.

how improvisation was important, both of equipment which was scarce and of the rules to enable all who wished to do so to take part, despite their incapacities.

> We have now got a tennis court and not at all a bad one. The net and racquets were provided for us by the Red Cross, and the poles for the surrounding net were cut by the men in the woods and the net itself we were lucky enough to buy off a fisherman for five francs. The court was opened by a Ladies' Singles between the Hon. Sec. of the local Red Cross and our landlady and has hardly been vacant since. We had a billiard tournament in which one-armed men got a start of 170 in 250 and which was won by Captain Coulston. And now we are in the midst of a fishing tournament. The fishing tournament and the tennis have been almost too successful, as it is at present almost impossible to get men to come for the walks we arrange in the lovely woods near us. In fact there was some talk on the part of my games committee of putting a time limit on the fishing tournament and allowing no one to fish for it before four in the morning.[100]

Another individual sport, in England enjoyed mostly by middle-class players, was golf. Officers interned in Montreux were able to join the golf club at Aigle. All British officers there were invited to be honorary members for a month. If they then chose to join, their membership subscription would be half the usual price. For those interned at Montreux, the boundaries within which they were allowed to wander freely were in a five-mile radius of the railway station. Aigle was twelve miles away but as that was where the golf course was, which was not considered to be out of bounds, membership extended the distance officers who joined the club could travel without permission.[101] A golf tournament for officers was held on the course there in the autumn of 1918.[102]

As some groups of internees, deemed less likely to recover from their injuries and illnesses, were repatriated home, it became more difficult to organize football and cricket games as the men not selected had got the impression that taking part in sport might spoil their chances of getting home, despite some teams bemoaning the loss of their best players to repatriation.[103]

Winter and mountain sports

Towards the end of the year, Switzerland was transformed from a green and sunny land to one covered by a thick blanket of snow; its lakes turned to ice with temperatures consistently below freezing, despite frequent blue skies and winter sunshine. The flat surfaces of sports pitches and tennis courts were then converted for use as ice rinks from November until the following spring.[104]

With no football or other games, the more adventurous among the internees turned their sporting interests towards less familiar activities, tobogganing, ice skating and skiing. For most of them, these sliding sports were a completely new experience. Among some of the officers, there might have been a few who had experienced winter sports as pre-war visitors to the Alps. Some German and French soldiers, especially those from Alpine regions, may have had experience of a mountain winter. Canadians would also have had experience of snowy winters lasting for months, but for most of the interned men an alpine winter was a completely new experience, offering either weeks of indoor confinement or new opportunities for sport and leisure despite the cold. When newly arrived as officer in charge in Interlaken, Major Ernest Collins visited Mürren to gain tips from the established centre there, his first impression was that it was freezing hard and all those who could ski were out and many others were learning.[105] The British and French internees' magazines give reports and images of winter sports activities, although this aspect of life is less prominent in the German publication. Evidence of German winter sporting activities is to be found in other sources, such as photographs and posters. A photograph album compiled by German internee Alexander Kirmmse in Engelberg contains images of sport in all seasons, including skiing, a ski race and mountain hiking.[106]

During their first winter in Switzerland, officers in Mürren took over the Palace Hotel ice rink. The 3.5-kilometre-long bobsleigh run was open to all internees. The British Interned Mürren Ski Club taught the men to ski and arranged tours and inter-hotel races.[107] The ski club included both officers and men; its chairman was Lieutenant Ralph du Boulay Evans (King's Own Shropshire Light Infantry), secretary Private Baillie and committee members Reverend J. D. McCready, Captain Edward Tristram R. Carlyon (10th Sherwood Foresters), Lieutenant Robert Henry Middleditch (Yorkshire Regiment), Private Foyster, Private Tyler and Arnold Lunn.[108] Officers subscribed 10 francs towards touring expenses; the lower ranks paid no fee. Skis could be hired through the club at 10 francs for the season. If a ski was broken, an extra 2 francs had to be paid before a replacement could be issued. For beginners there were lessons. A photograph of the Ski Club, dated November 1917, shows twenty-seven people.[109]

Those interned in Mürren were fortunate to have Arnold Lunn, a pioneer of the sport of downhill skiing, employed as an activities organizer. His father, Sir Henry Lunn, had started the Public Schools Alpine Sports Club as part of his tourism business, which ran several Swiss hotels, including the Palace and Grand Hotel des Alpes at Mürren. Arnold had spent much of his time in Switzerland since childhood and had been using skis since 1898 when he was a boy. In 1908 he founded the Alpine Ski Club, and in 1913 his book *Skiing* was published.[110] Lunn provided ski instruction and organized accompanied ski tours. The first excursion was to the foot of the Eiger Glacier with expenses borne by those taking part.[111]

Arnold Lunn was unfit for military service because of a leg injury from a climbing accident in Wales a few years earlier, an injury which left him with an open wound, which took twelve years to heal, and one leg two inches shorter than the other.[112] Perhaps this was an advantage when encouraging and teaching injured men to ski as he also had to adjust to life after serious injury. Being unfit for military duty, Lunn was fortunate to find a form of war work to which he was suited because of his involvement in his father's business in Switzerland. His first posting was among the wounded French officers in Montana.[113] Lunn was accompanied in Switzerland by his wife, Mabel, their infant son, Peter and a nanny. The family left London from Charing Cross station on 18 January 1916, so he was there to meet the first group of French prisoners to arrive from Germany. The Lunns organized the reception of the French, which required a great deal of administration, complicated by the health needs of the internees.[114] They then moved on, first to Montreux and then to Mürren where British prisoners began to arrive from July. Lunn was the managing director of the Palace Hotels in both Montana and Mürren.[115] The Lunn's, despite their seemingly privileged and safe position, were not exempt from the sorrows of the war. Two of Mabel Lunn's brothers were killed in action, one of Arnold's brothers was taken prisoner and held in camps in Germany and his other brother suffered a breakdown through trauma while serving in Mesopotamia. The work was not always easy; Lunn wrote to his mother in December 1916,

> Three or four times a week I take out skiing parties of officers, NCOs and men. This is a job which requires great patience and some little tact. You have so many people to deal with. ... There are the Swiss, the somewhat swollen-headed Dr Llopart (Swiss officer in charge in Mürren), the Colonel (Col Neish), the officers, the officers' wives. ... Regular Officers against one or two Canadian officers; one spends all one's time humouring people one would like to kick, or having violently to sit on people one rather likes.[116]

To keep his charges fit and also no doubt to pursue and share his own interest, Lunn arranged ski lessons and tests for both officers and ordinary soldiers, although he noted that most of the senior officers of the second batch of prisoners to arrive in Mürren skied well, reflecting their social background and pre-war lifestyles.[117] For those that wished, recently devised British Standard Ski

Tests were run following untested rules introduced during 1914. According to Lunn's secretary, Elizabeth Hussey, these rules formed a valuable test bed for discussions on technique after the war.[118] Lunn taught the internees a style of skiing originating in Scandinavia, using stem, Telemark and Christiania turns; the modern form of Alpine skiing was not yet in existence. Skiing at that time was for touring across country and an aid to mountaineering, with uphill climbs as important as sliding down. Unlike tobogganing and bobsleighing, skiing gave more freedom as at that time it was not done on prepared runs or pistes. At Mürren most of the officers and many of the men learnt to ski.[119] The internees in Mürren tried out Norwegian skis, even though these were unsuited to the steep slopes of Mürren. This didn't bother them as they had lots of free time in which to experiment.[120] On 19 February 1918, there was the first third-class Ski Test of the season, with Lunn and Marcel Kurz as judges, on a course on Winteregg Ridge from 'Khaki Cairn' to 'Test Finish'. The internees had renamed some of the landmarks; others were the 'Menin Gate', 'Kitchener's Crash', 'Hindenburg Line' (less formidable than it looked) and 'Regulars' Ramble'.[121] The third-class Test involved climbing 1,500 feet in twelve minutes. Style was taken into consideration; the habitual use of sticks to control the skis could lead to disqualification. Sliding downwards, the first 400 metres were steep and tricky, the remainder of the course was easy running through woods and shrubs. A candidate who could complete this section in twelve minutes could undertake any reasonable expedition with confidence. There were eight entrants in the test. All of them passed the uphill section, but although seven entrants completed the downward course only one of them, Captain Hall, managed to do so within the prescribed twelve minutes, even though he dropped his sticks. Sergeant Major Matthews broke a ski below a part of the course named 'Nose Dive' and was two and a half minutes over the time allowed. Major Barlow would have passed had the snow conditions been easier. Trooper Ormiston, Private Wright, Lieutenant White and Private Weaver did not complete the course quickly enough. Between 1916 and 1917, six internees and Mabel Lunn passed the second-class Ski Test in cross-country skiing, and nine passed the third-class Test. Captains Carlyon, du Boulay Evans and Sutherland, Lieutenants Franklin and Middleditch and Private Wells managed to pass both tests. Only one person took the third-class Test in 1918 as most who were interested had already passed the previous year.[122] A first-class test had not yet been devised, and so the second-class Test was the highest level of attainment. Those learning to ski and taking the tests were mixed groups of officers and men. In his report on skiing during the war, published in the *British Ski Year Book*, issued again in 1920 after a wartime break,

Arnold Lunn wrote that he thought it would have been 'a nasty jar to a Prussian officer to observe a senior British officer entering a ski test with three privates, and consenting to be judged by a Lieutenant and a civilian'. Even the republican Swiss, he thought, were a little surprised to see mixed parties of officers and men setting out for ski tours together but 'somehow, the atmosphere of the mountains is not conductive to military red tape'.[123]

From Mürren more confident skiers could enjoy skiing on the terrain around the village, making use of the Almendhubel mountain railway. The internees were grateful to the management of the Almendhubel for 'the very sporting way' they kept the railway open during the winter for the benefit of the interned.[124] From the top of the railway, internees and companions could come down on the toboggan run or ski.

Much of the information discovered about the activities of the group of skiers in Mürren comes thanks to the editorship of *British Interned Magazine* by ski and sport enthusiast Ralph du Boulay Evans. Evans, educated at Winchester School and at Cambridge, wrote in a humorous, at times sarcastic style but could also compose 'gentler, poetic prose'. Lunn wrote of him that he had inherited from his French ancestors 'Gallic wit and fire' and that he was 'a scientist with the soul of a poet'.[125] Evans also reveals his own admiration for Lunn in this mock-biblical piece which he wrote for the magazine:

> When the snow covered the ground ... then the prophet Lunn arose and spake unto his disciples, saying 'Arise, gird ye, get ye skis and come, we will climb up the hills and slide down again'. And the disciples of Lunn arose and girded themselves and bound the skis on their feet, and they climbed the mountains, and slid and turned, according to the words of the prophet Lunn. Then the prophet Lunn rejoiced greatly, and he sang a new song saying, 'The summer is past, and behold the winter cometh swiftly, and all men shall come unto me. For in summer all men do watch the footballers, playing with their football, but now they listen to my prophecies and will read the words of my book.'[126]

Ski tours offered opportunities to develop skills further after passing the tests. Skiing excursions, facilitated by special fares negotiated by Lunn, were offered by the local mountain railways.[127] Mr Liechti, manager of the Jungfraubahn and his assistant did everything in their power to make the trips a success.[128] One tour organized by the club was an excursion to Grindelwald on 17 February 1918. The skiers travelled part of the way on the Wengenalpbahn, on a stretch of line reopened specially for them by arrangement with the station master.[129] The more energetic members of the party donned skis and set off for Kleine Scheidegg, 'pursued by a volley of chaff from the "lazier" ones' who employed porters and had their skis carried up for them. Lunch was eaten on the verandah of the closed hotel before they set off downhill to Grindelwald. Snow conditions were not particularly good, and 'things were going badly for those in the rear owing to the "unselfishness" of Lunn who went ahead to show the way and took most of the snow with him. Four laggards in the rear amused the others by turning catherine wheels over precipices and other novel and entertaining evolutions.'[130] The scenery was too magnificent to pass by at speed, they claimed, so they took off their skis and walked the rest of the way. In Grindelwald they went for drinks in the Central Hotel where they met up with the Mürren curling team returning from games against Grindelwald.

The following month a large Mürren ski party enjoyed an excursion to the Jungfrau. They feasted on a breakfast of bacon and eggs at Wengen, tramped to the Eigergletscher station of the Jungfraubahn where they caught the train up to the Jungfraujoch from where they skied down to the Concordia Hut, their overnight accommodation, returning the next evening. A selection of comments, compiled by Evans, shows that the party had mixed feelings about the exhausting trip, comments such as:

> 'Simply hated it from start to finish'; 'Excellent'; 'The tunnel was as cold as charity'. 'Tried to get the porters to ski on to the Hut so as to have a fire started for when we arrived but all they did was tumble down in the snow'; 'Went down the slope like a dead fly falling down a window pane'; 'Lying on a table being fed with rum'; 'Could have cut the atmosphere in that hut with a knife'; 'The meat ration was good and sufficient'.[131]

These comments may give a clue as to why there was less enthusiasm for the next tour. Only Carlyon, Evans and Middleditch joined Lunn on the May ski trip, accompanied by mountain guides, Knubel, Bischoff and the Feuz brothers and porters to carry provisions.

The party reached the Jungfraujoch, where they slept, by train. On 18 May they crossed the Mönchjoch to the Finsteraarhorn Hut for the second night. Lunn was surprised by the amazing fitness of Carlyon who had lost an eye, Evans who had been shot in the arm and Middleditch whose leg had been broken by a shell; on one day they managed over twenty hours skiing, climbing and descending on the mountain to Meiringen.[132] Lunn wrote about this excursion for the *British Interned Magazine*, concluding it was 'altogether a most excellent trip, perhaps the finest ski tour that the writer has ever had the good luck to take part in'.[133]

In his many books, Lunn did not write much about his war work with the internees apart from his skiing relationship with the three British officers, Ralph du Boulay Evans, Bob Middleditch and Tristram Carlyon. 'To those war years I am indebted for the memory of a perfect friendship,' he wrote. Lunn and the three officers 'formed a ski-ing quartette, united by a love of mountains, of skiing and of passionate debate for we argued and quarrelled about a fine, confused array of themes, secular and divine'.[134] In Lunn's reminiscence work, *The Mountains of Youth*, he devoted an entire chapter to a single ski tour with his interned friends.[135] For Lunn, 'no expedition came within measurable distance of four perfect days spent with his three friends among the Oberland Glaciers', a memory that recurred again forty years later, in his 1958 book *The Bernese Oberland*, in which he informs readers that the three officers became his dearest friends.[136]

In the high Alps skiing is not confined to the winter months as snow lies on the peaks and glaciers all year round. In the late spring of 1917 three long glacier tours, led by Lunn, were undertaken. Parties of officers, non-commissioned officers and men climbed a fair number of skiable peaks such as the Ebenfluh, Gamilhorn, Mittaghorn and Oberaarhorn and crossed passes between Lötschental and the Grimsel.[137] In June 1917, Lunn with Captain Carlyon and Lieutenants Shillington and Evans, took a week-long skiing trip over the Jungfraujoch, via the Concordia Hut and the Rhone Valley.[138] It was through these ski tours that Lunn claims to have discovered the joys of spring skiing.[139] This ski tour convinced the party of the pleasures of summer glacier skiing; the ease of ascent on snow with a perforated crust, perfect for straight running owing to its excellent 'bite', was ideal for downhill Christianias and stemming turns.[140] On another tour, after the first night in a hut overlooking the Aletsch Glacier, the party was woken at 5.00 am by the guides struggling with the stove, a reference to the often invisible or anonymous Swiss men who made these tours possible. The skiers climbed much of the way on crampons, dragging their skis behind them on string attached to their rucksacks. The sun was so warm in June; they climbed shirtless, covering their faces with grease to avoid sunburn. After a couple of days, Lunn and Knubel split from the others to ski down to Grimsel while the rest continued to Kippel via the Grünhornlücke. The reason why Lunn and Knubel could not take the others with them was that the Grimsel area was fortified by the Swiss Army and so was out of bounds to internees. They were not left alone as they had guides, for whom they waited on the Concordiaplatz while they fetched provisions left the day before in the Concordia Hut. The two, plus the guides, went on to the Steiger Hut where they enjoyed views as far as Mont Blanc. Poor conditions on the return journey forced them to ski roped together before eventually taking off their skis and carrying them through a maze of crevasses down to green grass and wild flowers in the valley. Here the writer makes his first reference to the physical condition of the participants. 'Considering that not one member of the party, military or not, excepting of course the guides, could be considered perfectly fit, these two tours are a rather striking example of the use of skis in summer.' A third glacier tour in the beginning of July took them up the Ebenfluh and also the Gamilhorn, in what was possibly the first ski ascent of that mountain.[141] During the long winters, winter sport played an important role in occupying the internees as well as keeping them fit. Skiing for months at a time, many became quite proficient.[142]

These ski tours and the long, exhausting climbs the internees undertook before they could enjoy a run downwards are all the more remarkable when the injuries and disabilities of the participants are taken into account. Lunn often referred to the pain in his leg, which meant he had the problem of getting downhill on his one good leg, wearily dragging his lame limb.[143] Pain, though, is rarely mentioned by anyone in any of the descriptions of sporting activities. As already mentioned, Carlyon had lost an eye in battle and was imprisoned in Krefeld in Germany before coming to Switzerland. When

> Evans first arrived from Germany he could hardly manage an hour's climb. At the end of his first season he all but collapsed on the Great Scheidegg. ... He supported himself on two ski sticks, his head drooped. ... But he never gave in. If he set out to do a certain climb he arrived, abusive perhaps, but even when his body was still very ramshackle his spirit triumphed and somehow carried him to his goal. As I watched him striding down the road, I realised the great debt which many an Englishman owes to the little country which rescued them from barbed wire and restored them to health and the joy of life.[144]

At Leysin, where the internees were mostly tuberculosis patients, small groups were taken out almost daily for ski instruction by the local padré.[145] Skiers at lakeside Montreux could take a train to Les Avants and Sonloup, then run down the northern slopes to the lake at Clarens or cross to Malard and back to Les Pleiades from where there was a good run home.

Skiing was also an interesting and sometimes amusing pastime for spectators. Mrs Ormorod, an Oldham mother visiting her son Frank, courtesy of a Red Cross party, recalled on her return home:

> You could very soon tell the difference between an expert and a novice at skiing. It is really a splendid sight to see the Swiss people come down the sides of the

mountains – it is wonderful how they manage – for to me the skis look such clumsy things on their feet, but even the children manage them well. There is plenty of fun in watching a novice – he never gets far before coming down half-buried in the snow.[146]

Soldiers skiing in their military issue, uniform clothing, not really suitable for winter sports wear, gathered a lot of compacted snow on their garments if they fell and drying out clothes was a problem if they lacked a change of outfit. Letters home asked for more gloves and hats to give them spare pairs.

Not all the internees valued the opportunity to ski. In his report for the *British Ski Year Book*, Lunn wrote that the British Tommy did not take to skiing in any great numbers and that only about 20 per cent of the men who were fit to ski actually took up the sport with any keenness. Some of the men suspected that their officers wanted them to ski to keep them out of mischief. 'What use is skiing to the British working man?' asked one, who Lunn described as having Bolshevist tendencies.[147]

Skiing was not the only winter sport which had its enthusiasts among the internees. Most of the men preferred tobogganing, an easier activity for beginners. In Mürren, a female visitor noted the main sport was tobogganing. The toboggan track was reached by the Almendhubel mountain railway. The visitor preferred to watch, it being more fun to her to see others come tumbling down.[148] Another visitor, the mother of Private Harry Stock, had a go on a sledge but did not enjoy the experience and after one turn on the run refused to do it again. In his letter of thanks to his local newspaper, Stocks wrote,

> I got her to come down on a toboggan but could not get her to come down a second time. They have built a new railway, which goes straight up another 3,000 feet higher and there starts a toboggan run about two and a half miles long. I took her up on the railway but she would not come down on the run, so I came down on the run and met her at the bottom.[149]

The new railway Stock referred to was the Allmendhubel funicular which opened in 1912. Captain Hutchinson helped organize and promote tobogganing on the run.[150] Bobsleighs and sledges could be hired in the villages, where plenty were available, pre-war investments purchased in anticipation of tourists using them. In Engelberg, the results of a bobsleigh race with eight entries, gives evidence of this as most of the machines the teams rode had English names, such as Pepper, International, Peppermint and Tango. A pattern for a small bobsleigh was given to Chateau d'Oex internees, and they were looking into making some for sale.[151]

Officers at Leysin persuaded doctors to allow them a run on a bobsleigh. They got up two teams of five each, both of which included a female. The plan was to start out at 7.30 am, run down to a village four miles away where they would have breakfast, before continuing for a further six miles, returning by rail. For breakfast thirty eggs and bacon had been ordered, as the internees were all tired of bread and jam, the standard monotonous fare for breakfast in Swiss sanatoria. The trip didn't go as planned as the pilot of one of the bobsleigh teams overslept. The other team left without them and reached the breakfast place in fourteen minutes, although they had to pull the bobsleigh between 300 and 400 yards and give way to traffic on the road. They also had a narrow escape when they met a sleigh load of wood, hidden round a bend. To avoid a collision, the pilot steered into a bank. The first crew had already eaten breakfast by the time the bedraggled second team arrived, muddy and wet after having overturned. The second crew decided to walk home while the first continued the journey, returning by train.[152]

Sledging could be hazardous; the Leysin bobsleigh incident was not the only accident. French and Belgian internees were warned that winter sports could be dangerous after a Frenchman died following injuries received in a sledging accident. This tragic incident on 8 December 1917 killed Henri Arnoux of the 64 *Chasseurs Alpins* at the start of the descent from Salvan to Vernayaz in Valais.[153] Arnoux landed on a rock and died of internal injuries two days later in hospital in Martigny, leaving a wife and three children. Arnoux had been imprisoned since being wounded in January 1915 at Soissons and had been in Switzerland for a year before the accident. Swiss soldiers, with a rifle volley, ensured he had the honour of a military funeral.

After the death of Arnoux, internees were strongly advised in the *Journal des Internés Français* to have some prior training before launching themselves down the slopes for the first time. For sledging, as well as for skiing, they were told that learning ought to be done on a specified area of land where there was little danger.[154] It was in the interests of internees not to set off on ski excursions or long routes on sledges without careful preparatory exercises. Winter sportsmen were advised to avoid roads and busy paths with sudden contours, the route of which could present danger, not just to the slider but to other road users.

The French and Belgians in Engelberg organized winter sports activities as soon as the first snow appeared in November 1916. Luge, bobsleigh and skating runs were prepared and a committee formed to organize events.[155] They appreciated skiing but few of them actually did it, as, like most of the British, they were not familiar with winter sports. Sledging was most popular as it was easy to

Figure 6.3 French internees with a bobsleigh, skis and toboggan. Courtesy of Talmuseum Engelberg.

learn and didn't need expensive equipment. Sledges were readily available and the internees were happy with the existing 3 kilometre run.[156] In a luge race there in January 1917, twenty-two runners took part in the competition down the run from Gerschnialp. A few days later there was a bobsleigh race on the same track on 24 January, won by Soldier Thierry, Monsieur Huss and Sergeant Laborde.[157] This race was not exclusively for internees, as female names and that of a Swiss hotel owner and his wife were members of the teams of three.[158]

There were ski races under the auspices of the *Sport-Club d'Engelberg*, on 13 and 14 January 1917, in which internees could take part.[159] A 1 kilometre speed test reserved for internees was won by the Belgian, Puttevils; Lucas, another Belgian, came second and a Frenchman, Vial, third.[160] There were ten competitors in total, three Belgian and seven French.

The Germans who replaced the French and Belgians in Engelberg devoted themselves to sport. The officers liked to ski, and they organized various ski races. One of these was the first Central Switzerland Youth Ski Race which continued after the internees left. The Germans also liked ice hockey and bobsleighing. They formed an ice hockey club that carried on after their departure. Before the war, a bobsleigh run had been built in Engelberg, a facility used and developed by the Germans.[161] In these ways, the German internees played a role in developing the village as a winter sports centre. They had no problem integrating with local people through winter sports clubs as they were based in regions where their own language was spoken. At the Disentis Ski Club races, internees and civilians watched the racing and ski jumping. A special prisoners' race, *Anfängerrennen*, was organized for internees. Seven of them took part, racing over a distance of 1,500 metres. Those brave defenders of the Fatherland, swooped, dropping down until they finally landed among the cheers of their comrades, exclaimed the *Deutsche Internierten Zeitung*, but only one of them managed to reach the goal without falling.[162]

There are photographs of interned Germans as spectators at winter sports events, posing on bobsleds and skiing in Davos among the collection in the *Dokumentationsbibliotek Davos*.[163] A much-reduced season of winter sports, ice skating, bobsleigh, toboggan and ski races, continued at Davos throughout the war years. Tourists continued to come to Davos, although there were far fewer of them than in 1913.[164] At the Sanatorium in Davos Dorf sports equipment was available, which included skis, skates, sledges and an ice rink.[165]

Another winter sport, ice hockey was particularly popular with Canadians serving in the British army, who introduced the game to some of their British comrades. Teams representing the different internment centres would travel to play against each other and Swiss teams. The Chateau d'Oex ice hockey team beat one of the best Swiss teams, Rosey School of Gstaad 2–1. A couple of days later they were in action again in a tournament at Gstaad, in which the team succeeded in carrying off the Boorum Challenge Cup, after playing three matches in a single day, against Berne (5–1), Les Avants (3–2) and Rosey School (3–2). The following month there was another ice hockey tournament over two days in Caux on 2 and 3 February where the Mürren Canadian Hockey Team beat the Rosey team 8–0 and then drew a large crowd to watch them play against the Canadians of Chateau d'Oex in what was judged the best display of hockey seen so far at Caux. Chateau d'Oex beat Mürren 3–1 and went on to win the trophy after beating Berne 4–0 in the final. The results show that the standard of hockey played was variable; Chateau d'Oex and Mürren seemed equally matched, but in some games the results showed a wide discrepancy; Chateau d'Oex beat Bellerive 22–2 and against Caux they won 18–0.[166] This was due to the presence of Canadians among the internees in Mürren and Chateau d'Oex, places which also contained larger numbers of internees, making it easier to form teams and giving more choice of players.

On the way back from Caux on 4 February, the Mürren team stopped off at Chateau d'Oex to try and avenge their defeat of the day before. The home team were winning 2–1 at half-time. Although the game continued to be exciting, Mürren players were tired and the superior training of the Chateau d'Oex team was evident. Both teams were weary from the recent strenuous games of the Caux tournament. Chateau d'Oex went on to win 3–1. As a tribute to the success of the British Interned Hockey Club of Chateau d'Oex, the hotel keepers and businessmen of the district offered a challenge cup to be played for over the weekend of 16 and 17 February. Entries were received from many first-class Swiss teams. Before the war, Swiss hotel directors had realized the potential commercial impact of ice hockey, by organizing games for their guests and matches featuring top teams for them to watch.[167] Hotel owners played leading roles in the National Ice Hockey Federation.[168]

Other ice activities enjoyed by internees were ice carnivals, events that had been popular attractions before the war with tourists, such as the *Fête de Nuit* on the ice rink of the Hotel Cattani on 20 January 1917. These ice carnivals were popular attractions and on 11 February 1917 hotel owner and Engelberg's Mayor, Herr Cattani organized a skating festival. This event included an exhibition by 'professor of skating', Monsieur Huss, who performed some extraordinary figures, spirals and sitting pirouettes.[169] On 6 February 1918, there was an ice gymkhana at Mürren organized by Captain Hutchinson, with a mixture of sport in the form of speed racing contests, the spectacle of a Chinese lantern parade and the fun of a fancy-dress competition. Mrs Barlow, dressed as a Persian, won the ladies' prize with Mrs Warburton coming second as a white rabbit. For the men, Private Hickton won in his pirate costume, Major Barlow came second dressed as a 'red Indian' [*sic*] and Private Rhodes won third prize dressed as a flapper. Major Nutt's daughter won the children's prize for her Peter Pan costume.[170] Leysin had a skating carnival too. Ice skating was a popular activity, but as it was not usually competitive, there are few reports of it in the magazines although when a thaw stopped other sliding sports, *British Interned Magazine* could say of the rink in Chateau d'Oex, that it was little affected with the result that the rink was very crowded.[171] Major Ernest Collins, older than most of the internees, wrote to his brother in December 1917 that the skating rink in Interlaken wasn't quite ready but that he hoped to make use of it later.[172]

French and Belgian internees took part in a skating competition in Wengen on 13 February 1917. The races were said to be of general interest, and sometimes there was a lot of laughter because of the falls. The races included some of the light-hearted events of ice gymkhanas and carnivals, said to be unknown to the astonished French, for instance, the luge race with two people sitting back to back on a sledge, striving to move forward, their legs looking like those of frogs.[173]

Curling was another ice sport, played by some of the officers. On 17 February 1918 the Mürren curling team played in Grindelwald where they experienced their first taste of victory.¹⁷⁴ The Mürren team were Captain Hutchinson, Major Barlow, Mr Schlunegger and the skip was Captain Lister. The teams don't appear to be made up entirely of internees, as the four Grindelwald players all appear to have been Swiss.¹⁷⁵ In Wengen in March 1917, a team of French internees beat one of English officers by 19 points to 5, and in another game the French played a team of Swiss from Interlaken winning by 10 points to 5. A Wengen Swiss team also beat the British officers team from Grindelwald.

Of course, not all physical activity and exercise is competitive. The Alps are a perfect setting for walks and hiking, either alone or in groups. Rambling 'was the best antidote to the feeling of being "interned" that many suffered from'.¹⁷⁶ It could also be a distraction from drinking alcohol. The good work of the Mürren Temperance Society was commented on in the report of a trip on Lake Thun on 11 May. It was doing so well that Mr Clare White of the Royal Army Temperance Association agreed with the officer in charge that there was no need to form a RATA branch in Mürren which would have meant two temperance organizations competing with each other.¹⁷⁷ Connected to the Mürren Temperance Society there was the Total Abstinence Rambling Club with a large membership of teetotallers, that promoted temperance and good fellowship.¹⁷⁸ The Club, because of its tee-total nature, was the brunt of many jokes in the *British Interned Mürren* magazine, such as when they went for a ramble around Lake Brienz on 14 July 1917. The reporter couldn't resist the quip: 'They seem to be fond of lakes, but then water is strictly tee-total!'¹⁷⁹ Excursions to scenic destinations around the Bernese Oberland region, organized by the Club were popular. On Saturday 14 July 1917 a party of eighty-three enjoyed a trip to Meiringen, the Aare Gorge, the Reichenbach and Alpbach Falls and the lakeside village of Brienz. Arriving by train at Meiringen, the group had a refreshment break at the Bear Hotel. A local man acted as a guide to the Aaareslucht, describing it as 'one of the wonders of the world'. The Rambling Club were entertained by the singing of a party of Swiss women they met up with. The day out concluded with a boat trip on Lake Brienz back to Interlaken and the return train.¹⁸⁰ Not everyone enjoyed walking in groups; Major Collins, who often wrote letters describing his walks and wildlife he encountered, wrote to his father of the pleasure of walking alone instead of in groups as he had to do while imprisoned in Germany, which was pleasure enough without the fine surroundings and splendid weather.¹⁸¹

Hiking was enjoyed by all nationalities of internee. A group of Germans walked up Mount Pilatus in June 1917. There had been a lot of snow and avalanches early in the year, and the snow was still deep. The climb took five hours on foot. A stone fall delayed the group, which had to crawl up the steep final section.

Figure 6.4 British officers curling in Mürren. Courtesy of Adam Ruck, Kandahar Ski Club.

They reached the peak and the Hotel Pilatus Kulm at 7.15 in the evening, where they enjoyed a glorious view to the south and west. Even here, in this isolated location, there was a constant reminder of war, an ever-present grumbling and rumbling noise from the north-west, the sound of shooting in Alsace. The party slid down the slope for a quicker return journey, leaving their trousers dripping with water, remedied by lying down on their bellies in the evening sun.[182] Later in the summer, internee Josef Esser wrote describing a hike in the mountains around Steinegg, delighting in the idyllic walks and lakes nearby.[183] The Germans studying at the Internee Trade School in Chur, who spent their summer break hay making and cutting turf in the St Moritz area, made excursions into the Engadine at the weekend, visiting Piz Languard, Piz Rosatsch, Piz Lorvatsch and Piz de la Margna. Another trip took twenty-one German student internees from Berne up to the Jungfraujoch. Travelling beside Lake Thun, they passed the Niesen and Blumlisalp on the way to Interlaken where they caught the train to Lauterbrunnen where they joined the Jungfraubahn. 'Freed from the misery of this World War, how beautiful the world is,' concluded their report in the magazine *Deutsche Internierten Zeitung*. The party spent two hours among the ice and snow on the Jungfraujoch, returning through Grindelwald, appreciating the contrast between the cold white high above and the green meadows of cattle. The Wetterhorn and other mountains were golden in the evening sun; the article ended, 'It was the most beautiful day of our lives.'[184]

Some of the more adventurous officer internees were able to undertake some challenging climbs, despite their injuries. A lieutenant in the Durham Light Infantry, E. Angus Leybourne, managed to arrange four days away from his usual base in Chateau d'Oex, climbing in the Bernese Alps. A postcard to his fiancée, Constance Kirkup, tells her of his plans to climb on the Jungfrau that day, the Finsteraarhorn the next day and the Aletschgletscher the day after that. In looking forward to her visit, Connie anticipated taking part in sporting activities herself. Correspondence between the couple talks about tennis, horse riding, ice skating and skiing as possibilities. 'You ought to get skating when you are out so bring your skates, you can borrow skis here,' wrote Leybourne to Connie.[185] Connie did borrow skis, and she enjoyed herself immensely. She 'tumbled all over the show, but the snow was very soft on top, the worst of it was it stuck to one's breeks'. Connie wore a skirt that she said was usually around her neck but she also had on two pairs of breeches and her boots were 'top hole'.[186]

The correspondence between Constance Kirkup and her family shows how important Alpine sports were to internees, or at least some of them. Connie's first impression as she arrived in the Alps was of winter sports. When the train carrying her to Chateau d'Oex was nearing the destination, she saw through the window internees, including Leybourne, and civilians enjoying snow sports.

> As we climbed higher we saw the people tobogganing, and skating, and about halfway up the mountain, a crowd watching the finish of some bobsleigh races, and there, there was Angus, watching for me, he had just finished his race, and had come on to the platform to see if I was there.[187]
>
> I cannot give my reactions to the Life that greeted me at Les Avants, all were in holiday mood, winter sporting. Except for the khaki and the men who were wounded, armless or legless, or crippled, it was a pre-war winter sports holiday scene.
>
> Angus was in the next race, and when I saw his team of four coming down the run, iced, banked high at an angle at the corners, the yell that echoed round the hills as each corner was safely manoeuvred, and the final flash past the winning post out of a narrow avenue of pines, my heart stood still, but it was great and the English team won![188]

Leybourne and Connie were part of a group that had an outing to Caux to watch and take part in bobsleigh races. Leybourne and an American friend of his entered the races and won some small cups and medals.[189] Tobogganing was a popular pastime for the young couple. They borrowed a luge from Captain Barnes so they could enter the races. Leybourne entered the men's singles, and Connie and his sister Muriel entered the ladies' doubles.

> I don't think we won anything, we laughed so much, we landed in the snow drifts four times at the side, jumped up and pulled our luge onto the track again and off we went bumping down.[190]

Not only did internees and their visitors take part in winter sports, they enjoyed being spectators watching others compete. One Sunday, Leybourne, his mother, sister and fiancée all went to Gstaad, where hundreds of officers and men had gathered to watch a ski-jumping competition. It was a marvellous sight, Connie wrote, and they gasped when the first skier came down, 'especially when he crashed down to the bottom, turning somersaults'.[191]

For some of the more seriously injured, watching others take part in sport and enjoying their new-found or increasing fitness after suffering injury would cause heartache and sadness as their own disabilities were highlighted. A young man of twenty who had lost a leg is a reminder in Connie's letters of how seriously the war had affected some by inflicting life-changing injuries: 'Poor boy, sometimes he looks very sad and sick when he sees us going off on expeditions. It is dangerous for him on his crutches on the snow, it is so slippy.'[192] Leybourne himself had a leg injury, severed tendons in his knee, that was taking years to heal. When he climbed Mont Cray above Chateau d'Oex, Connie wrote that although he struggled walking downhill in deep snow, he was pleased to be able to do it with just one walking stick when he had needed two sticks the time he climbed it previously, evidence he was gradually recovering.[193]

Sports clubs did not confine their activities purely to sport but organized social events too. For instance, the Football Committee in Mürren held a smoking concert with songs, music and comedy entertainment.[194] When a group left Mürren to be repatriated, a farewell party with 300 guests was given by the Rambling Club.[195] In Engelberg, and no doubt elsewhere, there were social events following the ski contests. There was a family evening in the Bellevue-Terminus Restaurant after the ski races in 1917 with prize giving, then a musical evening and dancing in the Restaurant Bielialp following the ski-jumping competition the next day.[196]

By 1918, access to sporting facilities and playing fields was recognized in the Berne Accords between the French and German governments as a right for all prisoners and internees, sports provision was expected, just like facilities for sleeping, heating, dentists and hospitals. A minimum space for open-air exercise was required of at least 30 square metres a head or 25 square metres a head for groups of 200 or more. If there were more than 100 prisoners, a place had to be reserved for games and gymnastics, of 250 square metres for each 100 prisoners. It would be up to the prisoners to install the facilities themselves. Officers were allowed to go out for walks, providing they gave their word of honour not to go beyond the bounds that were set, according to Article 39 of the Berne Accord of 15 March 1918. They were allowed outdoors at any time during daylight inside an enclosure and for four hours a day beyond.[197]

All the internees were recovering from injuries, some serious and life-changing. Many of those taking part in sport were disabled and those who weren't had been confined for a long period of time and needed to redevelop physical fitness. It would have been difficult for someone who had lungs damaged by gas to take part in skiing or mountain excursions. Sledging though was seen as very good exercise that apparently only involved sliding along. Pre-war sanatoria patients with diseased lungs regarded it as a healthy, moderate form of exercise that did not involve too much effort.[198] 'Tobogganing is made for invalids' was the opinion of the sport that appeared in the *Davos Courier*, newspaper for English guests in 1888.[199] By 1914 it was less strenuous in larger resorts because there was no need to climb back up the hill as there were funiculars or trains at low prices for internees.[200] Most of the internees preferred to just go walking in groups, but some were too infirm. What does not seem to have been an issue that prevented or restricted involvement in sport was the amount of calories used up by strenuous exercise at a time when food rations were restricted to around 2,500 calories a day for working internees and 2,850 for those engaged in heavy manual work, assuming those not fit for work on 2,000 calories were not fit for sport either.[201] This may explain Major Collins' rapid weight loss that he wrote home about. This was a concern in Second World War prison camps, according to Midge Gillies in *The Barbed-Wire University*.[202] In Switzerland though, internees could supplement the ration provided by purchasing additional foodstuffs, although much was rationed, from local shops and cafes or contained in parcels sent from home. There was also the risk of serious injury to those whose broken bones or wounds had not fully healed but this does not seem to have been a deterrent either. Sport could rebuild self-esteem through the winning of competitions and trophies and acted as a diversion from bars and sexual frustrations. Reports of sporting events in the internee magazines reinforced its importance and enhanced the status of those who took part, especially those mentioned by name. By recreating physical strength, sport helped restore masculinity, by making demands on men's bodies and developing supposed warlike qualities. Sport established itself as an area where soldiers could build and express manliness.[203] Through sport, internees had social interaction, not just with each other but with local communities which allowed cultural transfer to take place. Competition between French, Belgian and British internees helped strengthen bonds between the allies and officers and other ranks.

Switzerland already had an established reputation as a place of healing with excellent medical facilities, particularly in the resorts where convalescent or ill tourists had sought cures, not just from physical ailments but from the cares of everyday life. Sport had developed here because of the need for diversion and exercise which was common to all forms of detention, whether voluntary or enforced.[204] Over a decade after the war was over, in 1929, the Geneva Conventions were modified to include the clause 'Belligerents shall encourage as much as possible the organization of intellectual and sporting pursuits by prisoners of war'.[205]

Notes

1 Tony Collins, *Sport in Capitalist Society*, Abingdon, 2013, p. 50.
2 Ibid., p. 54.
3 Madame von Duton to James Gray, 20 December 1917, private papers of James Gray, Imperial War Museum, Documents 12469.
4 Christian Koller, 'Sport Transfer over the Channel: Elitist Migration and the Advent of Football and Ice Hockey in Switzerland', *Sport in Society*, 20:10, 2017, p. 1391.
5 Ibid., p. 1397.
6 Collins, *Sport in Capitalist Society*, p. 83.
7 Ibid., p. 83.
8 Christian Koller and Fabian Brändle, *Goal! A Cultural and Social History of Modern Football*, Washington DC, 2002, p. 249.
9 Ibid., p. 331.
10 Ibid., p. 333.
11 Arnaud Waquet, 'Wartime Football, a Remedy for the Masculine Vulnerability of Poilus', *The International Journal of the History of Sport*, 29:8, May 2012, p. 1201.
12 Ibid.
13 Arnaud Waquet, 'Sport in the Trenches: The New Deal for Masculinity in France', *International Journal of the History of Sport*, 28:3–4, March 2011, p. 336.
14 Collins, *Sport in Capitalist Society*, p. 54.
15 Ketchum, *Ruhleben*, p. 221.
16 Ibid., p. 225.
17 Ibid., p. 226.

18 Ibid., p. 227.
19 Ibid., p. 225.
20 Ibid., p. 229.
21 Ibid.
22 Panayi, *Prisoners of Britain*, p. 192.
23 Ibid.
24 Ibid., p. 169.
25 Ibid., p. 190.
26 Ibid.
27 Ibid., p. 189.
28 Neil Hanson, *Escape from Germany*, London, 2011.
29 Ibid., p. 99.
30 Tony Mason and Eliza Riedi, *Sport and the Military, the British Armed Forces 1880-1960*, Cambridge, 2010, p. 206.
31 Bourke, *Dismembering the Male*, pp. 182–3.
32 Waquet, 'Wartime Football', p. 1209.
33 Mason and Riedi, *Sport and the Military*, p. 89.
34 Ibid., p. 104.
35 Bourke, *Dismembering the Male*, pp. 183–4.
36 Ibid., p. 180.
37 Waquet, 'Sport in the Trenches', p. 341.
38 Waquet, 'Wartime Football', p. 1200.
39 Picot, *The British Interned in Switzerland*, pp. 186–7.
40 *BIM*, No. 1, July 1917.
41 *BIM*, Vol. 2, No. 5, May 1918?.
42 Mürren Monthly Report, No. 10. June 1917 to the Officer i/c British Interned in Switzerland, p. 2, TNA FO383/329.
43 *BIM*, No. 8, October 1917.
44 Paillard, *Notes sur les événements politiques de 1914 à 1919*, p. 59.
45 *BIM*, Vol. 2, No. 4, May 1918.
46 Colonel Earle, SBO Chateau d'Oex, Report on workshops etc, September 1916, TNA FO 383/219.
47 Mürren Monthly Report, No. 3, 24 November 1916 to the Officer I/c British Interned in Switzerland, p. 2, TNA FO383/218.
48 *BIM*, Vol. 2, No. 6, July 1918.
49 *BIM*, No. 3, July 1917.
50 Ibid.
51 Ibid.
52 Ibid.
53 Ibid.

54 *JIF*, No. 6, 30 November 1916.
55 *BIM*, No. 7, September 1917.
56 *BIM*, Vol. 2, No. 8, September 1918.
57 *JIF*, No. 14, 27 January 1917.
58 *JIF*, No. 24, 7 April 1917.
59 *JIF*, No. 2, No. 9, 30 December 1917.
60 *JIF*, A2, No. 5, 2 December 1917.
61 *JIF*, No. 25, 14 April 1917.
62 *JIF*, No. 3, 9 November 1916.
63 *JIF*, No. 5, 23 November 1916.
64 *JIF*, No. 26, 21 April 1917.
65 *JIF*, No. 37, 7 July 1917.
66 *JIF*, A2, No. 9, 30 December 1917.
67 Ibid.
68 *JIF*, No. 24, 7 April 1917.
69 Ketchum, *Ruhleben*, p. 229.
70 Fuchs, 'Interniert im Appenzellerland', p. 65.
71 *BIM*, No. 3, July 1917.
72 Ibid.
73 Barton, *Healthy Living in the Alps*.
74 W. E. Hume-Williams, 7 October 1916, London, p. 2, Red Cross Papers, Imperial War Museum, Documents 10086.
75 Lieutenant Colonel Picot, Appendix to Monthly Report of officer in charge, British Interned in Switzerland, 30 November 1916, TNA FO 383/218.
76 Colonel Earle, Report on workshops etc, Chateau d'Oex, September 1916, TNA FO 383/219.
77 Mürren Monthly Report, No. 3.
78 *BIM*, No. 3, July 1917.
79 *BIM*, Vol. 2, No. 2, February 1918.
80 Ibid.
81 Paillard, *Notes sur les événements politiques de 1914 à 1919*, p. 59.
82 James Gray, private papers, IWM Documents 12469.
83 *Gazette de Döberitz*, No. 2, 1917.
84 H. D. Munyard, private papers, IWA Documents 10733.
85 Durrer, 'Internierte während des Ersten Weltkriegs', p. 101.
86 Photograph in Talmuseum Engelberg.
87 *JIF*, No. 38, 14 July 1917.
88 Picot, *The British Interned in Switzerland*, p. 187.
89 *JIF*, A2, No. 1, 4 November 1917.
90 Paillard, *Notes sur les événements politiques de 1914 à 1919*, p. 49.

91 *BIM*, Vol. 2, No. 9, 15 October 1918.
92 *JIF*, No. 38, 14 July 1917.
93 *BIM*, Vol. 2, No. 5, June 1918 and No. 7, 15 September 1918.
94 Captain A. Hargraves, SBO Laussane, Report, Ouchy, Lausanne, 24 July 1917, TNA FO 383/329.
95 Durrer, 'Internierte während des Ersten Weltkriegs', p. 101.
96 *BIM*, Vol. 2, No. 8, 30 September 1918.
97 Collins to his brother, 9 September 1918, Vevey, IWM Documents 15679.
98 *JIF*, No. 26, 21 April 1917.
99 *JIF*, No. 28, 5 May 1917.
100 Report of British Interned at Lucerne for July 1917, TNA FO383/329.
101 *BIM*, Vol. 2, No. 2, February 1918.
102 *BIM*, Vol. 2, No. 9, 15 October 1918.
103 *BIM*, Vol. 1, No. 7, September 1917.
104 *BIM*, Vol. 2, No. 4, April 1918.
105 Collins to his father, Hotel du Lac, Interlaken, 3 December 1917, IWM Documents 15679.
106 Alexander Kirmmse, photograph album, Talmuseum Engelberg.
107 *BIM*, No. 10, December 1917.
108 *BIM*, No. 9, November 1917.
109 Ibid.
110 Arnold Lunn, *Skiing*, London, 1913.
111 Lieutenant Colonel Neish, Report from SBO Mürren, 25 August 1916, TNA FO 383/218.
112 Arnold Lunn, *Mountain Jubilee*, London, 1943, p. 36.
113 Ibid.
114 Elizabeth Hussey, *Biography of Arnold Lunn, 1888-1974*, North Charleston, 2014, p. 40.
115 Arnold Lunn, *The Bernese Oberland*, London, 1958, p. 98.
116 Hussey, *Biography of Arnold Lunn*, p. 43.
117 Arnold Lunn, 'British Skiing during the War', *The British Ski Year Book for 1920*, p. 88.
118 Hussey, *Biography of Arnold Lunn*, p. 42.
119 Arnold Lunn, *The Mountains of Youth*, London, 1925, p. 132.
120 Amstutz, *The Golden Age of Alpine Skiing*, p. 56.
121 Lunn, *The Bernese Oberland*, p. 98; *BIM*, Vol. 2, No. 4, April 1918.
122 Lunn, 'British Skiing during the War', p. 89.
123 Ibid., p. 88.
124 *BIM*, Vol. 2, No. 3, March 1918.
125 Lunn, *Mountain Jubilee*, p. 37.

126 *BIM*, No. 9, November 1917.
127 Lieutenant Colonel Neish, report from SBO Mürren, 25 August 1916, TNA FO 383/218.
128 *BIM*, Vol. 2, No. 9, September 1918.
129 *BIM*, Vol. 2, No. 3, March 1918.
130 Ibid.
131 *BIM*, Vol. 2, No. 4, April 1918.
132 Lunn, *The Bernese Oberland*, p. 190.
133 *BIM*, Vol. 2, No. 10, October 1918.
134 Lunn, *Mountain Jubilee*, p. 37.
135 Lunn, *The Mountains of Youth*, p. 132.
136 Lunn, *The Bernese Oberland*, p. 190.
137 Lunn, *The Mountains of Youth*, p. 132.
138 *BIM*, No. 3, July 1917.
139 Lunn, *The Bernese Oberland*, p. 190.
140 *BIM*, Vol. 2, No. 7, July 1918.
141 *BIM*, Vol. 2, No. 8, August 1918.
142 Lunn, 'British Skiing during the War', p. 89.
143 Lunn, *The Mountains of Youth*, pp. 154–5.
144 Ibid., p. 154.
145 *BIM*, Vol. 2, No. 1, January 1918.
146 Ormorod, Visit to wounded military internee in Switzerland, IWM Misc 30(538), Documents 10086.
147 Lunn, *British Ski-ing during the War*, p. 87.
148 *A Trip to Switzerland in War Time* (anonymous internee's wife from Oldham), Red Cross Papers, IWM, Misc 30(538), Documents 10086, p. 5.
149 *Northampton Independent*, February 1917.
150 *BIM*, Vol. 2, No. 3, March 1918.
151 Colonel Earle, Report on workshops etc, Chateau d'Oex September 1916, TNA FO 383/219.
152 *BIM*, Vol. 2, No. 4, April 1918.
153 *JIF*, A2, No. 10, 13 January 1918.
154 *JIF*, A2, No. 9, 30 December 1917.
155 *JIF*, No. 6, 30 November 1916.
156 Durrer, 'Internierte während des Ersten Weltkriegs', p. 101.
157 *JIF*, No. 14, 27 January 1917.
158 *JIF*, No. 17, 17 February 1917.
159 *Les Internés de Guerre à Engelberg*, Kunstanstalt Brügger, Meiringen, c1917.
160 *JIF*, No. 14, 27 January 1917.
161 Durrer, 'Internierte während des Ersten Weltkriegs', p. 101.

162 *DIZ*, Heft Nr. 21, 10 February 1917.
163 Photographs, Dokumentationsbibliothek Davos.
164 *Davos Courier*, 13 May 1916.
165 Hoffman, 'Die Lehranstalt für internierte Kolonialdeutsche in Davos'.
166 *BIM*, Vol. 2, No. 2, February 1918.
167 Koller, 'Sport Transfer over the Channel', p. 395.
168 Ibid., p. 1396.
169 *JIF*, No. 17, 17 February 1917.
170 *BIM*, Vol. 2, No. 2, February 1918.
171 Ibid.
172 Collins to his brother, Interlaken, 23 December 1917, IWM Documents15679.
173 *JIF*, No. 18, 24 February 1917.
174 *BIM*, Vol. 2, No. 3, March 1918.
175 *JIF*, No. 2, 2 November 1916.
176 *BIM*, Vol. 1, Nr. 3, August 1917.
177 Mürren Monthly Report, No. 9, 24 May 1917 to the Officer I/c Switzerland, TNA FO 383/329.
178 *BIM*, Vol. 2, No. 2, February 1918.
179 *BIM*, No. 3, July 1917.
180 Ibid.
181 Collins to his father, Interlaken, 11 February 1918, IWM Documents 15679.
182 *DIZ*, Heft Nr. 40, 24 June 1917.
183 *DIZ*, Heft Nr. 52, 16 September 1917.
184 *DIZ*, Heft Nr. 53, 23 September 1917.
185 Lieutenant Elliott Angus Leybourne to Constance Kirkup, 29 November 1916.
186 From Constance Kirkup, 9 March 1917.
187 From Constance Kirkup, 26 January 1917.
188 Ibid.
189 From Constance Kirkup, 3 February 1917.
190 From Constance Kirkup, 10 February 1917.
191 From Constance Kirkup, 3 February 1917.
192 From Constance Kirkup, 10 February 1917.
193 From Constance Kirkup, 24 February 1917.
194 *BIM*, No. 8, October 1917.
195 *BIM*, No. 6, September 1917.
196 *JIF*, No. 14, 27 Janvier 1917.
197 *Accords entre le Gouvernement de la République Français et le Gouvernement Impérial Allemand concernant les Prisonniers de Guerre et les Civils*, Berne, 28 April 1918, Musé de Montreux, pp. 23 and 29.
198 Barton, *Healthy Living in the Alps*, p. 29.

199 *Davos Courier*, 1 November 1888.
200 *Les Internés de Guerre à Engelberg*.
201 Jones, *Violence against Prisoners of War in the First World War*, p. 241.
202 Gillies, *The Barbed-Wire University*, p. 56.
203 Waquet, 'Sport in the Trenches', p. 333.
204 Panayi, *Prisoners of Britain*, p. 189.
205 *Convention Relative to the Treatment of Prisoners of War*, Geneva, Chapter 4, Article 17, 27 July 1929.

7

Entertainment, relaxation, intellectual and spiritual well-being

Not all internees were fit or well enough or had the inclination to take part in sport. Even for those keen on sport, there was still a need for intellectual stimulation, especially during the winter when more time was spent indoors. Just as sports committees were created soon after the internees arrived, groups were formed to organize other amusements and entertainments. Among the internees were men who had particular skills or talents from before the war or gained during their time in prison camps. When the wounded men arrived in Switzerland, many of them already had up to eighteen months of experience of prison camp life and the various groups and societies that had evolved to help pass the time, which included education, sport, libraries, lectures, discussions, religious activities, music and drama. These experiences were common to both military and civilian internment. Ketchum, describing life at Ruhleben Camp in Berlin, where British civilians were interned during the war, referred to these groups as 'prison camp societies'.[1] In *Prisoners of Britain*, about the internment of German civilian and military prisoners during the 1914–18 war, Panikos Panayi devotes a chapter to prison camp societies in Britain, that were very similar in nature to those formed by British internees in Germany, described by Ketchum.[2] In military prison camps, as well as civilian, societies met a variety of intellectual and cultural needs of prisoners. These groups played a particularly important role for officers who were exempt from work and therefore needed to occupy their time, but evidence shows they appealed to prisoners of all ranks. Sport, work and education have been discussed in other chapters, so this one will focus on other pastimes.

In the prisoner of war and civilian internment camps, in all the belligerent nations, there were drama and music groups, which provided entertainment for audiences, occupation for participants and an opportunity to utilize and develop skills, rarely called upon since peace time, for those whose former lives had been interrupted by the war, some of whom had been actors, entertainers and musicians. Not only performers found an outlet for their talents, putting on a show or concert involved administration and organizational skills, art and design for advertising posters, programmes and tickets, costume, set and scenery design and practical skills in sewing, printing, carpentry and construction. Despite the lack of equipment and resources, prisoners' enthusiasm inspired them to improvise. Often the preparations were painstaking and what would normally be relatively simple tasks could take months due to the need to procure materials. For British military prisoners of war, held in Döberitz Camp in Germany, theatrical performances were a regular feature in the theatre they created, the 'Döberitz Empire'. Surviving souvenir programmes give details of the acts performing in the shows. There was an orchestra, singing, dancing and comedy and 'The Three Pierrettes', a name that suggests that this was a female impersonation act. Credits were also given to the stage manager, theatre manager, musical conductor, a pianist, scenic artists and the designer of the art work for the programme cover, who also helped with scenery.[3] Discussing captives during the later conflict of the Second World War, Clare Makepeace writes of the release watching a performance for a couple of hours could bring to someone living in deplorable conditions, a release that was just as welcome to the First World War prisoners.

> This is one of the reasons why theatrical entertainments were, for POWs, one of the most prized and valued aspects of their imprisoned lives. Those watching a play could drift off into a far-off world; those on stage could indulge in different material comforts and temporarily, become someone other than a prisoner of war.[4]

Not only performing arts and music featured in Döberitz, there was a camp magazine, the *Gazette de Döberitz,* which contained sections on the activities of the various sports clubs, reviews of shows at the Döberitz Empire, library opening times and church notices. It also featured artwork by talented artists and graphic designers.[5] Another Döberitz publication was *The Link*, a souvenir book, some of whose editors were men who were also involved in the theatrical productions.[6] Camp magazines provided a medium for writers, poets and artists to display their talents as well as for readers to pass the time and know what was going on in the camp. In the same way, interned prisoners in Switzerland had their own magazines, *British Interned Mürren*, later renamed *British Interned Magazine, Le Journal des Internés Français* and *Deutsche Internierten Zeitung,* published from 1917 until repatriation.

The reason so much has been discovered about the leisure activities of internees is thanks to these magazines. *British Interned in Mürren* (*BIM*) was initiated by Major Charley in June 1917. Produced in Mürren with financial help from the British Red Cross Organisation, the first issue appeared on 25 June and the second on 13 July 1917.[7] Its first editor was Lieutenant Hobbs and later Lieutenant Ralph du Boulay Evans. Until January 1918 stories were mainly about Mürren, but it widened its audience to the whole of the English-speaking internment community, changing its title to *British Interned Magazine*, edited by Evans and printed in Vevey.[8]

The French internees had a similar magazine, *Le Journal des Internés Français*, which was launched with a financial appeal in a circular letter of 11 July 1916. The letter told of the need to satisfy the internees intellectually and combat any sense of isolation. It referred to the papers produced in the military prison camps of Germany, such as at Gottingen which gave comfort, encouragement and discipline. Soon after the letter a leaflet announced that the magazine would be appearing soon.[9] Articles were written by internees and the publication included useful information. The editor was a writer with the pen name 'Paul Valentin', assisted by Jacques Mercoeur, a Belgian.[10] It cost 3.50 francs to internees, 6.50 francs to Swiss readers and 9 francs to receive a copy in the post, not enough to cover all expenses.

For German internees there was the *Deutsche Internierten Zeitung*, edited by author Hermann Hesse who volunteered for civilian service with the German embassy in Berne. By the middle of 1915 Hesse was in the department caring for German prisoners of war. With the help of Professor Richard Woltereck, he organized a book distribution centre, soliciting funds and books for prisoners and internees. He helped found the weekly journal, *Deutsche Internierten Zeitung* and a Sunday supplement in 1916, acting as co-editor until early 1919.[11] Belgian magazines were published under the name of *Le Beffroi, bulletin pour les internés belge en Suisse* in French and *Het Belfort* in Flemish, meaning the belfry; however, no more than five editions were published.[12] Fees from advertising supported all these magazines. The internee magazines followed the style and served the same purpose as trench papers such as the *Wipers' Times*, prison camp journals like the *Gazette de Döberitz* but with official announcements and information. There were also similarities with the Swiss tourist press, such as the *Davos Courier* and the *Engadine Express* for long-term visitors and patients.

Removed from the prison camps in Germany, France or Britain, the interned military men continued to come together to meet the cultural needs of the communities they were creating in Switzerland. Not only physical recovery and fitness were promoted, just as important was mental health and well-being.[13] When the novelty wore off, boredom was a problem which sometimes led to inappropriate behaviour. When the first batch of prisoners arrived in Chateau d'Oex from Germany at the end of May 1916, they were in such poor physical condition that they needed time to recuperate before any amusements were introduced. In the second group to arrive, the prisoners were less seriously ill as the worst cases had already left. The ground was prepared from the outset, so the later arrivals could be involved in various activities as well as work according to their capabilities, resulting in fewer disciplinary problems for this group from being left too long to their own devices.[14]

In contrast to the camps where they had been held before their transfer to Switzerland, the internees were no longer in a closed, all-male environment but were able to mix with women, local Swiss, volunteers providing a service to the wounded and the wives, mothers and daughters of internees whose families came out to stay or visit. The absence of women in prison camps meant that in theatre productions the female parts had to be played by men. In a closed society where the male prisoners had no contact with females, perhaps for several years, performers made every effort to make the women characters as realistic as possible, a form of impersonation known as 'mimesis', rather than the comedic mimicry of the pantomime dame.[15] Female impersonators became central to prisoner-of-war camp life during the First World War, and cross-dressing evolved from being a marginal activity into mainstream performance.[16] In Switzerland there was no need for cross-dressing due to the presence of women willing to join in the performances. Nevertheless, the practice of mimesis persisted in some performances. Photographs of the British Interned Variety Company of Chateau d'Oex show men dressed in female costumes. Among a group of performers in costumes such as comedy characters, Highland dancers in kilts, and a clown is an elegantly dressed 'lady' with her hand on the thigh of a smartly dressed young man sitting next to her. Another photograph is of a young couple, another smartly dressed young man wearing a shirt and tie with a young 'woman' leaning lovingly on his shoulder, perhaps a hint that some of these relationships were sexualized, either in the imagination or reality.[17] Male performers playing female characters was not something confined to British theatrical groups. Photographic evidence illustrates that German internees' theatrical performances also included cross-dressing and the Berne Internees' Theatrical Group performed two comedy plays in German in the Swiss capital on 23 November 1917, in which the female roles were played by Nicol, a French man. According to the *Journal des Internés Français* reviewer, Nicol knew how to give the illusion of reality to his role but was careful not to overact.[18]

Figure 7.1 German internees' theatrical group. Courtesy of Andrew Whitmarsh (www.switzerland1914-18.net).

Concerts played a big part in the social life of all internees, for whom they were a popular way to celebrate special occasions and frequently showcased the talents of women who joined in the theatrical activities of the internees as organizers, performers, musicians and audience members. Often the entertainments were charity events: the ticket price raising funds in aid of causes for those less fortunate or deserving of gratitude, such as Belgian refugees, prisoners of war still in camps, sick Swiss soldiers or the Red Cross. The musical and theatrical Variety Company of Chateau d'Oex put on shows in the *Grande Salle* to raise money for a fund to build a chalet for the region's *Colonie de Vacances* for children, as thanks for the friendly welcome they had received from local children on their arrival.[19] The first concert was on Saturday 22 July 1916. The Variety Company included an amateur theatrical group and a troupe of Scottish dancers, in demand for charity events in Geneva, Montreux, Basle, Lausanne and the Bernese Oberland, 'Their kilts, sporrans, and bearing were a never-ending joy to the spectators.'[20] These soirees were a great success; everyone wanted to see the Scottish dancers and the famous comic character Police Sergeant Raston.[21] The variety programme included one-act plays, comic and sentimental songs with the audience joining in the choruses.

Officers joined in the productions, some of which were said to be small masterpieces of directing and good taste.[22] Captain Irwin was put in charge of the variety entertainment in Chateau d'Oex although the group was started by the men themselves, but as was often patronizingly judged to be the case, 'the men without an officer to guide them get into stupid difficulties'.[23] In a couple of plays put on to entertain the internees in Chateau d'Oex, parts were taken by Lady Acton, Madame Hugh-Camp, Miss Rita Picot and Miss Nesta Sawyer, demonstrating that women of all classes were happy to join in.[24] During her long visit to her fiancé in Chateau d'Oex, Constance Kirkup kept herself busy in a Pierrot troupe, a task that involved not just dressing up and performing but practising hard every night after dinner from 9.00 pm to 11.00 pm for weeks before, as well as making stage hangings using a broken sewing machine, leaving everything to be made by hand. Her fiancé, Angus Leybourne spent his free time between the joiner's shop and the electric wires, rigging up footlights and a spotlight with different colours.[25]

Mürren had its own Variety Company that gave concerts at the Hotel Regina. These concerts were organized by Harry Hawthorne.[26] Another troupe, Mrs Bell's Concert Party, put on Minstrel shows.[27] The Palace Hotel closed in the autumn of 1917 due to the repatriation of many internees and heating problems; its remaining occupants moved into the Regina, leaving no room there for concerts. Entertainments then switched to the YMCA Hut and elsewhere.[28] Entertainers sometimes performed in other internment communities. A concert at the Kursaal in Interlaken by the Mürren internees' orchestra raised 200 francs for the relief committee for poor families of Swiss soldiers.[29] The Mürren theatrical group had permission to travel to Interlaken to stage a play, 'The Speckled Band', a trip that lasted three days as a heavy snowfall blocked the railway lines.[30]

When a concert was given by French internees in Grindelwald with music in the first half and a play in the second, *l'Anglais tel qu'on le parle* (English as it is spoken), the female roles were taken by Madame Picquet and Madame Moulin.[31] A concert at Boudry by the French theatrical group there, in aid of sick Swiss soldiers, featured several operatic arias, sketches and the piano playing of Mademoiselle Aubée.[32] On 17 June 1917, a concert for those soldiers leaving to be repatriated was held in Frutigen. Anna Jost played piano while Paul Darrass of the *Petit Casino* in Paris sang.[33] The concert included a popular patriotic play called *Servir* about a colonel willing to sacrifice all for France. A tombola drawn by Mademoiselle Paula Jost and Mademoiselle Gaspard was an added attraction, with 220 items for 300 tickets so there were many winners. A benefit concert organized by French internees, described as an ingenious means to occupy their leisure, took place in the Casino at Gimel in late 1917, with comic singer, Paudaran, singer Monsieur Gay Georges and Monsieur de Becque, with his voice *bien timbrée*. This show again featured the talent of female artistes, Mademoiselle Falconnier on piano followed by Mademoiselle Bretagne playing a Chopin prelude.³⁴ In Leysin, French soldiers organized *Poilus Revue*, a play in three acts of five scenes written by Monsieur Martin with Monsieur Revaldi, a tenor of the Grand Théâtre in Geneva taking part, on 13 April 1916 in the Grand Hotel ballroom. Swiss residents in the Lausanne area were invited to see the show, repeated weekly for three weeks.³⁵ The Hotel Sanetsch was the venue of a concert by internees and their families in Gsteig, where vocal and instrumental performances made it a night of joy and gaiety in an otherwise monotonous winter season, while at Wengen a violin solo brought a little laughter and French gaiety to a February evening.³⁶ At Yverdon internees organized a soiree in aid of Serbian prisoners of war in Germany and Swiss soldiers in need.³⁷ Belgian children and those of poor Swiss soldiers were the beneficiaries of a French play, *Les Nouveaux Pauvres*, put on in Montreux by *La Troupe de Théâtre* on 9 March 1918.³⁸ French and Belgian internees formed the *Théatre des Internés d'Engelberg* in June 1916, only a month after their arrival. Its aim was to help their unfortunate comrades, still imprisoned in Germany. Around six months after its creation the theatre group had made a net profit of 1,667 francs. A breakdown of its accounts show that of its income it spent 303.70 francs on the performances, 415.90 francs was paid into the theatre account, 228.70 francs donated to needy comrades, 228.70 francs given to prisoners in Germany, 290 francs to sick Swiss soldiers and 200 francs to the Red Cross in Geneva.³⁹ German internees also strengthened their relationships with local communities and each other through concerts and theatre groups, either taking part or as audience members. In Oberegg at the Hotel Bären, an entertainment evening with local hotelier and pianist Cäcilia Locher raised funds for the local soup kitchen and sick Swiss soldiers in the Appenzell region, a show repeated at Berneck.⁴⁰ Although concerts were held to raise money for charity, they did not always raise as much as anticipated. Major Collins wrote home from Interlaken that 'we gave a variety entertainment in the town last week for the hospital. It was quite successful but the expenses were more than we expected so I can't give the sum I'd hoped to the hospital.'⁴¹

Sometimes the entertainment included a film show as well as performances, such as the *Soirée récréative* in Weissenbourg on 22 November 1917.⁴² Cinema shows were organized as a different and novel diversion for the internees. The YMCA put on cinema shows for British internees in Leysin, Mürren and Vevey. Official war films were shown and an American serial called 'Pearl of the Army', featuring the silent film star Pearl White.⁴³ At Interlaken, French films were shown in the hall of the Apollo.⁴⁴

In Davos, where many Germans were interned, there was an effort to maintain at least a semblance of a winter season, of opera, theatre and balls, for the reduced colonies of sport and health seekers.[45] In 1913 there had been 1,138,201 nights spent by visitors in Davos, in 1914 1,003,561 visitor nights which declined to 726,633 in 1915, the first full year of the war. The numbers of actual visitors though had fallen by more than half, but people were staying for much longer, eighty days on average, compared with an average stay of fifty-nine days in 1913 and seventy in 1914.[46] Many of these visitors were said to be new to the resort. The local English language tourist newspaper, *The Davos Courier*, observed that the resort was maintaining the pre-war features of a social life and did not look less animated on the promenade.[47] During the first month of the German internees' arrival there was a symphony concert and Shrove Tuesday entertainment at the Belvedere to raise money to help poor French and Russians, presumably not aimed at a German audience, and also entertainment and dancing at the Kurhaus. German internees remained a minority among the visitors to Davos: in January 1917 there were around 5,000 cure, sport and soldier guests, of which only 1,232 were internees.[48] Even without the internees, the total was a thousand more than it had been a year earlier, showing that the presence of internees was not a deterrent to tourists, perhaps some of them came because of the internees, as family visitors who lodged in hotels. Entertainment was not exclusively for internees, local people were invited to a concert at the Hotel Rigiblick in Buochs.[49]

Classical music fans were well served in Switzerland as many variety shows included classical pieces or operatic arias. An orchestra of French and Belgian interned musicians, the *Orchestre Symphonique des Internés Alliés* (OSIA), under the leadership of well-known musician Marc de Ranse, gave forty concerts on a national tour during 1917.[50] Ranse, born in 1881, was a pianist, composer, organist, choir master and conductor. He had been wounded and was taken prisoner in Belgium, became ill in captivity and was sent to Montreux in 1916.[51] The orchestra toured the different Allied internment regions, in May 1917. The French violinist, Sailler, gave a performance in Interlaken in March 1917; he had been a prisoner in Heidelberg where he had also given concerts.[52] A gala concert for the benefit of the French Ladies of the Red Cross took place at the Apollo Theatre in Geneva, with the added attraction of a lottery.[53] At an internee evening on 8 August 1917, in the Hotel Belevedere in Davos the well-known pianist, Elly Ney accompanied Herr Rössel, the Davos concert singer, performing German songs by Liszt and Schubert.[54] There were British orchestras too: one formed in Chateau d'Oex and another in Mürren. In Chateau d'Oex's Anglican church the dedication of a new organ, a gift from internees, featured a recital on the instrument followed by a reception in the

Hotel Rosa.⁵⁵ Appeals for musical instruments were sent back to Britain, but some were found or purchased locally. A gift of 500 francs was donated by the chocolate manufacturer, Suchard of Neuchatel, for prisoners interned in Leysin to buy musical instruments for their orchestra.⁵⁶ A letter from Florence Bourne Wilder, honorary secretary of the Derby Prisoners' Aid Committee, appealed through the local newspaper to lovers of music in Derby on behalf of two Sherwood Foresters, one in Germany and another in Switzerland: Private A. Colledge in Giessen who wanted a violin and Sergeant Drummer Bowditch in Chateau d'Oex who, in his letter of request, wrote,

> I am writing these few lines asking if it is possible to send me an E flat piccolo with six keys as I should like very much to practice. It will take me at least two months to get in trim again. Then I dare say I could give our little band a lift.⁵⁷

Repatriation of some of the wounded caused disruption to musical activities, as regular practice required a stable group of people. At Meiringen, a small community of internees, the band had to be discontinued and the instruments stored awaiting new arrivals from Germany to replace those who had returned home.⁵⁸ Music was important as it helped morale and contributed to the well-being of musician and listener. For those who could not play an instrument, singing was a way of joining in with musical activities or entertaining themselves and their friends. 'Will you send me the words of *Jolly Good Luck to the Girl who Loves a Soldier?*' was a request sent by postcard from internee Cecil Walter to his friend Private Alf Gibbs.⁵⁹ Music raised the audience's spirits, such as in the concert in January 1918 at Seeburg:

> Again we lived in the happy pre-war days; again our souls felt stirred to greater things than hatred and revenge. For the time being war was non-existent, and only a great and glorious happiness flooded our whole beings. Miss Rich and Miss Doubleday [performers] can never quite realise what a feast their playing was.⁶⁰

Intellectually stimulating lectures, particularly those including slide shows, were another popular way to occupy an evening and perhaps learn something new. These lectures were intended to speak to the heart and intelligence of the internees. There was a panel of seventy-six French speakers, male and female, and presumably panels of British and Germans too.⁶¹ To illustrate their talks they used magic lantern slides. Some of the speakers travelled around the country giving the same talk in different internment centres. At Lungern and Fiesch a talk with slides was given while at Lauterbrunnen and Wengen Monsieur Concorda of Chaux de Fonds gave a lecture about Moscow.[62] In Fribourg Professor Girard talked about the formation of the mountains, *Monsieur* Schoderet spoke on the region of Gruyère and in Charmey and Châtel-St-Denis Captain Richard gave a lively talk on the subject of tax. Other subjects included the multiracial Turkish Empire, and Morocco.[63] In Interlaken a slide show presented images taken over the summit of Mont Blanc, on a traverse from Italy into France.[64] Lectures were a feature of the intellectual activities for the British internees too, such as Arnold Lunn's talk in Mürren on skiing in May 1918.[65] Because these slide shows did not feature sound, they could be circulated around the different regions of internment with narration given in the appropriate language.

Seasonal celebrations punctuated the year and marked the passing of time. Christmas was celebrated in all internment communities, in ways culturally appropriate to the regional traditions of those based there. The French-speaking Swiss organization, *la Commission Romande des Internés*, organized Christmas events in the seventy sectors where French and Belgians were interned.[66] For the majority who did not have family members with them during their internment, Christmas could be a sad day that brought back memories of happier times. It was said to be a time when children ran to the chimney to see what Little Jesus had put in their shoes but for orphans their father's shoes were missing.[67] The Swiss hosts tried to remedy this sadness. Hotel ballrooms and meeting rooms around Switzerland were decorated and provided with Christmas trees.

Celebrations included concerts, games and parties. Gifts were provided for internees and their children. A tombola system was a common method of deciding which internee received what gift. Chocolate and tobacco were usually given to all the men. In Berne, the Burgerhaus was said to be too small to hold the 350 *Poilus*, their families and invited guests. At the centre of the hall stood a magnificent, illuminated pine tree. The tables were loaded with pastries, chocolate and coffee with milk. The French ambassador thanked the hosts and compared the wartime struggle of France with the struggle of the Revolution during which times were just as difficult. Cries of *Vive la France* and *Vivent les Alliés* ended the party. In the Gruyères area a Christmas event was organized at Bulle. Young people from the Christian Union at Montreux arrived on skis to share the day with those they called their big brothers, making it a proper family festival with music, sketches, projections of the stars and carol singing around the tree. In Chailly there was a slide show on the history of Christmas around the world, songs and monologues and a tombola to distribute prizes to everyone on 23 December. The same slide show was shown in Diemtigen the following day, Christmas Eve, at the Hotel Hirschen with songs, a comedy

Figure 7.2 Christmas in Chateau d'Oex. Courtesy of Pat and Mark Esling (family collection) and Chris Twiggs (private collection).

play and a tombola. At Champéry there was a Christmas tree in the *Foyer du Soldat* for the benefit of internees' children. As well as a tombola, *Père Noël* was there, distributing gifts.[68] In Spiez the *Bonhomme de Noël* distributed toys to the children. An unusual festive entertainment was included in the Christmas Eve celebrations at Leukerbad when, as well as songs, there was a boxing match. Interlaken celebrated Christmas with a children's festival on the afternoon of 24 December, when the Countess of Dudzeele came from Berne to preside. It was a happy time for mothers and their children, with carols, poems, treats and gifts. Later on, the adult Belgian men enjoyed themselves as they gathered round the tree on Christmas Eve and Day, despite the electric lights on the tree fusing. Christmas Eve was the focus of festivities and gift giving among the protestant communities. Catholics celebrated mass on Christmas Day itself. In Weissenbourg there was a concert on Christmas Eve and mass in the Catholic chapel the next day, followed by a gathering around the Christmas tree with gifts for the children.[69] British internees received gifts of souvenir photograph books from Suchard, the chocolate company.

New Year was marked in Gunten by a *Fête de l'Entente*, with a banquet, songs and a tombola, organized by Mrs Cooke Daniels and Miss Martin, who ran the carpet workshop, a generous gesture accomplished with 'femininity and British grace'.[70] In Interlaken there was a New Year's Day party with a concert and another tombola and at Montreux an orchestral concert given by the OSIA in the

Figure 7.3 Souvenir photo booklet presented as a gift to British internees. Courtesy of Pat and Mark Esling (family collection) and Chris Twiggs (private collection).

Kursaal.[71] On New Year's Eve in Lauterbrunnen three young French internees, Teyssier, Chrétien and Margerard, disguised themselves as troubadours and went round the different hotels in the sector. They sang familiar songs, raising money for comrades in need.[72] Some German internees celebrated New Year, *Sylvesterfeuer*, in the Hotel Schweizerhof in Berne, where there was a special evening meal for them.[73]

National festivals were celebrated, often with the involvement of Swiss hosts, especially military events that called for a rifle fusillade salute as the internees could not carry guns. The King of the Belgians patronal feast was commemorated by those of that nationality in Montana on 15 November 1917 with a *Matinée Artistique*.[74] In Engelberg, King Albert's name day was celebrated with the help of French performers with a grand concert in the Kuranstalt. The Belgian queen's name day was also celebrated. The French celebrated their National Day on 14 July. In 1917 in Bagnes it was celebrated over two days, with an evening concert in the hall of the Hotel Giètroz with singing and music, followed the next day, a Sunday, by games.[75] At Fribourg there were songs from the school choir in the yard of the Villa St-Jean followed by speeches from Captain Bonafous. The *Societé Française de Fribourg* organized a reception in the hall of La Grenette, decorated in red, white and blue for the occasion. English and Belgian internees brought greetings; then there was a toast to Colonel Reynold who had presided over the internment of French soldiers in Fribourg in 1871. The day ended with musical entertainment and food.[76] In the

Bernese Oberland, at Lauterbrunnen, General Pau visited the internees on 14 July 1917. The station was decorated ready for his arrival, as were the dining rooms. Pau reviewed the French troops, made a speech and then looked at the Staubach waterfall. He enjoyed a dinner at the Steinbock Hotel where a choir sang the Marseillaise as he entered. Afterwards there was a concert before the General left for Wengen at 3.00 pm. In the evening there was another concert at the Steinbock for internees, their families and local people. In Wengen, Pau was presented with a tricolour bouquet by four-year-old twin girls; then he went on to the Hotel Falcon where a placard in French colours displayed welcoming wishes formed with daisies, the ingenious idea of Madame Dauziech, an internee's wife.[77]

For German internees *Kaiserfeier*, the Kaiser's birthday celebrated on 27 January, was their most important secular occasion, instrumental in the construction of a united German identity. In 1917 it was marked by Archduchess Marie von Mecklenburg's visit to interned students at the technical college in Zurich.[78] Kaiser Wilhelm's fifty-eighth birthday was celebrated in the Union Hotel in Lucerne, an event which opened with the musical march, *Adlerflug*, and continued with music through the evening as the internees enjoyed free beer and sausages.[79]

Figure 7.4 German internees celebrating at Schatzalp Sanatorium, Davos, 1917. Courtesy of Dokumentationsbibliothek Davos.

Among British internees, many religious or national commemorations were observed in a secular manner. St Patricks Day on 17 March 1917 was marked in Seeburg by a whist drive, dance and songs. On Good Friday there was another whist drive with prizes, followed by a dance and more whist on Easter Saturday and a fancy-dress ball on Easter Monday.[80] Anzac Day was celebrated by the Australians and New Zealanders at the Hotel Brunig in Interlaken with a dinner and entertainment.[81]

Used to entertaining holiday guests, most of the bigger hotels housing internees possessed large ballrooms. Soon they were put to use again for dancing. At the Hotel Alpenruh in Mürren, Commandant Captain Doctor Llopart allowed an extension of the time the internees were allowed out until 11.00 pm. Some of the ladies staying at the Hotel Regina joined them in dancing to the Mürren Orchestra.[82] There were also dances at Seeburg and a fancy-dress ball in Chateau d'Oex on 4 February 1918, where the curfew rules seem to have been suspended for the occasion. Dancing did not begin until 9.30 pm and continued until 3.00 am, with a supper served at midnight.[83] Over in Mürren, Mabel Lunn, assisted by a committee of officers and men, arranged a late night dance on 20 May 1918 in the Hotel Eiger, where the ballroom was decorated with festoons and flags. Supper was served at 11.00 pm and sixty guests danced into the small hours, thanks to the Commandant allowing several extensions of time.[84] The standard of dancing was improved by the Practice Dances Mrs Lunn organized which gave the men the opportunity to dance with a female partner, perhaps for the first time in years.[85]

After being released from prison camps, the internees enjoyed relative freedom for much of the day, in comparison to the time they had been imprisoned. Preventing abuse of that freedom and too much time spent drinking was a priority. Staying in a hotel, however comfortable, was always monotonous and impersonal. According to the *Journal des Internés Français*, internees dreamt of a familiar place, where they could rest after a days' work, somewhere away from their hotels where they would not be bored.[86] These well-being needs were met by a Swiss society, *Le Bien du Soldat,* that provided meeting places for the French and Belgians through the creation of *Foyers du Soldat,* where non-alcoholic drinks were available.[87] At Gunten, a foyer called *le Cercle des Alliés* was open by November 1916, thanks to the generosity of Mrs Cooke Daniels and Miss Martin. Its home was a well-furnished chalet, with a library, billiards and a space where internees could read or study. It had lecture rooms with teachers to help them learn languages, arithmetic and so on. The walls were decorated with photos of Allied Army generals; there was a bathroom and an electric kitchen where hot drinks could be made.[88] On the second floor were small rooms for letter writing and study. With electric light and heating throughout, it was a vast improvement on their actual homes for most ordinary soldiers. This was a model for foyers elsewhere. In Berne, *le Foyer du Soldat* was in the Hotel Eiger on Belpstrasse. It offered low-priced food, a lecture room and a library. It also had a room for fencing practice. By mid-1917 other centres had opened in Salvan and Bulle, and Interlaken had a foyer run by an American woman, which welcomed French, Belgian and British internees.[89] The foyers allowed the nationalities to mix socially. The *Journal des Internés Français* claimed that for the French three words of English and strong gestures were said to be vocabulary enough to communicate with their comrades from across the Channel. The YMCA had provided funds for this foyer and the *Commission Romande* the expertise. Every day, around 300 cups of coffee, 130 cups of cocoa and 110 cakes were consumed, a testament to its success.[90] A pianist played, Tipperary being a particular favourite tune, while the men chatted. There was billiards, played in a cloud of smoke, for most internees enjoyed a pipe and cigarette smoking was beginning to be common. Smoking was important and perhaps comforting, even to those who didn't smoke before the war, who perhaps had their first cigarette in the trenches and took to a pipe in captivity.

Similar informal facilities where British internees could relax without the temptation of alcohol were provided, also often under the auspices of the YMCA. These facilities were frequently run by women. Isabelle Leckie worked for the YMCA with British prisoners for three years. She organized canteens in Leysin, Mürren, Interlaken, Meieringen and Lucerne, a service for which she was awarded the Order of the Red Triangle, the symbol of the YMCA.[91] When Isabelle Leckie moved on from Leysin, she was praised by the senior British officer who said in his report that 'she worked very hard, was popular with the men, and all ranks regret her departure'.[92]

Foyers were opened throughout the regions of internment. At Lausanne, the YMCA branch was supervised by Mrs Carey, an English clergyman's wife, although the men ran it themselves.[93] Not all these establishments for the soldiers' relaxation were run under the auspices of the YMCA, Villeneuve, near Montreux, had the British Soldiers' Club and Chateau d'Oex the Grey Hut, supported by the Red Cross which served a similar function. The games, amusements, whist drives, debates and wood carving classes provided appropriate distractions as after two months of the Grey Hut opening, indiscipline offences were down by 90 per cent and cases of drunkenness almost nil. Not far from Chateau d'Oex was another foyer in Rougement, worked by a few English women and reported to be working splendidly and in constant use by the men. 'It is made as homelike as possible, the men know they are always welcomed, and they get good tea etc, plenty of books and papers, and they have a piano.'[94] Miss Bates, who assisted at the Rougemont foyer had also worked in French ones. Both were successful but, she believed, the one in Rougemont was doing more work. Interlaken had a small tea room which took the place of a Soldiers' Club by providing a convenient place to go when down from Mürren or other nearby centres.[95] It was looked after by two convalescent patients staying at Manor Farm on Lake Thun.[96] There were similar facilities for German internees, known as *Stube* (parlour), where they could relax. Above all, the foyers and YMCA huts offered internees a change of scene, a familiar homely place to relax in warm homely surroundings and somewhere to go to chat, play cards and other games and sometimes a place to study and learn.

The internees' spiritual welfare was met through facilities for religious worship and pastoral care. Each Christian denomination was catered for, and there was some attempt to meet the needs of Imperial and colonial internees. At Chateau d'Oex, Reverend Lampen, Anglican priest of St Peter's English church since 1907, had spent years in Switzerland. He wrote offering his services for the spiritual care of internees before the first batch arrived, an offer endorsed by his employer, the Colonial and Continental Church Society.[97] Lampen's work with the internees was voluntary as he received no additional stipend for this ministry. When the internees first arrived it was estimated that about half of them were strongly religious. For the first three weeks church attendance

Figure 7.5 German internees relax with friends, a drink and a smoke, Davos. Courtesy of Dokumentationsbibliothek Davos.

at St Peter's was around eighty to hundred, but after this initial enthusiasm attendance dropped while at the same time cases of drunkenness increased. A number of explanations were offered for this. One given by the men was that they had thanked God for their deliverance from Germany for three Sundays and that was enough. A second was that the Swiss Military Law concerning church going was put into operation. This rule was that church attendance was optional, but that those soldiers who went to church had to do so in the company of a corporal and march there in a parade, something that was resented and aroused widespread hostility among the men to church going. Those who did not go to church had to remain in barracks until 11.00 am. The immediate result was that church attendance fell to between forty and fifty. Then, in August, Chateau d'Oex was invaded by 'a crowd of undesirable visitors', Swiss people attracted to the village for a summer excursion by the novelty of meeting British soldiers. The men were subject to almost constant 'fêteing', being treated to teas and alcoholic drinks. Weekends were particularly popular with the visitors. Late night entertainments on Saturday were not conducive to church going on a Sunday morning, also a time when visitors liked to take them on outings and picnics in the neighbourhood. The internees were said to have been spoilt by the attention and flattery, although the novelty soon wore off and the number of visitors declined. Other reasons given for non-attendance at church reflect the crisis in faith caused by the Great War itself. Unbelief in the existence of God, or a deity, was becoming more common. Some of the men argued that if there was a loving supreme being, why did he permit this war and the horrors they had witnessed? 'It was a serious difficulty and an honest facing of facts,' said the report on St Peter's Church Chateau d'Oex. Some of the men who wished to attend faced the further deterrent of ridicule from non-churchgoers. Another reason for not going to church was the men's state of health while another problem, specific to Chateau d'Oex, was that the local British Committee that had run the soldiers' home, where they could relax and socialize, after some disagreement dissolved and handed over the running of the place and its work to the senior British officer, Colonel Earle. Lampen had been president and raised about £54 for a comfort fund, but the men hadn't realized this as it was administered by the Committee. The secretary, the internees' Scottish minister, refused to resign, and the men sided with him and retaliated by abstention from church services.

Most of the officers tried to set a good example by supporting the services, but this had little impact. It was noted that the men wished to revert to the religious liberty of England where many of them were never accustomed to go to church.[98] What is surprising about the circumstances described is that Reverend

Lampen seems to have been blamed for this state of affairs in the religious life of the internees and that soldiers' church attendance mattered to the War Office. It was said that on their arrival from Germany, the men were in a responsive mood but did not find comfort and spiritual guidance in the ministrations offered them. 'The right note was missing. The power is not given to everyone to be a leader and this was unfortunately lacking in the present instance.' Lampen, may have been well-suited to civilian work, but was said to lack the authority needed to work with soldiers. The military authorities suggested that Lampen be transferred elsewhere and a replacement sent to Chateau d'Oex, so Reverend Archibold Sewell was sent out.[99] This seems unfair to Lampen, given that he was working for nothing in addition to his normal duties and could hardly be blamed for the lack of faith among soldiers who had recently experienced the trauma of battle, injury and imprisonment. The British officer in charge at Chateau d'Oex came to the conclusion that only a military chaplain would have the necessary experience.[100] After the war Sewell wrote about some of the things the soldiers had experienced in an article entitled 'The Hun and His Prisoners: Some Impressions of an Army Chaplain' in a journal called *The Nineteenth Century and After*.[101]

Sewell worked hard to win over his charges in Chateau d'Oex. Every Wednesday he invited four Church of England men to tea and chat, different ones each time, and in this way began to become on friendly terms with them. There was also a Royal Army Total Abstinence group there, 120 members strong and having a good influence. After a year Sewell was able to report back, 'Suffice to say in summing up that you, Sir, need no longer be worried as to the state of affairs in this place.'

Mürren had the Reverend Campbell Bell, a retired British army chaplain living in Leysin and temporarily restored to the military establishment, conducting the spiritual ministrations in the English church there. Campbell Bell was licensed in this appointment by the Bishop of London.[102] He was appointed under arrangements with the Society for the Propagation of the Gospel on a salary of £250 a year. However after four months work, only £50 had reached him, Campbell Bell surmising that the SPG did not feel justified in using money, given chiefly for missionary purposes, although given the experiences in Chateau d'Oex, there could be seen to be as much need for missionary work among the internees as anywhere else.[103] To encourage men averse to formal worship, a free and easy song service was held on Sunday evenings in Mürren.[104] At the opening of the internment camp in Mürren there were 267 men belonging to the Church of England, 106 Roman Catholics, 49 Presbyterians, 27 other denominations such as Wesleyans and Baptists and 2 Jewish, numbers that would increase as further contingents of internees arrived from Germany.

Being part of a denominational group gave further opportunities for social activities, such as an excursion to Grindelwald, organized by the Church of England Missionary Society and the Sunday evening congregation.[105] The Bishop of Stepney made a visit and gave an account of the air raids on London to the internees in Mürren, although this may not have brought them much comfort or contributed to morale if their families seemed in danger.[106] Presbyterian worshippers had a resident minister in Mürren, Mr Sutherland, paid a stipend of £300 a year with a free house, who also served the Wesleyans and Baptists.[107] As in Chateau d'Oex, the men had Parade Services to church on Sundays.

Another Anglican clergyman in Mürren was Reverend Bulstrode, who reported in July 1917 that Sunday evening services continued to hold their own despite the attractions of the summer evenings, although he was disappointed with the number of communicants – scarcely any apart from Church Missionary Society members. About Leysin, Reverend Swann wrote,

> The men are very friendly and easy to get on with, though they need great patience and sometimes careful handling. The slight feeling of reserve and constraint with the Padre has gradually disappeared, and now, I think, we are perfectly at ease and understand each other pretty well. The number of communicants has been good since the confirmation. Before that there were none.[108]

A preparation class for confirmation ran regularly with twelve keen participants. The Sunday morning service was 'not at all bad. The men turn up quite well, there is a really good spirit and swing about it' but only about 40 per cent attended.

The *Mission Catholique Suisse*, based in Fribourg, provided funds to support Roman Catholics in their faith. These grants could be used to support priests and chaplains in their work or to provide candles, rosaries, prayer books and utensils for Holy Communion. Books suitable for Catholics to read were donated to libraries as there were concerns that the mainstream literature available was of an unsuitable nature.[109] These grants were available to Catholics, military or civilian, wherever they were imprisoned or interned, including Great Britain where the general libraries in internment and prison camps contained much that was thought dangerous to the Catholic mind.[110] The *Mission Catholique Suisse* compiled a short annual report on how the faith needs in the different internment regions had been met. In some regions there were few issues, as Catholicism was the religion of the canton and services were delivered in the language of the internees, as in Fribourg where French was spoken and the internees French and Belgian, but special measures were needed for Catholics interned in the protestant Reformed or Lutheran areas. The report for 1917 shows that there were five priests in the British sectors. Every Sunday there was a mass and sermon in English at Chateau d'Oex given by Father Neville who also had responsibility for Gstaad, until he was repatriated and replaced in 1918 by military chaplain Father Chapman. There were weekly services and mass at Mürren led by Father Fahy who also visited the sick and cared for Catholics in Interlaken where he visited every fifteen days. Mass was said regularly by Father Murphy at Leysin and Bougy. On top of these routine services, the Catholic priests in the British regions performed four funerals and eight marriages as well as Easter services during 1917 and seven funerals in 1918.

For 1,800 mostly Catholic Belgians there were three priests interned in Switzerland, who were repatriated in the autumn of 1917. The Belgian government sent out four more chaplains in June 1917, led by Monsieur Jauneau.[111] When the Belgians were spread out across Western Switzerland, organizing services was difficult. As they were transferred and concentrated in fewer centres work became easier for the four Belgian military chaplains at Clarens, Glion, Leysin and Gryon, where preaching was done in French. The Wengen and Lauterbrunnen areas were entirely protestant, and a Catholic priest working there had difficulties in paying his own expenses, as a grant of 750 francs received from the Swiss Catholic Mission did not cover his accommodation costs of 780 francs or any personal expenses.[112] French Catholics were stationed throughout French-speaking Switzerland, where forty-three resident chaplains gave mass across fifty-three parishes. Protestant French speakers could also attend existing Lutheran or Reformed churches. For the German internees the situation was simplified as they could attend regular services in the churches where they were interned which were mainly regions with a German-speaking, Catholic population. The needs of about 400 civilian Austro-Hungarians were also attended to by the Catholic Mission.[113] Some military priests arrived in convoys from the prison camps, others were sent out by their national governments.

As well as arrangements for the various Christian denominations, Leysin became a centre where troops of South Asian origin gathered because having a concentration of them made it easier to cater for their cultural and religious dietary needs. The British officer in charge there was Major Alexander of the Gurkha Rifles. He and some of the other officers who had been stationed in India had a knowledge of Hindi. In his report of July 1917, the general condition of the Indian soldiers was said to be very good although Tulbir Gharki of the Gurkha Rifles had died and been buried on 13 February 1917.[114] Major Alexander had enquired to the Swiss military authorities about the cost of cremation for deceased Hindu soldiers, including transport from Leysin to Lausanne. On finding that it would cost 470 Francs, he reported to Picot that, in his opinion, the expense was prohibitive and that cremation was not a matter of importance during war time. Picot agreed and communicated this decision to the War Office in London.[115] Nevertheless, when Sepoy Dalbahadar Thapa of the 2/8th Gurkhas died in Chateau d'Oex on 16 March 1917, he was given a funeral that included Hindu as well as military rituals.[116] According to an eyewitness account, the coffin in the grave was open. A Hindu officer put several coins at the side of the body, whose eyebrows were burnt. Then the soldiers threw a little earth on the body before the coffin was closed and the grave covered. A peal of the clarion concluded the ceremony.[117] Photographs show Thapa's funeral procession, led by Gurkhas and soldiers wearing turbans, immediately behind the flower-adorned hearse.[118] Although there were Muslim soldiers among the interned British and French colonial troops, no mention has been discovered as to any special facilities for their religious well-being.

Festivals, entertainment, recreation and faith provided opportunities for cultural transfer among groups with different backgrounds living together. The influenza epidemic brought an end to the social life of the internees during the latter part of 1918. Meetings, concerts, services, sports or anything that brought groups of people together were cancelled and anyone moving from place to place was subject to a period of quarantine.[119]

Notes

1   Ketchum, *Ruhleben*, pp. 35–57.
2   Panayi, *Prisoners of Britain*, pp. 166–99.
3   The New Döberitz Empire Programme, designed by Cecil A. Tooke, July 1915, AEF.
4   Clare Makepeace, 'Just Like the Real Thing', *History Today*, 67:12, December 2017, p. 46.
5   *Gazette de Döberitz*, No. 2, 9 May 1916, Papers of Corporal H. D. Munyard, IWM Documents 10733.
6   *The Link*, Döberitz, Easter 1917.
7   Mürren Monthly Report, No. 11, 24 July 1917, TNA 383/330.
8   Picot, *The British Interned in Switzerland*, p. 189.
9   Leaflet re: *Journal attiré des prisonniers de guerre Français et Belges hospitalisés en Suisse*, 1916, AEF.
10 Letter re: *Le Journal des Internés*, Lausanne, 11 July 1916, AEF.

11 Joseph Mileck, *Hermann Hesse: Life and Art*, California, 1981, p. 71.
12 Draenert, *Kriegschirurgie und Kriegsorthopädie in der Schweiz zur Zeit des Ersten Weltkrieges*, p. 145.
13 *Coventry Evening Telegraph*, 4 July 1918.
14 Picot to the War Office, Berne, 1 September 1916, TNA FO 383/218.
15 Makepeace, 'Just Like the Real Thing', p. 46.
16 David A. Boxwell, 'The Follies of War: Cross-Dressing and Popular Theatre on the British Front Lines, 1914-1918', *Modernism and Modernity*, 9:1, 2002, p. 4; Iris Rachmaninov, 'The Disruptive Comforts of Drag', p. 363, quoted by Makepeace, *Captives of War*, p. 115.
17 Photographs, papers of Corporal H. D. Munyard, IWM Documents 10733.
18 *JIF*, A2, No. 5, 2 December 1917.
19 Paillard, *Notes sur les événements politiques de 1914 à 1919*, p. 47.
20 Picot, *The British Interned in Switzerland*, p. 189.
21 Paillard, *Notes sur les événements politiques de 1914 à 1919*, p. 47.
22 Ibid., p. 48.
23 Colonel Earle, Report on the workshops at Chateau d'Oex, September 1916, TNA FO 383/218.
24 *Newcastle Journal*, 16 September 1916.
25 From Constance Kirkup, 10 February 1917.
26 *BIM*, No. 3, July 1917.
27 *BIM*, Vol. 2, No. 4, April 1918.
28 *BIM*, No. 7, September 1917.
29 *BIM*, No. 5, August 1917.
30 Collins to sister, 8 March 1918, IWM Documents 15679.
31 *JIF*, No. 23, 7 July 1917.
32 *JIF*, A2, No. 5, 2 December 1917.
33 *JIF*, No. 23, 7 July 1917.
34 *JIF*, A2, No. 5, 2 December 1917.
35 *Tribune de Lausanne*, 9 Avril 1916.
36 *JIF*, No. 17, 17 February 1917; No. 18, 24 February 1917.
37 *JIF*, No. 18, 24 February 1917.
38 *JIF*, A2, No. 23, 7 April 1918.
39 *JIF*, No. 14, 27 January 1917.
40 Fuchs, 'Interniert im Appenzellerland', p. 61.
41 Major E. R. Collins to father, 11 February 1918, IWM Documents 15679.
42 *JIF*, A2, No. 5, 2 December 1917.
43 *BIM*, Vol. 2, No. 8, 30 September 1918.
44 *JIF*, No. 18, 24 February 1917.
45 *Davoser Blätter and Courier*, 8 January 1916; *Davos Courier*, 15 May 1916.
46 *Davos Courier*, 25 March 1916.

47 *Davos Courier*, 8 April 1916.
48 *Davoser Blätter*, 27 January 1917.
49 *DIZ*, Heft 52, 16 September 1917.
50 *JIF*, A2, No. 23, 7 Avril 1918.
51 *L'Orchestre symphonique des Internés Alliés*, http://www.notrehistoire.ch/medias/3224
52 Collins to sister, 8 March 1918, IWM Documents 15679.
53 *JIF*, No. 6, 30 November 1916.
54 *DIZ*, Heft Nr. 50, 2 September 1917.
55 Letter from Constance Kirkup, 10 March 1917.
56 *Feuille d'Avis*, Lausanne, 20 May 1916.
57 *Derby Daily Telegraph*, 30 August 1917.
58 *BIM*, No. 9, November 1917.
59 Cecil Walter to Private Alfred Gibbs of Leicester, 24 October 1916.
60 *BIM*, Vol. 2, No. 2, February 1918.
61 Jaccottet et al., *Au Soleil et Sur les Monts*, p. 235.
62 *JIF*, A2, No. 5, 2 December 1917.
63 *JIF*, A2, No. 16, 17 February 1918.
64 *JIF*, No. 18, 24 February 1917.
65 *BIM*, Vol. 2, No. 4, May 1918.
66 *JIF*, A2, No. 10, 13 January 1918.
67 *JIF*, No. 3, 9 November 1916.
68 *JIF*, A2, No. 10, 13 January 1918.
69 Ibid.
70 *JIF*, A2, No. 12, 20 January 1918.
71 Ibid.
72 *JIF*, A2, No. 10, 13 January 1918.
73 *DIZ*, Heft Nr. 21, 10 February 1917.
74 *JIF*, A2, No. 5, 2 December 1917.
75 *JIF*, No. 40, 28 July 1917.
76 Ibid.
77 Ibid.
78 *DIZ*, Heft Nr. 50, 2 September 1917.
79 *DIZ*, Heft Nr. 21, 10 February 1917.
80 *BIM*, Vol. 2, No. 4, May 1918.
81 Ibid.
82 *BIM*, Vol. 2, No. 2, February 1918.
83 Ibid.
84 *BIM*, Vol. 2, No. 5, June 1918.
85 *BIM*, No. 4, May 1918.
86 *JIF*, No. 2, 2 November 1916.
87 Walle, 'Les Prisonniers de Guerre Francais Internés en Suisse (1916–1919)', p. 59.

88 *JIF*, No. 3, 9 November 1916.
89 Ibid.; No. 38, 14 July 1917; A2, No. 5, 2 December 1917.
90 *JIF*, A2, No. 6, 9 December 1917.
91 *Walsall Advertiser and South Staffordshire Chronicle*, 2 February 1918.
92 Major Alexander, SBO Leysin, Monthly Report from Leysin, 29 June 1917, TNA FO 383/229.
93 Captain A. Hargreaves, 1/5 Battalion 13th Light Infantry, SBO Lausanne, Report 24 July 1917, TNA FO 383/330.
94 Miss Bates to Mrs Crozier, Rougement, 10 August 1916, TNA FO 383/218.
95 Monthly Report from Chateau d'Oex, November 1916, TNA FO 383/219.
96 Report from Interlaken, June 1917, TNA FO 383/229.
97 J. D. Mullins, secretary, Colonial & Continental Church Society, to the Under-Secretary of State for Foreign Affairs, 13 May 1916, TNA FO 383/215.
98 Picot, Report on St Peter's Church Chateau d'Oex, October 1916, TNA FO 383/219.
99 Ibid.
100 Revd Archibald Sewell to Chaplain General, Chateau d'Oex, 11 July 1917, IWM, FO 383/329.
101 *Belfast Newsletter*, 4 December 1918; *The Scotsman*, 4 December 1918.
102 Picot to War Office, 1 July 1916; War Office to Lt-Col. Picot, 4 August 1916; D. D. Cubitt of the War Office to under-secretary of state at the Foreign Office, 13 August 1916, TNA FO 383/217.
103 Picot, Report on Church of England, Mürren, October 1916, TNA FO 383/219.
104 *BIM*, No. 3, July 1917.
105 *BIM*, No. 5, August 1917.
106 *BIM*, Vol. 2, No. 8, 30 September 1918.
107 Picot, Report on Church in Mürren etc, October 1916.
108 Ibid.
109 Records of the Mission Catholique Suisse, 31, AEF.
110 Vincent Steinhurst to Mission Catholique Suisse, 15 October 1917, AEF.
111 Mission Catholique Suisse, Report 1917, 1918, AEF.
112 Wengen Broniolas de Laliski, 8 August 1917, Mission Catholique Suisse, AEF.
113 Mission Catholique Suisse, Report 1918, 14 March 1919, AEF.
114 Commonwealth War Graves, Vevey.
115 Picot to War Office, Berne 18 July 1917, TNA WA 383/329.
116 Picot to War Office, Berne, 23 March 1917.
117 Paillard, *Notes sur les événements politiques de 1914 à 1919*, p. 58.
118 Photographs, papers of Corporal H. D. Munyard, IWM, Documents 10733.
119 *BIM*, Vol. 2, No. 7, 15 September 1918.

8

Family life and relatives' visits

Estimates have put the total number of prisoners of war in the First World War at up to 9 million. By the end of March 1915 there were 37,000 British prisoners alone held in Germany. British schemes to provide assistance to the prisoners were entirely voluntary with the War Office refusing to take responsibility for the work of the Prisoners of War Help Committee until September 1916 when an official Central Prisoners of War Committee was established.[1] Local voluntary committees raised funds and sent food parcels to prisoners from their neighbourhood. When the Finance Committee of the Leicester, Leicestershire and Rutland Prisoners of War Committee met in November 1917, there were forty-seven people present, all male, including four representatives of the Trades' Council representing the town's trade union and labour movement.[2] In Leicester the Executive Committee of 27 included only 6 women, whereas 87 out of 133 voluntary workers, who did the practical tasks, were female.[3] Nearly £500 a month was spent sending parcels to 236 men. By the end of August 1916 over 21,000 parcels had been despatched, and the treasurer's statement showed a credit balance of £1,290, indicating the level of support for and hard work of the organization.[4]

> The work has from its very outset evoked the unbounded confidence of the town and communities of Leicestershire and Rutland. The large number of grateful letters received from prisoners and their relatives gives ample proof that the work has inspired the profound and heartfelt gratitude of the men who, for longer or shorter periods, have had the misfortune to be incarcerated behind the wire entanglements of a German Prisoners' Camp. The Committee therefore appeal for a continuance of that generosity from every section of the community which in the past has rendered the work, though at times arduous and extremely difficult, a real patriotic labour of love.[5]

Appeals for money raised funds for the Committee's work, such as that in December 1917 when the Leicester, Leicestershire and Rutland committee set itself a new target of £30,000, its original one of £20,000 being too low for the increasing number of prisoners to be supported. Ordinary people in warehouse, office and factory collections donated to the appeal.[6]

In France, women were encouraged to contribute to the morale of men serving on the front line by sending them parcels and letters as soldiers from the invaded regions often received no news from their families, an initiative known as *marraines de guerre* (war godmothers). The first of these schemes was started in January 1915 by Marguerite de Lens at Versailles.[7] Her *La Famille du Soldat* organization put soldiers in touch with volunteer letter writers. Other initiatives soon followed, publicized by the press, with immediate success. Each *marraine* or godmother adopted a *filleul* or godson and wrote to them regularly throughout the war, sometimes following their internment in Switzerland. Although these were mostly platonic or friendly interactions, sometimes they evoked suspicion as popular culture began to sexualize these relationships.[8] The image of these godmothers as easy girls offering themselves to a soldier deprived of sexual relations tarnished their reputation in the eyes of some. Fears were also raised that the *marraines* might be spies working for the enemy. There were similar initiatives in other warring countries, where women began penfriend relationships with soldiers who sometimes may not have had family members to write to them. The relationship between the *marraines* and French soldiers does not seem different from that of women of other nationalities who wrote to soldiers.

As well as the new burdens and responsibilities of war work and their ongoing domestic and childcare role, women had the additional stress and worry about their husbands and sons facing danger in battle or, even worse, the grief of bereavement. For women whose sons or husbands were taken prisoner there was perhaps relief that they would no longer be on the front lines but additional worries appeared about what conditions they were kept in, hardships they may be enduring or whether they were fed adequately. For those whose men were wounded and taken prisoner there were anxieties concerning their health and whether they were receiving appropriate care and medical treatment. Some men were missing in action which meant that their families had to both accept that they may be dead and never return yet also retain a hope that they might turn up in a hospital or prison camp somewhere. Hearing that a husband or son might qualify for internment and medical care in Switzerland was a massive relief for anxious families.

As soon as rumours emerged that prisoners might be interned in Switzerland, wives with the financial means began to make enquiries about joining their husbands in the Alps.[9] Even before any agreement regarding an exchange of

British prisoners from Germany and Germans imprisoned in Britain had been reached, letters began to arrive in the War Office, such as this one from Mrs Eden Vansittart written on 17 March 1916 when exchanged French and German prisoners were already in Switzerland:

> I have been advised to write to you to ask if there is any likelihood of English officer Prisoners of War being sent from Germany to Switzerland. My husband, Colonel Eden Vansittert, who was badly wounded on Sept 26th and is now at Crefeld, was told by the Camp Commandant on Dec 21st that as his lungs are effected from his wound and the exposure he suffered before he was picked up by the Germans that he would be sent to Switzerland almost at once.[10]

Mrs Vansittart received a reply from the under-secretary of state for the Foreign Office, expressing the Secretary of State Sir Edward Grey's regret that he was not in a position to make a definite statement regarding the transfer of British wounded prisoners.[11] At this point, no agreement had been reached between the German and British governments. When the exchange of prisoners between Germany and Britain finally took place, officers who could afford to do so were allowed to rent their own accommodation and have their wives and children join them. This led to rumours that some hoteliers were particularly interested in accommodating rich internees whose relatives were most likely to visit.[12]

Lieutenant Colonel Picot saw that it was beneficial for officers to be able to have their wives and families with them. In his account, *The British Interned in Switzerland*, Picot took credit for introducing the idea of close relatives of men of the lower ranks being able to visit.

> It struck me as eminently desirable that NCOs and men should also, if feasible, have an opportunity of seeing their wives or members of their families, and I addressed myself to the War Office, in the hope that arrangements in this sense might be made. Lord Northcliffe approved and promoted the idea in *The Times*.[13]

The Swiss, too, approved of these visits. Major Edouard Favre emphasized in his report *l'Internement en Suisse*, 'We cannot sufficiently insist on the happy influence exercised by the visits of relatives. By this means a living contact with the family, that basis of all social life, is re-established.'[14]

An article appeared in the press on 16 June 1916 with the capitalized headline 'INTERESTING TO RELATIVES'. It was reporting the secretary to the War Office's announcement that relatives of British prisoners of war interned in Switzerland who wanted to visit were requested to apply for permission at the Military Permit Office, 19 Bedford Square in London. Only near relatives of prisoners were eligible and only if they could show they could afford the return journey and other expenses incurred during their stay. When the Military Permit Office replied positively, applicants who already had a passport had to obtain a visa from its office, allowing them to leave the UK. Those who had no passport had to get one from the Foreign Office.[15] A list containing the names, regiment and wives' addresses of the first batch of twenty-four married men wanting their spouses to come out to Switzerland for one month was compiled during July 1916, soon followed by a list of forty-nine more names for the second batch.[16]

In Britain, the arrangements for the visits were the responsibility of Harold Wilkins while examination of local conditions in Switzerland were done by W. R. Ellis Hume-Williams, member of parliament for the Bassetlaw Division and Central Prisoner of War Committee member. He travelled to Switzerland in September 1916 to ensure that all arrangements for the visits of relatives were satisfactory.[17] He visited the places where British men were interned and, with the sanction of the Swiss authorities, secured accommodation for fifty relatives in Mürren and fifty more in Chateau d'Oex. From Autumn 1916, two parties of sixteen to eighteen women accompanied by two conductresses left London each week to travel out to Switzerland.[18] It was only possible to send one relative per prisoner, and each woman sent out by the Central Prisoners of War Committee had to return at the end of a fortnight. The Soldiers' and Sailors' Families' Association supervised the departure of the relatives from their homes. In case of delays the YWCA arranged accommodation in London or Southampton. Each relative was placed under five days of medical observation before leaving England, as required by the Swiss government, to prove they were free of illness.[19] These brave women set off by boat across the enemy submarine-infested English Channel and then travelled through the night by train across war-torn France for just a fortnight's visit, but they were happy to do so to be able to see their loved ones again. 'Only fourteen days' visit? Yes, but I would have come if only for an hour' was one woman's response. Another said, 'The bairns think I have gone to fetch their daddy home. I just let them think it.'[20] Unmarried internees were not forgotten and were allowed to have their mothers visit them. Miss Bates, a woman working with British internees in Rougemont, wrote,

> Those who know best are all in favour of helping them if it can be managed, because it is felt that to have relays of decent women, relations and relations of comrades would have a good moral effect. They are naturally in the way of many temptations, they are surrounded by sympathy and kindness, a vast amount of perhaps injudicious petting, and so it is not wonderful if Tommy's head gets a little turned. He is such a good sort and deserves help, such a lot of help, for the

contrast between their sufferings in Germany and their comfort now makes him a little liable to get into trouble, and the trouble is drink, a very easily obtainable refreshment, and poor men they are all suffering from neglected wounds and are a mass of nerves.[21]

It is understandable that better off families would find the money to visit their interned sons, husbands or fiancés in Switzerland. What is more surprising is that these visits were seen as so important back home that the Red Cross and local committees that raised money and sent food parcels and gifts to prisoners of war now focused some of their fundraising on paying for women's visit. Most cities, towns and counties in the UK had these organizations. The Leicester Committee was pleased to learn that eleven of the men they assisted were among the prisoners transferred from Germany to Switzerland. At its Executive Meeting on 1 September 1916, the chairman, Reverend Moss, reported that a number of letters had been received from them conveying the men's appreciation of the kindness shown to them during their imprisonment in Germany. The question of arranging for any of their wives who wished to visit their husbands in Switzerland was approved, and the secretary, George Clarke, made the arrangements.[22] After the Committee's AGM on 2 April 1917 the local newspaper reported,

> A further interesting feature of the work has been in connection with the interned men in Switzerland. In conjunction with the British Red Cross the committee were instrumental in arranging for visits of ten wives and mothers to Switzerland. Their stay extended over a fortnight and their entire expenses were paid from their home and back again. A small sum of money was also given to them for emergencies. £25 5 shillings was received and expended in this way.[23]

The British Red Cross Society's scheme to send visitors to interned men was promoted widely by *The Times* and local newspapers, which helped with fundraising nationwide. Trips were estimated to cost about £12 each from England, Scotland, Ireland and Wales.[24] A national scheme for raising money for injured troops, some of which was used for the visits, was Lord Kitchener's National Memorial Fund which raised a total of £264,000, including £1,000 donated by Lord Tredegar.[25] Lord Derby gave £200 to the fund for Lancashire men, Fenwick Harrison offered to pay for fifty women to travel with a donation to the Lord Kitchener fund, managed by Sir Hedley Bas. Bas received many requests to be included in the first party of wives and mothers and remarked, 'It is really quite pathetic how anxious these wives and mothers are to go out to their men folk.' Preference was given to the very poorest who could not possibly go otherwise.[26] Lord Justice Sir Robert Younger, who drafted the codes for POW treatment in future conflicts, offered to pay for fifty visits to Switzerland at £12 each.[27] The British Red Cross Society also supported the visits. It became a matter of local pride in some places that funds should be raised locally with no recourse to the national scheme. There were twenty-nine Birmingham men in Switzerland, and wives of thirteen of them applied to visit. It would have been 'unworthy of Birmingham if the cost of visits were met from elsewhere', decided the Executive Committee of the Lady Mayoress Depot for POWs of Birmingham; sufficient money was needed to cover the expenses of these thirteen cases and donations could be given to Mr G. O. Howard Smith of Waterloo Street. One person donated £100 to this committee, whose membership included Mrs Neville Chamberlain.[28] Advertising the scheme was a 'good source of revenue because the romance appealed to the emotions of the public'.[29] The financial record of the British Red Cross Society for the year end, October 1917, shows £12,187 received from the public in donations to the fund for 'relatives' visits'. The total expenditure of the Red Cross on the visits was around £15,000, an average of £25 per visitor, a reasonable figure, according to Picot, when wartime conditions were envisaged.[30]

As soon as the proposal to fund family members to visit internees in Switzerland was made public, women began to make enquiries. Hundreds of letters were sent by applicants; by October 1916 there were 500 cases to be dealt with.[31] One woman wrote, 'I have six sons serving the King'; she pleaded to be allowed to see her son who was interned in Mürren. Another wrote, 'I am most anxious to see my husband as he was reported killed, so it would be like seeing him back from the grave.'[32]

Preparations to receive the visitors were organized by the Red Cross, with cooperation between the International and different national sections of the organization: 'Everything is ready, at Mürren and Chateau d'Oex. Accommodation is ready at both. Soldiers will be allowed to leave their residence and join their wives in very comfortable quarters for the duration of the visit.'[33] In Leysin, husbands were allowed to sleep out three nights a week during the visits but had to be in their hotels for the midday meal. Four francs a day was allowed for the maintenance of soldiers and that was accepted by the owners of houses where the men joined their wives. At Mürren 5 francs was charged because it was more difficult and costly to get food up there.[34]

Women fortunate enough to be chosen to make the trip were given a list of things to take with them:

a) One hat and coat and skirt – on. Plain and serviceable. No feathers on hats.
b) One spare pair of boots or shoes – thick.

c) One or two changes of linen.
d) One spare skirt.
e) Two or three blouses.
f) Handkerchiefs, sponges, brush, comb etc.
g) Warm knitted coat and scarf desirable.[35]

A cloak, rug or gollosh boots could be borrowed if the traveller did not possess her own. The women were told what not to take with them: No presents except quite tiny ones, which they had to take home again with them. No chocolates, biscuits, cake or provisions of any kind would be allowed through the frontier of Switzerland. In Switzerland, they were to clean their own rooms but could pay to have their underwear washed. Wives were requested to refrain from all discussion of politics and questions regarding the war with the Swiss.[36] They were reminded that the interned men were not allowed beyond the boundary of the area to which they were assigned without the commanding medical officer's permission and that going to public houses was forbidden to the internees except during their free hours. Alcoholic drinks were forbidden in the bedrooms and meeting rooms. Unmarried internees were not allowed to visit the rooms of married ones.

The internees decided who they wanted to visit them, and the British Red Cross Society organized travel arrangements in Britain. The first party of twenty left London from Waterloo Station bound for Southampton and a boat to Le Havre on Saturday 30 September 1916. The party included sixteen wives and a bride-to-be, Miss Lilian Spencer of Croydon, who was engaged to Private Ernest Baylie. Additional expenses for the men's temporary transfer to stay with their wives were defrayed by the Red Cross Society.[37]

The arrangements for the women's travel included a Channel crossing from Southampton to Le Havre, where they were met in the morning for breakfast and then took a train to Paris. In Paris they stayed overnight in the Hotel d'Iena. The Channel crossing itself could be hazardous and often unpleasant, making it particularly frightening perhaps for women unused to travelling by boat or ship. The account of Katherine Furse, who had been a regular long-term visitor to Switzerland with her father John Addington Symonds since the 1880s and was now playing a leading organizational role in the Red Cross, mentions the dangers and delays caused by the presence of German submarines outside Southampton.

Katharine Furse and her assistant Miss Elsie MacSwinney were appointed to conduct and chaperone the party to Chateau d'Oex. Furse wrote that they set off on the journey 'like a triumphal march, with a press photographer and three journalists'.[38]

> At Southampton there were rumours the boat would not be able to sail because there was a German submarine waiting outside the harbour. For two nights and days we remained on the boat, as, having gone through passport formalities, no passengers were allowed to land, even though we were moored alongside the quay. It was an uncomfortable time, as there were some 500 passengers on a steamer built to hold 300, but the wives were wonderful and settled down quite happily, helping mothers with their children and patiently watching all that went on. We did succeed in getting permission to land on the third day, in order to get some exercise. We ran round Southampton, and that evening we were allowed to sail, reaching Havre safely and going on to Paris where we were received with great enthusiasm by the British Red Cross Society being shown the town and given an excellent dinner at the Gare de Lyon. We had a pathetic party of quiet, reserved women, expressing little interest in anything, while our reporters took every opportunity of telegraphing to announce any item of news they could squeeze out of us, in order to keep up the excitement at home.[39]

No doubt the travellers were tired, perhaps anxious about the possibility of Zeppelin raids on Paris and worried about how their menfolk would be when they met again after sometimes two years apart. They travelled across France by train from Gare de Lyon through the night to the border station of Vallorbe, just inside Switzerland. At Vallorbe where the party stopped for coffee, there was a crowd of Swiss waiting to welcome them, just as there was when a train load of internees arrived. From this point 'the wives began to notice things, discussing the muddle of the war and the thickness of the coffee cups', which reminded Furse of the complaints at home about the thickness of hospital cups, 'with thin cups being almost a gauge of respectability'. From Vallorbe they set off on the final stage of the journey to Chateau d'Oex. By now, the reporters' telegrams must have been more and more intense, wrote Furse, describing the suppressed impatience of wives going to meet their husbands, but

> poor women, they were far too tired and muddled after four nights out of bed, and with all the changes of habits and customs and all the questions asked of them by our Pressmen and by the people who met them at every station, to take much notice of what went on, or where they were, but I know that there was anxiety in the hearts of that carefully-chosen first band of pilgrims as to how they would find their husbands.[40]

The press had generated public interest in the visits through campaigning for donations, so the reporters were eager to get the first reports back to their newspapers ahead of their rivals. Once the group was safely delivered to Chateau d'Oex and had been reunited with their husbands and sons, the women were handed over to the care of the authorities there. For Furse, vivid impressions were the number of healthy young Swiss men everywhere, and the electric light in the village at night. She had become accustomed to only seeing young men in uniform at home and groping her way around darkened streets. Although it was a relief to be away from the war, its results were terribly apparent in the officers and men interned at Chateau d'Oex – so many were crippled or sick and all were nervy.[41] Furse left for home and the responsibilities of her usual work after a couple of days, leaving the party in the care of Elsie MacSwinney. The group stayed at Chateau d'Oex for two weeks.

Extreme tiredness was normal for the women travellers, Major Ernest Collins, interned in Interlaken, wrote home that

> all the ladies who have come to see and live with their husbands have been so exhausted that they have to spend two or three days in their beds on arrival and now shiver with cold.[42]

After the success of the first party to travel to visit their husbands, parties of women travellers across war-torn France became a regular occurrence. A party of eighteen women that left for Switzerland in November 1916 had a pleasant cross-Channel voyage and train ride through France. One of those in the party was the wife of Private Grant of the Territorial Gordon Highlanders from Aberdeen who was one of the first 150 men to be sent to the front from his regiment. He had lain on the battlefield a couple of days before he was found by a German who tried to put a bullet through his head and left him for dead. Next day another German found him and took him to a dugout where he lay up to his neck in water. The German went to look for another to help him and the two took him to a hospital where he was treated, showing how survival after being wounded could depend on chance and the mood or nature of the soldier who found an injured man. Asked about her husband by a reporter from the *Aberdeen Evening Post*, Mrs Grant remarked,

> Oh yes, I found my husband very well, though unable to use his right arm, twice shot through, once in battle and the next time when he held his arm up to defend himself from a German bullet aimed at his head as he lay helpless on the battlefield.[43]

Private Grant, she said, was being well treated by the Swiss as regards clothing and food. Mrs Hurworth of Alveston was also in a party that left in November 1916. Her husband, a sergeant in the West Yorkshire Regiment had been taken prisoner in August 1914. He had been badly wounded in the face and was waiting to undergo a delicate operation by Swiss surgeons. While imprisoned in Germany, Hurworth had received regular parcels from the Derby and Derbyshire Prisoners of War Help Committee which helped him and other men to survive. The Mayor and Mayoress and a few friends came to see Mrs Hurworth off at the station.[44]

The women visiting Switzerland came from all over the UK. Mrs Ormorod was the first to travel from Oldham and on her return offered to give a talk to other women in the Red Cross Sewing Meeting there. This offer was turned down as it would not raise much money for future visits and so Mrs Ormorod found herself addressing a large public meeting to raise money for future work. She gave a talk recalling her experiences on her trip to visit her son, Frank, in Mürren. She left home on 11 December but was delayed in London for a week through a mistake with her passport. This did not appear to spoil the trip very much as it was Mrs Ormorod's first visit to London where she visited the main tourist sites of the capital, while staying in the YWCA hostel on Bedford Square. The party she joined left London for Southampton and the eight-hour overnight crossing to Le Havre on 19 December. Mrs Ormorod described a rough sea crossing causing sickness. When her Red Cross party arrived on board their ship,

> supper was ready for us and we did our best to eat, but the boat was far too wobbly even to enable us to feel hungry. The Stewardess asked us to get settled down as soon as we could for she was afraid we should have a rough time. The rule was the younger ladies take the upper bunks, so of course I classed myself one of these. When she was leaving us she promised to come and see how we were doing during the night, and she told us that if the boat did happen to lurch, just to hold tight. We had not been long out before we did have to hold tight, and 13 out of the 16 were very soon busy. To be eight hours on a sea like that, well to say the least, was not pleasant, but you soon get over it when you get off the boat.[45]

They were met from the boat by Red Cross vehicles at 7.30 am and taken to the YWCA. They had a guided tour of Le Havre and then after tea took the tram to Paris where they stayed overnight before a guided tour of the French capital. On top of the Arc de Triomph was an anti-aircraft gun, and outside Les Invalides were guns and aeroplanes captured from the Germans. All afternoon the booming of guns could be heard. At the border they had no trouble going through French and then Swiss customs.[46]

For French relatives to visit their family member it was a slightly less complex process as no sea voyage was necessary, and it did not involve crossing another country. To travel to Switzerland, applicants for passports needed proof of identity and evidence of who they wanted to visit. They had to state their relationship, such as wife, parent, child, guardian, foster parent or evidence of adoption. The travellers needed to show they had enough money to pay for the return journey and the expenses of their stay. On producing evidence at the railway ticket office that they were a close relative visiting an internee in Switzerland, they would be given a half-price ticket for their journey across France. The ticket price was reduced by 75 per cent for the poorest. Even with these reductions, the cost of the journey was quite high. Poor applicants could receive financial help to visit military internees by applying to a charity, *L'Oeuvre de la Colonie Suisse de France*, which was under the patronage of the Swiss legation.[47] Families of civilian internees could apply to a different office. To simplify the formalities, family members returning from visits were exempt from the requirement to have their passport stamped at a French consulate before their return, provided she or he returned to France within fifteen days by the same point on the border that they crossed on the outward journey.[48]

Like the British wives and mothers, the parents, wives and children of French internees could receive support to enable them to travel to Switzerland to visit their wounded relatives. *L'Oeuvre de la Colonie Suisse de France* in aid of French military internees in Switzerland, created on 17 May 1916, was an initiative of Swiss people living in France, led by Monsieur Lardy, the Swiss minister in France and made up of Swiss groups in Paris. The society helped families get travel documents from the Swiss Consulate and for poorer people to travel at a quarter of the usual price on French railways to the border. They were then issued with a free return ticket, from the frontier stations to the place of their relative's internment, valid for up to forty-five days on Swiss railways. In addition the families received a small allowance to help towards the cost of their stay. They were also supplied with two letters of recommendation, one for the station master at the frontier station and the other for the Swiss *Commandant de Place* at the place of internment. By February 1917, out of 12,000 French soldiers interned, the organization had helped 2,600 of them, military and civilian.[49]

The French also looked forward to their families joining them. The writer Jacques Rivière, serving in the French army, was imprisoned at Königsbrück where he lamented in his diary that he felt like a meadow crushed to the ground.[50]

He sent his wife Isabelle a telegram from Zurich on 14 June 1917 saying simply that he had arrived in Switzerland and that a letter was to follow. After another telegram the next day, telling Isabelle that he was about to travel to Lucerne, she feared he was being taken back to Germany. Her worries were unfounded, and the next day a postcard was sent by Jacques telling her his new address in the Hotel Edelweiss in Engelberg. Isabelle wrote in her diary that she grasped the telegram as if it were the train that could take her to him. The letter prompted her to begin the necessary steps in the complicated process of obtaining a pass which she optimistically hoped to get in five days at the earliest. As she wrote this news in a letter to her husband, dated 19 June 1917, Isabelle said her hand was trembling so much she could hardly write.[51] Rivière hoped that being with his wife and children would rescue him from his depression. He wrote to her that materially speaking he was a free man but that he did not really understand how as it had happened so suddenly. It was as if his body had been released from prison but his soul had not been given back to him. He longed for his 'precious princess' to come to him.[52] The Hotel Edelweiss where Rivière was accommodated was just for soldiers so he looked around for lodgings for himself, his wife and child. Luckily he found two rooms to rent in Haus Gletscherblick. The owner of the house and their four children lived on the upper floor. Frau Stohr, whose home it was, spoke French and so helped the Rivières to settle, the children of the two families becoming constant playmates.

Wives and relatives of German internees could travel to Eastern Switzerland without problems in 1916 and 1917, but this became more difficult as the war progressed and the German economy became more strained and transport difficult.[53] Some German wives and children remained with their husbands after the war ended, awaiting repatriation, some until August 1919.

Soon after the first British internees arrived in Switzerland and it was confirmed that they could receive visitors, the question arose of whether there would be any objection to the marriage of an interned soldier to a British subject in Switzerland. There was none according to Swiss law.[54] The reply, a few days later, was that the Army Council saw no objection to the marriage referred to, provided no objection was raised, either by the Swiss authorities or the officer in charge of British prisoners interned in Switzerland and that the marriage was solemnized in a valid form, recognized by the Swiss.[55] The first wedding of a British officer in Switzerland took place in Berne on 14 November 1916. The bride was Miss Florence Golbourn Tarry, daughter of Major George Tarry of the Leicestershire Regiment. Miss Tarry married Captain R. W. Thomas of the Munster Fusiliers from Castletown Roche in Ireland. He had been severely wounded in the throat at Mons and imprisoned in Germany for two years. His new wife moved out to live with him in Berne.[56]

As well as wives and mothers, fiancées were encouraged to come on the funded visits to Switzerland but were expected to marry during their stay. For the British, these marriages were 'off strength', meaning the new wives were not considered part of the military establishment.[57] Miss E. Carpenter of Deptford received a letter from Miss Lean of the British Red Cross Society and Order of St John of Jerusalem Joint War Committee containing a proposal on behalf of Lance Corporal H. Munyard interned in Mürren. The organization had received a letter from Munyard asking that Miss Carpenter might be allowed to visit him and, as the couple were not yet married, if Miss Carpenter would be willing to go to Switzerland to marry him if they could arrange it.[58] Miss Carpenter obviously said yes, as she received a second letter on 2 May 1917 from Janette Lean:

> Will you please note, party to Switzerland will leave London on 9th. Will you therefore be ready by Tuesday 8th? I will send you instructions as to where you are to report by Friday night's post. As you are going out to Switzerland to be married will you please be sure to bring your birth certificate with you, also your fiancé's birth certificate if you have not forwarded them to Switzerland.[59]

The couple were married on 22 May in Berne, their wedding photograph includes six to eight brides, showing that several weddings were organized around the same time and some part of the celebration was shared.[60] The couple were soon parted again, as the new Mrs Munyard had to return home with the Red Cross party, a fact noticed by other internees as a sentence in *British Interned Mürren* magazine, marked with an 'X' by Munyard, said, 'What is a certain corporal going to do now "Happy" has gone away?'[61]

For women who were not visiting a husband or son, it could be difficult to get a passport and a visa to cross France if they had no plans to marry during the visit. Lieutenant Angus Leybourne and Constance Kirkup discovered this soon after Angus arrived with the first contingent in Chateau d'Oex. Leybourne and Connie were just friends when Angus first wrote to her from the Grand Chalet at Rossinières, on 9 June 1916, inviting her to come out as a friend of the family to see him on a 'small holiday'.[62] 'There are girls galore here already, but I like them from the north with something in 'em, none of your Folkestone flappers for me', he wrote.[63] Leybourne proposed to Connie by letter in September, and he continued to urge her to come to see him now that she could travel as his fiancée.[64] His unsuccessful applications for Connie to visit continued to meet with red tape, because Connie's visits were not to involve their marriage. In his appeal to the senior British officer in Chateau d'Oex and to Lieutenant Colonel Picot, Leybourne provided a newspaper cutting as evidence of their engagement and pleaded that 'the question of the date and place of my marriage I must reserve as the course of the war in the next few months influences matters considerably'. He also explained that there would be no problem with Connie being alone as his mother and sister were out there and that they proposed to remain in the country.[65] Leybourne went on to explain that Miss Kirkup's application for a passport had already been refused and pointed out the unfairness of this 'as soldiers' wives and fiancées are brought out here freely at the public expense, I would respectfully urge, that I myself as an officer should not be debarred from this privilege when my case implies no expense to the state', a possible misunderstanding of how the funding, basically charitable, worked. Picot gave in to these pleas and wrote to the secretary at the War Office in London to say that 'I have no objection to Miss Kirkup coming out. She seems to be in every way desirable and would be under the care of Lieutenant Leybourne's mother'.[66] It was January 1917 when Connie finally left for Switzerland, travelling in the company of a Red Cross party as she was alone. She arrived on 27 January where she remained until the end of May.[67]

For the French, there were three different regulations, issued in Circular Number 10 of the army. Those who were active or recommissioned officers or NCOs had to send a request for authorization to the French government, under its laws relating to the marriage of servicemen. Soldiers from the reserve or territorial army, officers, NCOs and troopers had to contact the consulate concerned to obtain the necessary documents. An unusual third way of getting married was introduced to enable soldiers who were away to marry women left behind, especially those who were pregnant. This was marriage by proxy. Authorization from the Minister of War and the Minister of Justice had to be obtained. The interned soldier was then invited to sign an application and a power of attorney. The power of attorney or proxy had to be signed either at the chancery of one of the French consulates or before a notary or competent Swiss officer. This meant that the bride and groom did not have to be together for the marriage to be legally recognized. An advantage of this was that the wife and any children would be eligible to claim separation allowances from the government. Unfounded fears of an increase in illegitimacy rates, of babies fathered by soldiers, led the French government to allow soldiers to marry by proxy, provided they could prove a previous sustained commitment to the mother. The government also approved legislation that permitted the legitimization of children of soldiers even if the father was killed.[68] France had adopted a policy of pronatalism, designed to encourage and support French women to have children, due to fears of a declining birth rate, an idea made stronger by the devastating loss of life in battle.[69]

Once fiancées began to arrive wedding announcements and reports appeared frequently in the internee newspapers. Lieutenant Middleditch, a skiing companion of Arnold Lunn, was married quietly in Berne on 20 September 1917, and his wife was transferred to the Mürren garrison.[70] Not all the weddings were quiet; many were communal affairs involving fellow internees, staff and friends, often standing in for families who were unable to make the journey. The wedding of Sergeant Matthews of the 2nd Royal Dublin Fusiliers to Miss N. Marshall of Hampshire on 21 November 1917, was delayed as the bride had to stay in Paris for several days due to the frontier between Switzerland and France being closed, something that happened periodically depending on the situation of the fighting. After the usual formal ceremony in Berne, the couple were married by Reverend McCready in Mürren. The bridal party arrived at the church in a sleigh drawn by enthusiastic friends while the groom and his best man, Sergeant C. F. Lewis of the 32nd Australian Infantry, waited at the church. The bride, dressed in white crepe-de-chine and carrying a large bouquet of white chrysanthemums, was given away by the army schoolmaster K. G. Spendlove and attended by bridesmaid Miss M. Williams, dressed in blue. After the ceremony 'a very jolly wedding breakfast' was held in the Hotel Bellevue. The toasts, speeches and good wishes were many and enthusiastic. Sergeant and the new Mrs Matthews left the same afternoon for a honeymoon in Vevey and Geneva.[71]

A week after the Matthews wedding, on 28 November 1917, Lance Corporal Challis of the Kings Own Yorkshire Light Infantry married Miss Buckley of Bradford at Interlaken. The weather being exceptionally fine, many internees were present. After the service the bride and groom were surprised to find that the horses had been taken out of the shafts of their carriage and a number of their friends were waiting to pull them to the Hotel des Alpes for their wedding breakfast where the speeches and toasts were said to be very good, particularly the groom's reply to the toast for the bride and bridegroom. Lieutenant Corporal Strachen of the 48th Canadian Highlanders was best man and Private Clay of the same regiment as the groom gave the bride away.[72]

The bride was dressed in a costume of dark blue and a grey hat, with a bouquet of white flowers, when Miss Somers of Glasgow married Lieutenant J. K. Bell of the Canadian Infantry at the English church in Vevey in February 1918. The groom was supported by Lieutenant Wallis, and the bride given away by Captain F. C. Rose of the Lincolnshire Regiment. Pension Miremont hosted the reception to which many friends were invited. The couple's honeymoon was in the mountain village of Les Avants.[73]

There were plenty of weddings taking place, a fact alluded to in a humorous announcement in *British Interned Murren* in August 1917:

> Will the Red Cross kindly let us have the fiancées more in instalments. When the Civil Registrar had to marry six couples at once a short time ago, he was so overcome that he had to go away in the middle and change his collar.[74]

Perhaps the article is referring to the day, or another like it, when six couples were married in Mürren.[75] One of them was Jack Perry Taylor of the 4th Leicestershire Regiment who married Agnes Atkinson whom he had met in his home town of Leicester. The couple were married in a civil ceremony in Berne on 17 May 1917, followed by a wedding in the English church in Mürren on 23 May.[76] Taylor had joined up as a volunteer with other members of his football team who played on Victoria Park. He was injured at the Hohenzollern Redoubt, shot in the right wrist and lost a finger on his left hand. Left out all night, he packed his wound with mud to stop the bleeding. He was eventually found and taken to a German hospital before being sent to Mannheim Camp.[77] Following the weddings, all six couples shared a crowded reception in the ballroom of the Palace Hotel.

Wedding celebrations also punctuated internment life for French internees. Before the war it had been the dream of newly-weds to come to Switzerland, the classic honeymoon destination, on the banks of a beautiful lake with a background of majestic mountains. The generosity of the Swiss allowed internees to have this dream come true, claimed the *Journal des Internés Français*, when in May 1917 Sergeant Courtois Valentin of the 122nd Infantry Regiment married Marguerite Balcou in the Berne Catholic Church. Their honeymoon was spent by Lake Thun.[78] In June 1917 the Catholic Church in Yverdon was the venue for the nuptials of Captain Mazars of the 142nd Infantry Regiment and Elisabeth Paffie. The groom, who was studying in Neuchatel, had been seriously wounded at the beginning of the war at Lauterfingen in Lorraine.[79] Sergeant Pierre Fargue's wedding to Ida Wellig took place on 28 November 1917 and the new young husband and his wife looked forward to their approaching repatriation back to France.[80]

Weddings also performed a communal function for German internees. At the marriage of Captain Werner and Gertrud Neubert in Ragaz as well as family and friends coming out for the event, a choir of internees serenaded them on

Figure 8.1 The wedding of Jack Taylor and Agnes Atkinson, Mürren, May 1917. Courtesy of Pat and Mark Esling (family collection).

the eve of their nuptials and sang Psalm 22 at the church.[81] Three weddings were announced in the German magazine *Deutsche Internierten Zeitung* in March 1917 and a further three in June. At Oberegg relations of senior NCO Ganter and Fraulein Trauung were all assembled for a wedding that had to be delayed while the bride awaited her papers which had not yet arrived.[82] Another groom was Heizer Geisler of *SMS Blücher*, a ship that had taken part in the bombardment of Yarmouth, Scarborough, Hartlepool and Whitby in 1914, before being sunk in January 1915 at the Battle of Dogger Bank. Geisler was lucky to have been recovered by a British ship as a German Zeppelin began bombing, forcing rescuing ships to withdraw, leaving between 747 and 1,000 casualties to drown. Geisler looked forward to happier times when he came from Berne to Walzenhausen church with his bride who joined him from Germany. The couple then lodged with a Swiss family. In Davos, soldier Wilhelm Zehender married Ida Gurdner on 7 March, Junior NCO Alfred Paulick wed Beda Neumeister on 20 March and on 29 June there was a double wedding when soldier Heinrich Rathert married

Figure 8.2 Wedding reception for six British couples, Palace Hotel, Mürren, May 1917. Courtesy of Pat and Mark Esling (family collection).

Frederike Heuer from Minden in Westfalia and Erich Meier wed Martha Funke from Selbilz on 29 June.[83] In St Gallen Paul Müller married Annemarie Niemann on 26 June.[84] Some couples were lucky enough to have family members present. When Captain Werner von Sichart of the 12 *Jägerbattallion* married Gertrud Neubert of Dresden on 25 July 1917, the officiating clergyman was a friend of the bride's family, Pfarrer Schuknecht, who had come to Switzerland especially to perform the ceremony at Ragaz. The parents of the bride and the mother and brother of the groom were also there, as well as friends and other interned officers.[85]

Most internees were young and many not yet married or courting. Meeting a Swiss woman and having a relationship was something some internees aspired to. When a group from Seeburg were transferred to Vevey the band played 'The Girl I Left Behind Me' and, according to a report in *British Interned Magazine*, 'those unable to pick up lady friends here are wondering if they will have more luck down South'.[86] While young Swiss men were away from their homes on service, the presence of internees was a source of conflict for local girls who, by giving favours to prisoners, could be accused of having dissolute morals in inflammatory newspaper articles, which alleged that some might be giving more than food and favours. They feared above all that girls and women had hearts too tender, urging or enticing internees who were weak, physically or psychologically, to commit immoral acts or behave improperly.[87] Some of these conflicts led to disorder and violence, for example, the brawl in a Herisau dance hall between local men and German internees in October 1917. Interactions between internees and local women were a cause of consternation for both the individual national authorities and the local Swiss population, particularly the young men absent on military service. The enthusiasm shown to internees on their arrival was not always unanimous, and some authorities feared it might be a potential source of trouble to public order. Free time spent in bars and cafes could present opportunities for liaisons with local women as well as drunkenness. One British internee, Private Jimmie Green, a cockney of the Middlesex Regiment, was said to be 'a great favourite with the ladies and during the summer was often seen accompanying them on rambles over the hills in search of wild flowers'.[88]

The possibilities for romance were evident from the time the first internees began to arrive. The poet from Nidwald, Isabelle Kaisser wrote a pamphlet in 1916 about the arrival of German wounded in the Lucerne area. According to Kaisser's observations, she believed some of the guests would remain after the war and settle down in Swiss homes since they did not drink at the fountain of freedom in vain. Young Swiss women would feel warmth and affection for the interned men, for in the warm circle of sympathy, many flames ignited, silent holy fires, spinning invisible bonds from heart to heart. The path from compassion to love is not far and compassion blooms towards the prisoners on all sides. These romantic words were followed by a warning, that in the soul-stumbling block of first love, it is hard enough for a good marriage to overcome the diversity of the characters without adding the dividing scruples of nationality, race and religion, and many conflicts have already and will result.[89]

Sometimes relationships between interned men and local women led to marriage, such as that between Wilhelm Hormann from Bremen and Emma Stauber of Teufen whose wedding ceremony was on 9 August 1917.[90] Another relationship that developed into marriage was between Walter Strutz and Emilie Geprägs of Lichtensteig, St Gallen who were married on 18 August 1917 at the evangelical church in Trogen.[91] French internee, Sergeant Emile Fornage, of the 5 *Tirailleurs Algériens*, interned at Pension Victoria-Vevey married a local girl, Marie Zenhäusern of Tour de Peilz.[92] A Swiss woman, Edmée Cordier-Moennat, described as a charming and pretty Genevan, was the bride of Captain Charles de Laréa, of the 154th Infantry Regiment. The groom wore his dress uniform, with a red feather in his cap and epaulettes with gold fringes for the occasion. On his cheek was a large scar, a souvenir of a serious wound received near Verdun. Among the large crowd of guests in the church were French, Belgian and Swiss officers.[93] Another Frenchman, Georges Pansard married Amélie Duay of

Sembrancher in Bagnes on 8 July 1918.[94] Among the British internees, Corporal Joseph Miller of the 1st Cheshire Regiment married Madamemoiselle Emilie-Louise-Henriette Witwer of Renens near Lausanne on 27 June 1918 at the Church of St Jean in Lausanne. The groom was manager of the Vevey Soldiers' Club.[95] Privates Edward Varley and Albert Tidy married Mürren sisters, Anna and Martha Huggler. The Varleys became better known among the internees as the Whiteleys as they kept a shop. Whiteley's was a well-known London store of the time. When the British internees left Chateau d'Oex for home on 4 December, they took with them twenty local women who left to find a new home abroad as wives of former prisoners of war.[96] There must have been similar numbers of marriages between internees and Swiss in other internment communities.

These marriages were sometimes met with disapproval. An article in the *Journal des Internés Français*, published in February 1918 after several marriages between internees and local Swiss women had already taken place, emphasized that the patriotic duty of a French soldier did not include marrying a foreigner. The writer claimed that he understood the state of mind of young men, leaving for war between the ages of twenty-five and thirty, seeing the fruitful years of their youth going by, and knew the pain of their loneliness. A few Swiss girls made good French wives and were made welcome in the homeland, but this should always be an exception. Every Frenchman who marries a Swiss bride would be sacrificing the marriage hopes of a French girl. He would also perhaps be damaging the preservation of the French race. Internees were urged to wait until they returned home to marry as French women were waiting, saving their fresh, simple souls, generosity and exquisiteness for them.[97]

Not all relations between internees and Swiss women ended happily. Among the reasons for punishments given for breaches of discipline or 'crimes' as they were termed by the British military, absence featured frequently, second only to drunkenness. Absence could have been to get out to buy alcohol but could also have been in order to meet up with women. For instance, Corporal C. Ashford of the 1st Welsh Fusiliers was absent without leave in Leysin between 28 and 31 March 1917. When asked if he had anything to say, Corporal Ashford replied, 'I knew if I asked for leave, it would be refused me – I therefore went without leave.' The senior British officer in Leysin, Major Alexander, already knew that Ashford had been to see a woman who had since left Leysin but with whom Ashford had been on intimate terms. Ashford was demoted because of the risk to discipline if non-commissioned officers set such a poor example of lack of self-control.[98] A military tribunal found Thomas Fitzhenry of the 2nd Irish Guards, interned at the Palace Hotel in Mürren guilty of the attempted rape of a young

Swiss woman, Miss von Allmen, who had accompanied him on a toboggan ride from Almendhubel in January 1917. Medical evidence verified her accusation, and Fitzhenry was sent to prison in Interlaken for fifteen months and to pay 39 francs 20 centimes in costs.[99]

Not all the marriages were with fiancées coming from the home country or with local Swiss women. Switzerland offered opportunities to meet other women of the internee's own nationality visiting, staying or working there. There were female teachers, for whom the possibility of finding a match was acknowledged officially, but it had to be a match with a partner of the correct social class. Female teachers employed to work with internees were forbidden to marry any soldier below the rank of sergeant. Major Collins, interned in Interlaken and then at Vevey, met his wife Margaret Sotheron Estcourt in Switzerland. Margaret was in Switzerland on leave from her work in France on account of her health. She was staying with her interned brother, Captain Estcourt of the 'Greys', and his family who rented a flat near Vevey but had moved into Major Collins' hotel as the flat was too small for them all. Collins wrote to his parents describing Margaret,

> She is 38 years of age and no pretence of good looks though she must have been very pleasant looking before the war as a photo of her shows, but her mother died when she was about 20 and she has the family to look after in her place and during the war she has been a scullery maid in a hospital and after was cleaning out the wards, then a clerk in the munitions at the War Office and finally canteen work in France in charge of French and American soldiers, so you see she has been through the mill and I think it was that which was the great attraction to me. I am of course very happy and if this comes off, I feel the reward is more than ample for all the trials and disappointments I have suffered during the last four years.[100]

The wedding did indeed 'come off', and Major Collins, aged forty-eight, married Margaret Alice Sotheron Estcourt on 25 March 1919 at Long Newnton in Wiltshire.

Mothers were able to visit their sons. It is hard to imagine the joy of Mrs H. Stock of Kettering when after over a year of grieving for her son, Harry, missing presumed dead, she received news that he was in Mürren. Harry had been wounded, losing an eye and having a hand shattered and was taken as a prisoner to Germany. For Mrs Stock, at the age of sixty it was a big journey for her as well as a memorable one. She had never before been to London, where the group of women travellers met up. Among her thrilling experiences were a day in Paris, a toboggan ride and a railway climb up a mountain amid snow and ice. Harry had a pass to go to Interlaken to meet her where the party changed trains.[101]

Another visitor was the mother of nineteen-year-old Private Frederick Albert Terry of the 7th Battalion Northamptonshire Regiment from Desborough. Terry was wounded in the leg at Loos in the autumn of 1915 when he was picked up by a German soldier and taken to hospital in Cologne. After he was sent to Switzerland he was looked after along with other internees by a Miss Hannah, who came over from England. Mrs Emma Terry was selected for a funded visit and was able to go to her son who had left school at fourteen to work as a clicker in the shoe trade. Without the financial support offered, a corset maker married to a boot maker with a young family, Mrs Terry would have been unable to afford the journey. Switzerland's beauty made a lasting impression on Emma Terry, memories of which she passed down to her children and grandchildren. A century later, her eighty-year-old granddaughter, Frederick's child Doris, unborn at the time of the visit was able to recall that Emma travelled to France by boat, leaving a three-month-old baby at home, a very brave thing to do during the war, she said. Although Doris had never been to Switzerland herself, she was able to recall her mother talking about the magnificent sight of a gorge, which Doris was able to accurately describe as like 'a big cave with waterfalls going through it', based on her mother and grandfather's stories. She even used the phrase 'one of the wonders of the world' even though she did not know the name of the place. This was probably the Aare Gorge at Meiringen, sometimes described in publicity as one of the world's wonders.[102]

These stories of wives, mothers and fiancées travelling out to visit internees remained in the public eye throughout the rest of the war, showing that the media and perhaps the public did not tire of these stories, a positive change from the usual war news. It was not only the press back home that reported on these family visits. The internees' magazines are a source of information about the women who came out to Switzerland, their activities and sometimes their marriages and births of babies while they were there. The arrivals and departures were diligently reported in each edition. In the *British Interned Murren* magazine, changes reported in the married establishment at the Bellevue Hotel during July 1917 were that Mrs Pugh, Mrs Coats and Mrs Wellings had returned to England and the latest arrivals were Mrs Coggins and Mrs Seymour. Mrs Wellings had married bandsman Private Wellings during her visit. Mrs Taylor, wife of Private 'Cuthbert' Taylor of the 4th Leicesters was remaining in the village a little longer at the Alpina. There were also some mothers staying among them and so 'Privates Walker, Wright, Samson and Sapper Mainwaring were the happiest of boys in the Palace Hotel'.[103] Later in July, there was a complete change of faces at the married people's tables at the Bellevue. The old party were all safely back in England, and they now had the pleasure of the company of Mrs Reynolds and Mrs Harris who was visiting her son. 'Our congratulations go out to sailor Jack and his wife, as she is one of the August party, and it is only now, after eleven months' weary waiting, that he has had the happiness of seeing his good lady.'[104] A month later a party of relatives had just left: Mrs Howe, Mrs Buckle, Mrs Wells and Mrs McDougal departed as Mrs Richardson arrived to visit her husband Private Richardson. Corporal Drewitt had just married his fiancée with the service conducted by Reverend Bulstrode. There were four ladies at the Palace: Mrs Reid, Mrs McVicar, Mrs Gee and Mrs Richards. Private Fiskin was congratulated when his wife joined him after twelve months of waiting, a visit that was referred to as a holiday for them both.[105]

Whether a relative might visit Switzerland depended not just on the funds raised by local committees but on the accommodation available in the resorts, where hotels were often full to capacity with interned men. For the wealthy officers' families this was not such a problem as they could make their own arrangements, in private lodgings or rent a house or chalet, however, accommodation for NCOs was said to be limited. To restrict the numbers who might go on the funded visits four key rules were in place: Only one relative per prisoner could go; no children under sixteen; the prisoner himself was to select the relative he wanted to visit; the visitors were to spend no more than fourteen days in the accommodation.[106]

The arrival of a party of visitors was always eagerly awaited and internees expecting someone were allowed to meet them from the train. The men in Mürren were allowed a pass to go down to Interlaken, where the party had to change trains from the mainline service to the narrow gauge railway. Sometimes a party was held up because of weather or war conditions, a great disappointment to those who had come to meet them.[107]

Once in Switzerland, for the women travelling with the Red Cross, the time was spent almost as if it were a holiday, only these visitors were not the usual class of tourist. For those who arrived in winter, there were winter sports, something totally unfamiliar to working-class women, particularly the mothers in whose youth there had been no such thing. Even so, they enjoyed watching, and some of the more adventurous had a go themselves. For instance, Mrs Ormorod in her talk given in Oldham told her audience that the main sports were tobogganing and skiing, and that there was a toboggan track 3,000 feet above Mürren, reached by the Almendhubel mountain railway. Although you were supposed to go up on the train and down on the track, Mrs Ormorod did not like the idea of the toboggan. She preferred to look on as she found it

Figure 8.3 Internees and some wives in Mürren. Courtesy of Pat and Mark Esling (family collection).

more fun to see others come tumbling down, either on skis or sledges.[108] This was also the view of Harry Stock's mother when she visited the same place, but at least she did have a go at sledging, but when Harry wanted her to go on the long run down the Almendhubel, although she went up on the train with him, she preferred to return the same way and meet him at the bottom, just like any other mum on holiday with her boy.[109] Internees were given leave and accompanied their visitors in sightseeing. Mrs Ormorod and Frank had a day in Interlaken, which she preferred to Mürren as it was more level and had more walks about, probably because it was winter and only one street was cleared of snow in the higher lying village. The 'boys' were even allowed to accompany their mothers or wives to Berne on the first leg of the return journey, where they had lunch together and a guided tour of the city, including the Bear Pit and the place from where bread, 1,300 packages daily, was sent to prisoner-of-war camps in Germany. In Berne one of the mothers said to her son, 'Do you like it?' because he stood and looked about him so much. 'Like it?' he replied, 'Today I feel a free man – this is the first time I have seen a street since I went to Germany.'[110]

The scheme enabling relatives of British prisoners of war to visit Switzerland was judged a successful initiative. At the end of the first period of eighteen months in which these visits had taken place, a communication to the Admiralty in London said the visits had 'proved the greatest boon to British prisoners of war in Switzerland and their relatives and the Council is of the opinion that it is undesirable to prohibit these visits in future'.[111] They also benefited the family members able to make the journey, many of whom had endured a couple of years or so of stress, worrying what would become of their wounded or ill son, husband or boyfriend, in a prison camp and perhaps simultaneously struggling with exhaustion, trying to meet the demands that a war economy and total war made on them personally plus the fear of Zeppelin air raids. 'Mürren is very bracing and it did me good' was Mrs Ormorod's verdict; 'I have felt very much better since the holiday.'[112]

For the families of officers, the trip was less of a holiday and more of a change of abode. Their lifestyle was much like that of the pre-war colonies that made the Alps their home for months at a time, both for health reasons and for sport. One report went as far as to say that 'in some respects the life is somewhat reminiscent of some of the smaller hill stations in India', with its little circle of English people.[113] These women joined in with the social life of the internment community. Constance Kirkup joined some of the Chateau d'Oex internees in a Pierrot troupe, taking part in theatrical performances to entertain the internees and often took lunch in local cafes such as Madame Pittel's at Chateau d'Oex, who she said must have been making a fortune with all the British internees as everyone beetled up there in the afternoon.[114] In many of the amateur dramatic performances, the female parts were played by women, a big change from in the prison camps where men had to dress up to cover the feminine roles.[115] The wife of the Earl of Stair and her children accompanied her husband in Chateau d'Oex adding the sound of upper-class accents to the mixture of middle-class officers' relatives. Some of the officers' wives started a successful canteen for the men. A request was sent to England on their behalf by Colonel Earle, the senior British officer there, to ask for a gramophone and records to be sent out to improve the experience of their 'customers'.[116] This was perhaps the tea place, run by two or three ladies, designed to keep the soldiers away from drink in the long winter evenings, opened at the request of Colonel Earle.[117] Women were also a welcome addition to the dances that were held regularly. At the Palace Hotel in Mürren, Arnold Lunn's wife, Mabel, organized successful Practice Dances made more pleasant by the number of ladies present, 'who so kindly helped to make the evening a success.'[118] Mrs Lunn even managed to get the internees late leave so they could stay out and enjoy themselves longer.[119] Families of well-off officers were very welcome in the internment resorts as they had more money to spend and paid more than the military for their accommodation from their own resources.

Wives of French internees were also engaged in the communities that they had joined. Appeals were made by the French Service of Internment and the Ladies of the Embassy in Berne, for wives in Switzerland to work to help the wounded.[120] Women organized and worked in the Ladies' Workrooms of Vevey, Lausanne, Villars, Engelberg, Interlaken, Chempery, Spiez, Clarens, Montreux and Interlaken, making garments for soldiers at the front and refugees evacuated from northern France, as well as layettes for new babies. Vests and knickers for evacuee women and flannel vests for little boys were needed urgently. Finished items were sent to the Committee of Evacuees in Zurich. Items for wounded soldiers were sent to the central committee in Berne. The women also helped procure the money and resources for the workrooms through concerts and other fundraising initiatives. Between April 1917 and February 1918 about 7,250 garments were made.[121]

On the day of the French *Fête National*, 14 July 1917, women and children were involved in celebrations and their preparation. At Martigny both French and Belgian families went to the cemetery to put flowers on the graves of deceased comrades before enjoying a family dinner, while at Wengen the wife of an internee created a placard of welcoming wishes made out of flowers for their guest General Pau.[122]

As the war progressed, travel to Switzerland became more difficult. Major Collins, now in Vevey, tried to dissuade his relatives from coming to visit him because of possible problems on the way.

> You must not think of coming here at present; firstly your journey may take any length of time, probably at the least 10 days; all the officers' wives who are just beginning to arrive have had terrible experiences in closed boats, trains and hotels, many have had to stop two weeks in Paris where conditions are such as you have been [un]accustomed to for many years and where prices at ordinary hotels are enormous. One good lady had to pay £38 for herself and child for a week's stay; secondly you may get stopped at Lyon for an indefinite amount of time on the border. The heating of all these places is very indifferent owing to restrictions on fuel, to say nothing of being in a strange land where the language is not one you know and eating a strange diet which might easily make you unwell.[123]

For French women, travelling and moving to Switzerland was a much easier process than it was for the British who needed passports and a visa in order to make the Channel crossing. The French only had to cross a land-border into Western Switzerland where their men were interned in a region with which they shared a common language. Some managed to cross into Switzerland illegally, without going through the proper procedures.[124] Many had lost their homes, as large areas of north eastern France were occupied by Germans or devastated by fighting. The high numbers of French women in Switzerland brought problems with resources. Work was needed to help the wives of internees in need at childbirth for instance. A charitable organization gave them all a layette and 50 francs if the expectant mothers sent their names to Madame Provot in Berne giving their expected date of confinement.[125] Some military workshops were directed to make baby clothes, to be sent to each region for women in those places.

As well as weddings new babies were born to some of the women who had been able to remain in Switzerland with their spouses. Lieutenant and Mrs Russell celebrated the arrival of a daughter on 15 September 1917.[126] The following month Lieutenant and Mrs Melurg welcomed a baby girl, born at Vevey on 27 October.[127] Births were a regular occurrence among the French; for instance, Hubert Dantel, the son of Corporal Albert Dantel, interned at Tour de Peilz, was born in early 1918 around the same time as a little girl, Odette was born to internee Monsieur Baugran and his wife.[128] Three French births were announced in December 1917: There was little Augustine-Louise Monard, daughter of a soldier interned in Goldiwil; Louis Phillippe of Gstaad became the father of Simone and one more French person appeared in the Interlaken area when Ernest Métivet became the first born of a family it was hoped, according to the journal, would be numerous.[129] Madeline Richard also came into the world, whose interned father had been a teacher of history and geography at the Lycée Valenciennes and was now running courses at Lausanne.[130] Later the same month, a cradle came into use in another internee home, declared the *Journal des Internés Français*, when Monsieur and Madame Martin had a son, Marcel, born in Bulle.[131]

Many French wives brought their children with them, of course, and they needed facilities for their education and well-being. Some of the children from invaded regions of France and Belgium had had no teaching since the beginning of the war, more than two years earlier. At Frutigen there was a school for the children of French internees in the Hotel Bellevue, fully equipped with tables, benches and blackboards, led by teacher Henri Trégan, assisted by Raymond Krémer.[132] Another school for French children opened in 1916 at Leukerbad with six pupils.[133] At Weissenbourg the internees' children at the school there gave their teacher, Monsieur Brun, a magnificent inkwell carved from wood as a Christmas gift.[134] Other schools were in Grindelwald, originally based in the Hotel Belvedere but relocated to two rooms in the local village school, in Spiez, furnished by donations from local hotels, where there were fifteen boys and girls attending and in Interlaken for French and Belgian children.[135] These schools were in regions where the language spoken was the Swiss-German dialect, and so there was no existing French medium schools they could attend.

Every internment community had Christmas celebrations and parties. Entertainment and games for families were a feature everywhere, and presents were provided for all the children. These events were given particular attention in the *Journal des Internés Français*; for instance, at Boudry, on 20 December 1917, there was a Christmas party and concert with a mug of chocolate, cake and toys for the children. On the same day at Lauterbrunnen, there were many women present at a show organized by the *Commission Romande* for families at Christmas. At Chailly the *Commission Romande* organized a Christmas tree for the internees and their children so they would not be deprived of their festival on 23 December, and on Christmas Day in Champéry there was a Christmas tree in the *Foyer du Soldat* for the benefit of internees' children with a visit from *Père Nöel* who distributed toys and treats to 'those dear children', one of whom commented that it was much better than at home, as at home we never see *Père Nöel*. At Interlaken there was a children's festival on Christmas Eve with carols, treats and gifts, while at Wilderswil, at the Hotel Bären, a tree was loaded with treats and a thousand flames, the little ones' eyes were wide open in delight, with charming exclamations from their little mouths when the gifts were distributed.[136]

Figure 8.4 German internees, accompanied by women and children, enjoy an outing. Courtesy of Dokumentationsbibliothek Davos.

Fewer British children were present owing to the difficulty in obtaining travel documents and the potentially frightening, if not perilous, journey across the Channel and war-torn France; 'All along the route both ways you never lost sight of the fact there was a war on.'[137] Many of the wealthier officers, who could have their families live with them, would have their children in boarding schools back in Britain and working-class visitors were only there for two weeks, without their children. As the war progressed and resources became scarcer, it became more difficult for German women to travel, although many internee wives had made the journey across the border by 1917. Evidence of a female presence in the regions housing German wounded internees is provided in the pages of the soldiers' magazine *Deutsche Internierten Zeitung*. At an internee evening concert of German songs and poems in Davos in August 1917, seated among the men dressed in their field grey uniforms, the light clothing of their wives made a colourful picture.[138] When *Herr Kapitänleutnant* Lecher left Switzerland to go back home on 28 August 1917, he took his wife with him. Some were not so lucky. The wife of *Felwebelleutnant* Lau never did return to her home. She died and was buried in Walzenhausen.[139]

As education and training programmes got underway, some women came out to Switzerland to act as trainers and educators, but this was resisted by the Prisoners of War Department in London when requests were received for Voluntary Aid Detachment workers to teach typing and shorthand. 'A woman who had been working constantly for two years and was in need of a change and rest might possibly be sent. She would have a few hours' work each day, as the men would not be in a fit state to stand more than that at a time.'[140] Lieutenant Colonel Picot's opinion was that no ladies were required for work among interned prisoners in Switzerland, a view in which the War Office concurred.[141] Nevertheless, there were women working as instructors with the British internees. Some of them were already resident in Switzerland. One such was Madame Boutibonne of Wilderswil who taught wood carving to classes of twenty-five British internees.[142] There were also Mrs William Cooke Daniels and Miss Martin, English women who not only taught carpet making to British internees in a workshop at Gunten that they funded themselves but also entertained French soldiers at an event they called a *Fête de l'Entente*.[143] As well as female relatives of internees, Swiss women took part in entertainment as performers, organizers and funders. Mademoiselle de Corneville of Lausanne provided Christmas presents for the French children of fathers interned in Salvan.[144] One place internees were unlikely to meet women was in their hotels as owners were advised not to employ female staff.[145]

The presence of so many women, children and other family members in Switzerland made internment there a completely different experience from the homosocial closed communities of the prisoner-of-war camps. Those women who stayed longer than the fortnight long visits organized by the Red Cross were expected to contribute to the life of the internment communities and reports of their visits boosted morale at home, so they could still be seen to be helping in the war effort for their country. For many working-class women, visiting their sons or husbands broadened their experiences beyond anything they had previously known or perhaps even imagined. Travelling by boat to a foreign country, witnessing evidence of battle as they crossed France and the contrast of this to the Alpine beauty of Switzerland, was a life-changing experience, never to be forgotten.

Notes

1. Arthur Marwick, *The Deluge – British Society and the First World War*, London, 1965, p. 176.
2. Leicester, Leicestershire and Rutland Prisoners of War Committee (LLRPWC), Special Finance Committee, November 1917, pp. 34–5, ROLLR, 14D35/245.
3. *The Great War 1914–1918: Leicester, Leicestershire and Rutland Prisoners of War Committee*, Organized by the Churches, Leicester, 1919, pp. 36, 106–7.
4. LLRPWC, Executive Meeting, 1 September 1916, ROLLR, 14D35/24.
5. *Leicester Daily Mercury*, 3 April 1917.
6. LLRPWC Finance Joint Committee, 10 December 1917, ROLLR, 14D35/24.
7. Sylvaine Messerli, 'Dossier: Un Interné et sa Marraine de Guerre', *Passé Simple*, No. 32, February 2018, p. 8.
8. Susan R. Grayzel, *Women and the First World War*, Harlow and London, 2002, p. 48.
9. Picot, *The British Interned in Switzerland*, p. 183.
10. Mrs Eden Vansittert, Hove, 17 March 1916, TNA FO383/215.
11. Under-Secretary of State to Mrs Vansittert, 22 March 1916, TNA 383/215.
12. Bürgisser, 'L'humanité comme raison d'Etat', p. 284.
13. Picot, *The British Interned in Switzerland*, p. 183.
14. Major Edouard Favre, *L'Internement en Suisse*, 1917, quoted in Picot, *The British Interned in Switzerland*, p. 186.
15. *Western Daily Press, Aberdeen Mercury*, 16 June 1916.
16. List of Married People – Men Wanting their Wives Out for One Month, undated, TNA FO 383/217.
17. W. E. Hume-Williams, *Report on Conditions of British Interned in Switzerland*, 7 October 1916, IWM Red Cross Papers, Documents 8762, Box No: Misc 26 (473).

18 *Newcastle Journal*, 13 October 1916.
19 *Nottingham Evening Post*, 23 September 1916.
20 Picot, *The British Interned in Switzerland*, p. 184.
21 Miss Bates, foyer for English prisoners, Rougemont, to Mrs Crozier, 10 August 1916, TNA FO 383/218.
22 LLRPWC, Executive Meeting, 1 September 1916, ROLLR, 14D35/24.
23 *Leicester Daily Mercury*, 3 April 1917.
24 *Dundee Courier*, 2 September 1916.
25 *Western Daily Press*, 5 September 1916.
26 *Nottingham Evening Post*, 1 September 1916.
27 James Crossland, *Britain and the International Committee of the Red Cross, 1939–45*, Basingstoke, 2014, p. 33; *Birmingham Daily Post*, 4 September 1916.
28 *Birmingham Gazette*, 14 October 1916.
29 Katharine Furse, *Kind Hearts and Pomegranates*, Glasgow, 1940, p. 338.
30 Picot, *The British Interned in Switzerland*, p. 185.
31 *Newcastle Journal*, 13 October 1916.
32 *Western Daily Press*, 5 September 1916.
33 Captain E. W. S. Faljambe, senior medical officer, Leysin, December 1916, TNA FO 383/219.
34 First World War Red Cross Papers concerning interned, IWM Documents 8762, Box No: Misc 26 (473).
35 List of Articles Required for Visit to Switzerland, Corporal H. D. Munyard, IWM Documents 10733.
36 Red Cross papers re soldier internees in Switzerland and prisoners of war, IWM Documents 8762.
37 *Yorkshire Evening Post*, 27 September 1916.
38 Furse, *Kind Hearts and Pomegranates*, p. 338.
39 Ibid., p. 339.
40 Ibid., p. 340.
41 Ibid.
42 Major Collins to sister, 23 December 1917, IWM Documents 15679.
43 *Aberdeen Evening Post*, 11 December 1916.
44 *Derby Daily Telegraph*, 2 November 1916.
45 Mrs Ormorod, Account of a visit to wounded military internee in Switzerland, 1917, IWA Misc 30(538), Documents 10086.
46 Ibid.
47 Stéphanie Leu, 'Visiting French Internees in Switzerland during the First World War: Women in the Construction of National States (1915–1918)', in Lucia Aiello, Joy Charnley and Mariangela Palladino (eds), *Displaced Women: Multilingual Narratives of Migration in Europe*, Newcastle upon Tyne, 2014, p. 153; *L'Interné – organe collectif des prisonniers de guerre*, No. 10, 10 Avril 1917.

48 *JIF*, No. 6, 30 November 1916.
49 *JIF*, No. 17, 17 February 1917.
50 Georg Dufner, 'Sergeant Jacques Rivière, Kriegsinternierte 1917', *Engelberger Dokumente 7*, Engelberg, 1979, p. 10.
51 Dufner, 'Sergeant Jacques Rivière, Kriegsinternierte 1917', p. 11.
52 Ibid., p. 12.
53 Fuchs, 'Interniert im Appenzellerland', p. 64.
54 Grant Duff to War Office, 27 July 1916, TNA FO 383/217.
55 War Office to Grant Duff, signed D. D. Cubitt, 10 August 1916, TNA FO 383/217.
56 *Yorkshire Evening Post*, 29 November 1916.
57 Mürren Monthly Report, Sheet 4, July 1917, TNA FO 383/230.
58 Janette Lean, British Red Cross Society and Order of St John of Jerusalem in England, Joint War Committee, Pall Mall, to Miss E. Carpenter, 66 Tanners Hill, Deptford, 20 March 1917, IWM Documents 10733 H. D. Munyard.
59 Lean to Miss E. Carpenter, 66 Tanners Hill, Deptford, 2 May 1917, IWM Documents 10733 H. D. Munyard.
60 Molly Ford (daughter of H. D. Munyard), *Mum and Dad's Story*, family document, IWM Documents 10733 H. D. Munyard, undated.
61 *BIM*, No. 3, July 1917.
62 Lieutenant Elliott Angus Leybourne, Rossinière, 9 June 1916, Leybourne family correspondence on temporary loan to Durham County Record Office (Durham at War).
63 Leybourne, Rossinière, 10 June 1916.
64 Leybourne, Rossinière, 4 September 1916.
65 Leybourne, Rossinière, 20 November 1916, TNA FO 383/217.
66 Picot to War Office, November 1916.
67 Constance Kirkup, 20 May 1917.
68 Grayzel, *Women and the First World War*, p. 66.
69 Margaret Darrow, *French Women and the First World War: War Stories of the Home Front*, Oxford, 2000, p. 208.
70 *BIM*, No. 7, October 1917.
71 *BIM*, No. 10, December 1917.
72 Ibid.
73 *BIM*, Vol. 2, Nr. 3, March 1918.
74 *BIM*, No. 4, August 1917.
75 Oral testimony of Mr Taylor's granddaughter, interviewed in April 2017 and photographic evidence in her private collection.
76 Copy of entry in Berne marriage register, 1917, in private collection of Jack Taylor's family.
77 Oral testimony of Mr Taylor's granddaughter, Pat Esling, interviewed in April 2017.
78 *JIF*, No. 31, 26 May 1917.
79 *JIF*, No. 32, 2 June 1917.

80 *JIF*, A2, No. 6, 9 December 1917.
81 *DIZ*, Heft 46, 5 August 1917.
82 *DIZ*, Heft Nr. 28, 31 March 1917.
83 *DIZ*, Heft Nr. 28, 31 March and Heft Nr. 42–3, 15 July 1917.
84 *DIZ*, Heft Nr. 42–3, 15 July 1917.
85 *DIZ*, Heft Nr. 46, 5 August 1917.
86 *BIM*, Vol. 2, No. 7, 15 September 1918.
87 *Neue Züricher Zeitung*, No. 1584, 6 Oktober 1916.
88 *BIM*, No. 7, September 1917.
89 Isabelle Kaisser, *Unserer deutschen Kriegsgäste am Vierwaldstädtersee*, 1916, p. 6.
90 Fuchs, 'Interniert im Appenzellerland', p. 65.
91 *DIZ*, Heft Nr. 52, 16 September 1917.
92 *JIF*, A2, No. 5, 2 December 1917.
93 *JIF*, No. 5, 23 November 1916.
94 *JIF*, A2, No. 40, 28 July 1917.
95 *BIM*, Vol. 2, No. 6, July 1917.
96 André Paillard, *Notes sur les événements politiques de 1914-1918 à Chateau d'Oex*, 1919, no page.
97 *JIF*, A2, No. 17, 24 February 1918.
98 Major R. D. Alexander, SBO Leysin to Lieutenant Colonel Picot, Officer in Charge, British Interned in Switzerland, Leysin, 10 April 1917, TNA FO 383/329.
99 *Tribunal Militaire Territorial I*, 19 April 1917, NA FO 383/329.
100 Major E. R. Collins, Vevey, 1 October 1918, IWM Documents 15679.
101 *Northampton Independent*, February 1917.
102 Doris Panter, Oral reminiscence of the daughter of Frederick Terry of Desborough, interviewed May 2016.
103 *BIM*, Issue 2, July 1917.
104 *BIM*, Issue 3, July 1917.
105 *BIM*, Issue 5, August 1917.
106 *Sunday Post*, 8 October 1916.
107 *BIM*, No. 5, August 1917.
108 Mrs Ormorod, Account of a visit to wounded military internee in Switzerland, 1917, IWA Misc 30(538), Documents 10086.
109 *Northampton Independent*, February 1917.
110 Mrs Ormorod.
111 Army Council to the Admiralty 29 November 1917, TNA FO 383/219.
112 Mrs Ormorod.
113 Report on Hospitals and Establishments in Switzerland where British soldiers are interned drawn up by Colonel C. H. Thurston and Lieutenant Colonel Forrest after a visit carried out at the request of Lieutenant Colonel Picot, Officer I/c British Interned Switzerland. 1917, TNA FO 382/330.

114 Constance Kirkup, 10 February 1917.
115 *Newcastle Journal*, 16 September 1916.
116 Adelaide Livingstone, *Report of visit to Switzerland*, 1 October 1916, TNA FO 383/219.
117 Hume-Williams to secretary of the POW Dept, 28 November 1916, TNA FO 383/219.
118 *BIM*, No. 4, August 1917.
119 *BIM*, No. 5, September 1917.
120 *JIF*, No. 22, 24 March 1917.
121 *JIF*, A2, No. 16, 17 February 1918.
122 *JIF*, A1, No. 40, 28 July 1917.
123 Major Collins to mother, 19 December 1917, IWM Documents 15679.
124 Leu, 'Visiting French Internees in Switzerland during the First World War', p. 152.
125 *JIF*, A2, No. 16, 17 February 1918.
126 *BIM*, No. 7, October 1917.
127 *BIM*, No. 9, November 1917.
128 *JIF*, A2, No. 16, 17 February 1918.
129 *JIF*, A2, No. 6, 9 December 1917.
130 *JIF*, A2, No. 7, 16 December 1917.
131 *JIF*, A2, No. 9, 30 December 1917.
132 *JIF*, A2, No. 16, 17 February 1918.
133 *JIF*, A2, No. 9, 30 December 1917.
134 *JIF*, A2, No. 10, 13 January 1918.
135 *JIF*, No. 17, 17 February 1917, No. 32, 2 June 1917; *L'Interné - organe collectif des prisonniers de guerre*, No. 10, 10 April 1917.
136 *JIF*, A2, No. 10, 13 January 1918.
137 Mrs Ormorod.
138 *DIZ*, Heft Nr. 50, 2 September 1917.
139 *DIZ*, Heft Nr. 52, 16 September 1917.
140 Adelaide Livingstone, *Report of visit to Switzerland*, TNA FO 383/219.
141 Secretary of POW Dept, 22 November 1916, TNA FO 383/219.
142 Colonel F. O. Neish, SBO at Mürren, Report on workshops etc, 5 October 1916, TNA FO 383/218.
143 *JIF*, A2, No. 12, 20 January 1918.
144 *JIF*, A2, No. 10, 13 January 1918.
145 *Règlements Divers et Instructions sur l'Alimentation des Prisonniers de Guerre Internés en Suisse dans la Région de Montreux*, La Léman, 1916.

9

Going home and conclusion

Despite their beautiful surroundings, having plenty to keep them occupied and the companionship of friends and perhaps even family, internees of all nationalities longed for peace and to go home. A common and emotive photographic image of the time was of groups of French soldiers on the shore of Lake Geneva, saluting their country or gazing longingly across to France, visible on the other side of the water.[1]

Not all internees had to wait until after the Armistice to return home. Those who had shown no improvement in their conditions since they arrived in Switzerland were examined by Swiss medical officers and repatriated home during 1917 and 1918, which made room for other wounded prisoners coming from military camps in Germany, France and Britain.[2] The official numbers of British repatriated in September 1917 were 86 officers and 774 other ranks.[3] Every detail of the return home of wounded soldiers had to be agreed between the warring nations, including the routes to be taken. When the first internees left Chateau d'Oex or Mürren crowds came to see them off at the station. A letter signed by repatriated Colonel Neish, on behalf of grateful former internees, offered their warmest thanks to the Swiss nation for the hospitality they had received during their stay, with their sincere wishes for her prosperity both now and in the future.[4]

The homecoming of internees was almost as newsworthy as their arrival in Switzerland had been. The return of Bombardier Eales of Long Buckby in Northamptonshire was celebrated in his local newspaper. Eales told the reporter that his homeward journey was in a party of 415 comrades. He arrived in London on a Monday and was taken to hospital, where he stayed until the Thursday when he was allowed to go home to Long Buckby which he described as 'like heaven'.[5] Eales struggled to realize that his terrible experiences were in the past. A great luxury and surprise, for him, was to have white bread again at last after having only black bread for years.

For those not chosen for repatriation, life in Switzerland took on a more melancholy aspect for a while. Friendship groups had been broken up, and pastimes, sports and cultural activities were affected as team members left for home. Some of those left behind wondered whether taking part in physical activities had made them appear to be in better health than they actually were and if it had been counted against them during the selection process. Ironically sports clubs commented on the loss of their best players due to repatriation. The original editor of the *British Interned Mürren* journal was repatriated, and a new editor took over the magazine, renamed *British Interned Magazine* from January 1918.

> Everyone in Mürren is talking about the Exchange [of prisoners]. Those who have passed are packing their kits and those who have to stay are grousing. We hope that those who are going will not have to wait so long or be subject to as many disappointments as the majority a year ago. With hotels shutting down and numbers going home, and rumours of when and where we go for the winter, no one knows what to do nowadays. At present it seems the world will end at the end of August. We wish the war would end but that is past hoping for.[6]

The repatriated prisoners were replaced by fresh batches of wounded arriving from prison camps. Groups of German prisoners arrived, including 60 new internees in Davos, prisoners of France on 28 July 1917, replacing some of the 300 who left Switzerland on 8 June.[7] On 28 November 1917 a group of 81 British officers and 326 men arrived from Germany, some of whom had been prisoners for over three years.[8] The officers went to the district around Montreux, and the rest divided between Chateau d'Oex and Mürren. The next day, another contingent of 200 British, including 27 officers arrived in Switzerland from Germany, a third of them destined for Mürren.[9] In March 1918 some French internees, over the age of forty-five, were repatriated and travelled back to France by boat across Lake Geneva from Ouchy to Evian under the first Berne Accord. French prisoners arrived regularly from Germany, including a large party in early April 1918.[10] New contingents continued to arrive in Switzerland until the autumn of 1918.

As French internees left Switzerland they were given a leaflet with a farewell message from the Swiss, addressed to those whose hearts were assumed to be filled with joy and happiness at seeing their homeland once again, although some internees may have been reluctant to leave because of relationships, their work or interrupting their studies. The leaflet offered sincere fraternal wishes and rejoicing that for many of them, the stay on Swiss soil had brought better health and made possible their return.[11]

The war's end did not come as a total surprise as there was access to news in Switzerland, as Major Collins wrote home on 4 November 1918,

> One can hardly keep pace with the map, Austria, Bulgaria and Turkey all out of it, and now for the Hun and the Hun only. I only hope he won't give in just yet. I want to see our armies in his beastly country which I wish may be razed to the ground.[12]

The first internees to realize the war had ended were those based around Lake Geneva who could hear the celebrations, pealing church bells, rifle volleys and cheering taking place in France from across the other side of the Lake. Major Collins wrote home the next day, and in his letter he conveys not unqualified joy at the coming of the longed for peace but a sense of melancholy or a feeling of having missed out.

> The bells have just stopped ringing and the town is shouting and singing various national anthems as they did last night on the receipt of the news of the armistice. What a collapse it has been but I'm glad to see that the British army reached the ground beyond Mons, thereby ending their victories where they began their defence in 1914. Here I am, still in exile, and missing all that I wanted to see; England under war conditions, women working as they never have before in our history, and the great day of the final defeat of Germany. We could hear the guns firing in France across the Lake yesterday and I longed to be there to see how the people took it. Kismet. I feel that I, the trained soldier of your family, have done less for his country than any of his brothers and it is a rather bitter thing after 26 years work.[13]

On 11 November 1918 there were 25,614 prisoners of war interned in Switzerland: nearly half of them, 12,555, were French. On 13 November France demanded the return of its internees without delay. They began leaving on 25 November, and by 10 December 11,800 men and 1,750 officers had left. The signing of the Armistice annulled the Berne Accords, agreed between France and Germany in March and April 1918 and ended internment for the French, Belgian and British. The last of the Allies had left Switzerland by the spring of 1919. However, the German internees had to wait longer to return home, some of them until almost the autumn of 1919. Around 8,700 Germans including a few Austro-Hungarians, former prisoners of France and Belgium remained until under Swiss pressure, they were allowed to leave from 14 July 1919.

The last of them departed between 1 and 12 August 1919.[14] For the Swiss, awaiting final repayments in settlement for bills and expenses and the outcome of a court case over overpaid salaries, internment issues dragged on until 22 January 1922 when the Federal Council announced that compensations had been settled in full.[15]

Until the Armistice the conduct of the British interned in Chateau d'Oex had given no cause for serious complaints but on the evening of 11 November (Paillard's manuscript says October, but this may have been an error) some tipsy Tommies caused disorder in the village by unexpectedly attacking some of the local inhabitants. Fights broke out on all sides, and from that day there was a sense that discipline was lax and that the British officers themselves could no longer control their men. Sadly, this left a bad memory in the area for a while, although the Swiss realized it was only a minority whose unacceptable behaviour infected the others. Among the internees were some excellent young men, Paillard claimed, whom the people of Chateau d'Oex would have been happy to see again. The internees left Chateau d'Oex on 4 December 1918, taking with them twenty local girls. The whole population of the village was at the station to see them off with a lively farewell.[16]

This break down of discipline was not confined to the British internees. The number of escape attempts by Germans increased significantly after the Armistice and those who made it to Germany were no longer returned, contrary to agreements.[17]

At the same time as discipline appeared to break down, there was serious political and labour unrest in Switzerland, with strikes in some cities and regions. The war had brought economic difficulties to Switzerland, and there were demonstrations against the high cost of living and food shortages. Swiss soldiers were called away to these areas to quell what some saw as a potentially revolutionary situation, with the Bolshevik Revolution in Russia fresh in their minds and similar scenarios happening in Germany and elsewhere. 'There are big strikes going on in northern Switzerland which has stopped traffic. Luckily for us, this canton and the next voted against strikes so things locally are normal but all the men and most of the doctors are away on "mobilization" against the strikes,' wrote Major Collins to his father.[18] This may partially help to explain the breakdown of discipline, if much of the Swiss military presence had disappeared.

Shortages in Switzerland meant that internees returning home were not allowed to take certain items with them, things they may have wanted to take home as gifts or as keepsakes for themselves. The Swiss government strictly forbade the export of five categories of articles:

1. All articles of food and drink, including chocolate.
2. Cigars, cigarettes and tobacco.
3. Fats, oils, soap, candles, perfumes etc.
4. Clothing, woollen, cotton and linen stuffs.
5. Leather articles such as shoes, boots, gloves, etc.[19]

The ban on taking clothing and leather articles applied only to new things, not items worn or in a soldier's personal wardrobe. Notices clearly explaining the rules were posted in all centres of internment, and men were verbally reminded of them. Some of the men still tried to get round the rules by smuggling such goods away with them, contraband which was discovered when their luggage was searched by Swiss customs officials. If an internee acknowledged having forbidden articles in his luggage, the items would just be sent back to Switzerland at his own expense. If he were convicted of attempting to hide contraband items from the customs officials, his repatriation could be suspended unless he could guarantee payment of any fine imposed. Anyone under arrest for any crime, awaiting court martial or already sentenced would not be released until his punishment was completed.[20]

A booklet on repatriation published by the Swiss showed the routes by which internees would travel out of Switzerland, the reverse journey to those which had brought in prisoners of their opponents. For the Allies, trains of those interned in the regions of Lucerne, Zurich, Mürren and the Bernese Oberland would converge in Berne. From there they would travel onwards to Fribourg and Lausanne. Those based in Jura, Yverdon, Montreux, Leysin, Chateau d'Oex and Bex would meet up in Lausanne. From Lausanne the trains would take them on to Geneva where they would cross the border into France. German internees interned in Lucerne, Berne or Basle districts converged in Zurich from where they headed for Constance via Emmishofen where they were joined by Germans from Davos and the St Gallen region.[21]

Once the Armistice was signed, arrangements for prisoners of war to go home began almost immediately, following agreements made for the repatriation of prisoners of war and civilians at the International Armistice Commission at Spa in Belgium. Article 10 of the Armistice Treaty obliged Germany to release all Allied prisoners immediately but was indefinite about when German prisoners would be released.[22] Tens of thousands of men had to return home, a logistical challenge, necessitating a supply of food and additional fuel for transport. Of the many prisoners in Germany, some were to be sent through Switzerland if they were in the south of the country, others by river, train or marching to the North Sea and Channel ports, some via Holland. The French internment officer in Berne was anxious that French prisoners should be repatriated from Germany via Switzerland as he was worried about the political situation in Germany and the disorganization of the old battle front.[23]

The Swiss Internment Service began to prepare for the earliest possible date for the repatriation of Belgian, French and British interned prisoners. British ambassador Sir Horace Rumbold communicated regularly with the Foreign Office in London about the terms agreed for repatriation. The first communication on 12 November reaffirmed that prisoners should remain under Swiss discipline pending their departure.[24] There were also questions asked regarding civilian internees, who were now free to leave. The French Legation notified the Swiss government that all French-interned prisoners would be repatriated forthwith under the relevant clause of the Armistice, and Rumbold received permission from London to organize the departure of the British on 15 November. General Hanbury Williams made arrangements with the Swiss for the anticipated repatriation of British soldiers by the end of November.[25]

On 22 November, Rumbold wrote to the Foreign Office that the head of the Prisoners Section of the Federal Political Department of the Swiss government had been informed by the German Legation that Britain had consented to the repatriation of German prisoners interned in Holland under the terms of the Armistice. Switzerland was now anxious to wind up the entire internment organization and considered the absence of reciprocity only applied in enemy countries and that under the Hague Convention of 1918, all prisoners of war interned in neutral countries were eligible for repatriation. There would be difficulties regarding Germans held on behalf of the French in Switzerland as there was no agreement between Germany and France with similar terms to the Hague Agreement.[26]

Plans were made to send home British internees by late November; however, the repatriation of the British from Switzerland was delayed owing to a coal shortage.[27] Arrangements were made with the French to carry British prisoners, as well as their own, across Switzerland using French rolling stock and coal, 1,000 tonnes made available for the repatriation. Coal, about 40 tonnes, designated for the transport of parcels to prisoners of war was diverted for use for the repatriation of British soldiers.[28] British soldiers interned in Switzerland left for home over four consecutive days from Tuesday 3 December. By the following Saturday the internment scheme for the British had come to an end, although men with tuberculosis, not well enough to travel, or those working in official employment stayed behind for a while longer.[29]

Once the internees had left Switzerland, the accounts relating to their internment costs had to be closed down the next day. Any soldiers remaining behind because they were unfit to travel or had work to do were placed under the authority of the Berne region. Swiss officers were paid for only a few days after the end of internment. Equipment used, motor bikes, cars, bicycles, horses and fodder became the property of the central quartermaster. Some of it was used by the Swiss Army but much of it was sold off.[30]

When the British internees left Chateau d'Oex, the Grey Hut that they had used for recreation was donated to the *Colonies de Vacances* with a financial contribution of 3,000 francs towards the costs of holidays.[31] The internees had also provided a new organ for St Peter's Church, a lasting legacy still used by worshippers a century later.

During the period of internment eighty-eight British and Dominion soldiers died in Switzerland, sixty-one before repatriation; the others were among those who were unfit to travel and remained behind in sanatoria after the war. The last British deaths were those of Captain Edward Lawlor, who died on 8 January 1921, as a delayed consequence of a gas attack, Lieutenant Thomas Herbert Rudd of the RAF, who died of tuberculosis on 19 February 1921 following a gas attack in 1915, Lieutenant Raymond Martlew of the Tank Corps, who died on 4 June 1921, Lieutenant Henry Reginald Best, who died on 13 August 1921 after contracting tuberculosis in France and Rifleman Daniel Key who died of pneumonia on 5 December 1921. The bodies of all eighty-eight were exhumed from their original burial places across Switzerland and reinterred in the Commonwealth War Graves plot in St Martin's Cemetery in Vevey during 1923.[32] In Leysin cemetery there is a memorial to the internees who died there. For the German internees there is a memorial to those who died and were buried in the grounds of the Seehof Sanatorium near Davos Dorf.

As well as the return home of interned soldiers, the British government negotiated the transfer of 10,000 British prisoners of war from camps in Bavaria, Wurtemberg and Baden in Germany to Switzerland, around twenty-eight train loads, with a request that they stay there for a few days before their return to the UK.[33] Although they gained permission to travel by rail across Switzerland, the Swiss would not allow the trains to stop on their territory. As an alternative GHQ in France agreed that, after passing through Switzerland, the British former prisoners were to be directed to a rest camp at St Germain au Mont d'Or, near Lyon, and arrangements made with Switzerland to supply food for the journey there.[34] French prisoners travelled home via Switzerland too, among them were some small groups of British.

When the soldiers who had been interned in Switzerland arrived back in Britain they were treated in the same way as any other soldier returning from the

Figure 9.1 Programme of homecoming ceremony for Leicester prisoners of war and internees, February 1919. Courtesy of Pat and Mark Esling (family collection) and Chris Twiggs (private collection).

war. Like many others who had been captured, not all of them saw themselves as heroes because they felt they had not done enough to help their countries. 'When I do return, I want to return quietly and not with a crowd to meet me. I feel I have done so little in this great crisis that there is nothing to make a fuss about,' confided Major Collins to his family.[35]

Across the UK there were welcome home celebrations. In Leicester there was a celebration organized by the Leicester, Leicestershire and Rutland Prisoners of War Committee for local repatriated prisoners on 1 February 1919. Following a parade and welcoming speeches from local civic dignitaries, the men were treated to a high tea of roast beef, boiled beef, ham, tongue, pickles, beetroot, cakes, pastries, jam, marmalade, bread and butter, while the band of the 4th Volunteer Battalion of the Leicestershire Regiment played popular tunes.

Each returning prisoner of war received a letter from King George V:

> The Queen joins me in welcoming you on your release from the miseries and hardships, which you have endured with so much patience and courage. During these many months of trial, the early rescue of our gallant Officers and Men from the cruelties of their captivity has been uppermost in our thoughts. We are thankful that this longed for day has arrived, and that back in the old country you will be able once more to enjoy the happiness of a home and to see good days among those who anxiously look for your return.[36]

Conclusion

This book has investigated the experiences of Belgian, British, French and German wounded soldiers transferred to Switzerland for internment rather than continued imprisonment by their nation's enemies. Internment in the neutral state of Switzerland had significant differences from that in countries that were at war, although there were also similarities between the daily life of military prisoners of war, interned civilians in prison camps and those interned in Switzerland. The most important difference was that in a neutral country internees were not confined behind walls or fences but in this case were lodged in hotels with relative freedom within geographical limits and could go beyond those boundaries with a pass giving special permission. As a neutral country, Switzerland could not incarcerate prisoners of war and had no enemies. Those selected for internment had to agree not to try to leave under the threat of being returned to a prison camp on enemy territory and the potential loss of the privilege of internment to all wounded prisoners in future.

As in all forms of internment, routines were important to pass the time. Work and sports, theatre, music and education were all important aspects of military, civilian and neutral internment that could help maintain discipline and prevent boredom and associated psychological problems. Perhaps more surprising is how similar the life of internees in Switzerland was to that of health seekers and tourists in the health, summer and winter sports resorts, the peace time occupants of the hotels in the internment regions. Like the internees, visitors to Alpine Switzerland, including the British for whom many hotels catered, stayed for several months or even years at a time. They came for their health or as companions of health seekers and formed their own communities or colonies. To pass the time, these English colonies, joined by other nationalities, formed committees to organize entertainment and sports events in ways similar to the interned prisoners. In the mountains for long periods, sanatoria patients and visitors lived in closed communities, even though they were not prisoners. Unlike tourists but similar to those hoping for a cure to tuberculosis, the internees could not leave at the end of the season. Internees had no choice in where they stayed, another difference to tourists. Another important dissimilarity was their social class. Pre-war tourists in the Alps were from the affluent middle and upper classes who could afford to spend long periods of time living in a hotel. Internees were from all social backgrounds, mostly lower class, although segregated by rank within their accommodation. This was the first time large numbers of working-class men and their wives and mothers who visited them had stayed in Swiss hotels and resorts.

Internees were not in a homosocial environment, a difference to imprisonment in military or civilian camps. They could meet with women in local communities and have their own family present or visit them for a holiday. Wives, fiancées, mothers and sisters could all play a role in the life of the internment communities, taking part in sport, leisure activities, theatricals, volunteering and, importantly to their Swiss hosts, bringing in extra revenue through their hotel bills and spending in local businesses.

In Switzerland care was taken to rehabilitate internees with life-changing injuries through medical treatment, therapies, exercise, education, training and employment. This built on existing Swiss medical expertise and utilized sanatoria facilities. Everyone of the internees was wounded and perhaps disabled or disfigured in some way which could build a sense of solidarity between them, help make them less self-conscious and enable them to grow in awareness and confidence before returning home to the stares of communities where, at least before the war, disabilities were unusual.

Another aspect of internment was the cultural transfer between local people and the internees of different nationalities, backgrounds and faiths, including Hindu and Muslim. For rural Swiss, even those in tourist regions, it was often the first time they had encountered people from Asia or Africa with their specific religious and cultural needs. Entertainment also facilitated cultural exchanges, such as the Scottish dancers in their kilts, cross-dressing performers, humour, songs or perhaps introducing classical music to some soldiers for the first time. Sharing each other's seasonal celebrations with their various regional traditions could have contributed towards the twentieth-century development of national festive traditions. Foyers and YMCA huts allowed men of different regions and nationalities to socialize, encountering strangers from different cultures as equals and comrades.

Sporting activities had a major impact and helped popularize and diffuse football, ice hockey and, to a certain extent, winter sports. Physical activity played a vital role in the rehabilitation of mutilated bodies or the regaining of strength and fitness after years of confinement. As in military and civilian internment camps, sporting achievement contributed to the redevelopment of self-esteem and could enhance the status of those with talent. Through sport, there were opportunities to play against teams or players of different nationalities among the allies and in Swiss clubs. Sport also allowed cross-class bonding with officers who facilitated or took part in some events. As in other military environments, sport could also be used as a disciplinary tool, giving men something to occupy their time and energies to prevent discontent, as a diversion from inns and alcohol consumption or potentially be withheld as a punishment.

During their internment, the wounded soldiers could increase the possibility of finding alternative employment after the war through vocational training and general education programmes. These courses were especially beneficial to those whose life-changing injuries meant they could no longer go back to their previous jobs or those with little formal education who lacked basic skills. Developing literacy and numeracy was important for anyone who might have to take up a desk job. Driving lessons and mechanic training would equip some men with important and necessary skills to work with motor vehicles which were rapidly replacing horse-drawn transport by the time of the War. Higher education allowed students to continue studies that had been cut short. Employment in Switzerland, in agriculture, industry or business reintegrated internees into the routines and discipline of work and also provided experience and an opportunity to try out new skills.

For the Swiss, the internment of wounded and sick prisoners of war in Switzerland gave their neutrality a clear humanitarian and positive role, at the same time as giving its citizens in the 25 cantons a common cause that helped bring them together and strengthen a national identity, despite linguistic and cultural differences. The economic benefits for tourism, particularly the hotel trade, saved the industry from disaster and brought in much needed cash flows that allowed many businesses to survive. The presence of citizens from warring nations gave the Swiss, dependent on imports, some bargaining power in relation to imports of food and coal. Even so, attitudes towards internment were not always positive, especially as the war continued and rationing and shortages caused resentment from some Swiss who perceived that internees and their relatives were being allocated food and other resources that could have gone to local people. However, the presence of internees from both sides of the conflict enabled the Swiss to keep their supply lines open and continue to receive imports, albeit diminished in quantity. Other Swiss feared that because internees were allowed to undertake some form of work wages would be undercut or depressed, even though, with most younger Swiss men away on military service, there would have been no one to do the work, particularly on farms, and internees were paid a smaller amount and were much less productive than an able-bodied, experienced worker.

Altogether, during the War 67,726 wounded or sick prisoners of war had been interned in Switzerland: 37,515 French, 4,326 Belgians, 4,081 British and over 21,000 German plus around 600 Austro-Hungarians. Apart from a short period in the summer of 1918, there were never more than 30,000 simultaneously interned. The Swiss newspaper, *Oberländische Volksblatt*, reported in January 1918 that foreign countries reimbursed Switzerland with 5 million francs a month for the accommodation of internees.[37] By the end of the war the Swiss state treasury had an excess of 800,000 Swiss francs from internment, showing that looking after the internees had financial as well as political and humanitarian advantages, although calculations claim only 150,000 francs were left after all expenses had been paid out, not an especially large amount, although the hotel industry was estimated to have gained a vital 134 million francs in revenue.[38] The Swiss had made many large lump sum payments, but repayment was made in instalments and hospitals had an ongoing deficit.[39]

It is important to remember that internment in Switzerland involved only a small minority of prisoners out of a total of up to 9 million held in camps around Europe.

The research for this book has shown that the behaviour, interests and activities of all nationalities of internee were similar. They shared the same conditions of internment in their various regions. Despite the idyllic surroundings, they longed for their families and to go home. Whether they realized it or not, they all shared a common enemy and that was war itself. Switzerland offered a release to prisoners, a chance to heal from their wounds and perhaps adjust to a new way of life. As one 'broken repatriated man' wrote in gratitude to the Leicester Prisoners of War Committee,

> I've had two real thrills in my life. The first when I saw your parcel. The second when I steamed into Switzerland an exchanged prisoner and saw the laughing, cheerful, singing Swiss girls with their supply, for the English prisoners, of cigs and sweets.[40]

Notes

1. Jaccottet et al., *Au Soleil et Sur les Monts*, p. 11.
2. *Newcastle Journal*, 28 July 1917.
3. *BIM*, No. 6, September 1917.
4. *Dundee Evening Telegraph*, 13 September 1917.
5. *Northamptonshire Mercury*, 21 September 1917.
6. *BIM*, No. 5, August 1917.
7. *JIF*, A2, No. 23, 7 April 1918.
8. *Sheffield Evening Telegraph*, 29 November 1917.
9. *Western Times*, 30 November 1917.
10. *JIF*, A2, No. 23, 7 April 1918.
11. *Aux Internés Quittant la Suisse*, leaflet produced by La Commission Romande des Internés, 1918.
12. Collins to his father, 4 November 1918, IWM Documents 15679.
13. Collins to his mother, 12 November 1918, IWM Documents 15679.
14. Bürgisser, 'L'humanité comme raison d'Etat'.
15. Draenert, *Kriegschirurgie und Kriegsorthopädie in der Schweiz zur Zeit des Ersten Weltkrieges*, p. 291.
16. Paillard, *Notes sur les événements politiques de 1914 à 1919*, p. 75.
17. Draenert, *Kriegschirurgie und Kriegsorthopädie in der Schweiz zur Zeit des Ersten Weltkrieges*, p. 290.
18. Collins to his mother, 12 November 1918, IWM Documents 15679.
19. *Important Notice regarding Repatriation*, Major de la Harpe, Vevey, 5 March 1918, Musé de Vieux Montreux.
20. Notice signed by Col Hauser, Chief Medical Officer, General Headquarters, 14 May 1918, Musé de Vieux Montreux.

21 *Repatriation – instructions générales concernant les transport d;internés de rapatriés*, c1918, Musé de Vieux Montreux.
22 Jones, *Violence against Prisoners of War in the First World War*, p. 260.
23 Sir Horace Rumbold, to Foreign Office, 26 November 1918, TNA FO 383/330.
24 Rumbold to Foreign Office, 12 November 1918, TNA FO 383/330.
25 Rumbold to Foreign Office, 18 November 1918, TNA FO 383/330.
26 Rumbold to Foreign Office, 26 November 1918, TNA FO 383/330.
27 Rumbold to Foreign Office, 22 November 1918, TNA FO 383/330.
28 Berne Rumbold, 29 November 1918.
29 Rumbold to Foreign Office, 3 December 1918, TNA FO 383/330.
30 *Ordre relatif à la liquidation des Regions d'Internement de l'Etente*, Quartier-Général, 22 Novembre 1918.
31 Paillard, *Notes sur les événements politiques de 1914 à 1919*, p. 76.
32 Commonwealth War Graves Commission, www.cwgc.org, accessed 27 May 2018.
33 Rumbold to Foreign Office, Berne, 28 November 1918, TNA FO 383/330.
34 J. A. Corcoram, War Office POW Dept, to Rumbold, London, 4 December 1918, TNA FO 383/330.
35 Collins to his father, 21 July 1918, IWM Documents 15679.
36 King George V to returning prisoners of war, addressed to Pte A. Gibbs, 1st Leicester, 1918.
37 *Oberländische Volksblatt*, 25 January 1918.
38 Bürgisser, 'L'humanité comme raison d'Etat', p. 279.
39 Draenert, *Kriegschirurgie und Kriegsorthopädie in der Schweiz zur Zeit des Ersten Weltkrieges*, p. 291.
40 *The Great War 1914–1918: Leicester, Leicestershire and Rutland Prisoners of War Committee*, Organized by the Churches, Leicester, 1919, p. 23.

Bibliography

Books

Amstutz, Max. *Die Anfänge des alpinen Skirennensports/The Golden Age of Alpine Skiing*, Zurich, 2010.

André, Maurice. *Leysin – Station Medicale*, Pully, 2002.

Barton, Susan. *Healthy Living in the Alps, the Origins of Winter Tourism in Switzerland, 1860-1914*, Manchester, 2008.

Bourke, Joanna. *Dismembering the Male: Men's Bodies, Britain and the Great War*, London, 1996.

Collins, Tony. *Sport in Capitalist Society*, Abingdon, 2013.

Crossland, James. *Britain and the International Committee of the Red Cross, 1939-45*, Basingstoke, 2014.

Desponds, Liliane. *Leysin – Histoire et renconversion d'une ville à la montagne*, Bière, 1993.

Furse, Katharine. *Kind Hearts and Pomegranites*, Glasgow, 1940.

Gillies, Midge. *The Barbed-Wire University, the Real Lives of Allied Prisoners of War in the Second World War*, London, 2011.

Grayzel, Susan R. *Women and the First World War*, Harlow and London, 2002.

Hanson, Neil. *Escape from Germany*, London, 2011.

Hussey, Elizabeth. *Biography of Arnold Lunn, 1888-1974*, North Charleston, 2014.

James, Trevor. *Prisoners of War at Dartmoor: American and French Soldiers and Sailors in an English Prison during the Napoleonic Wars*, Jefferson, 2013.

Jones, Heather. *Violence against Prisoners of War in the First World War: Britain, France and Germany 1914-1920*, Cambridge, 2011.

Ketchum, J. David. *Ruhleben, a Prison Camp Society*, Toronto, 1965.

Koller, Christian and Brände, Fabian, *Goal! A Cultural and Social History of Modern Football*, Washington DC, 2002.

Lloyd, Clive. *The Arts and Crafts of Napoleonic and American Prisoners of War, 1756-1816*, Woodbridge, 2007.

Lunn, Arnold. *Skiing*, London, 1913.

Lunn, Arnold. *The Mountains of Youth*, London, 1925.

Lunn, Arnold. *Mountain Jubilee*, London, 1943.

Lunn, Arnold. *The Bernese Oberland*, London, 1958.

Makepeace, Clare. *Captives of War, British Prisoners of War in Europe in the Second World War*, Cambridge, 2017.

Marwick, Arthur. *The Deluge – British Society and the First World War*, London, 1965.

Mason, Tony and Riedi, Eliza. *Sport and the Military, the British Armed Forces 1880-1960*, Cambridge, 2010.

McDill, John R. *Lessons from the Enemy – How Germany Cares for Her War Disabled*, Philadelphia, 1918.

Neiburg, Michael S. *Soldiers' Lives through History*, Westport, 2006.

Panayi, Panikos. *Prisoners of Britain, German Civilian and Combatant Internees during the First World War*, Manchester, 2012.

Roper, Michael. *The Secret Battle – Emotional Survival in the Great War*, Manchester, 2009.

Wilkinson, Oliver. *British Prisoners of War in First World War Germany*, Cambridge, 2017.

Chapters in an edited collection

Boxwell, David A. 'The Follies of War: Cross-Dressing and Popular Theatre on the British Front Lines, 1914-1918', *Modernism and Modernity*, Vol. 9, No. 1, 2002.

Bürgisser, Thomas. 'Internees (Switzerland)', Peter Gatrell, Oliver Janz, Heather Jones, Jennifer Keene, Aalan Kramer and Bill Nasson (eds), *1914-1918-online. International Encyclopedia of the First World War*, issued by Freie Universität Berlin, Berlin, 29 September 2015, DOI:10.15463/ie1418.10735

Bürgisser, Thomas. 'L'humanité comme raison d'Etat: l'internement ds prisonnier de guerre étrangers en Suissse pendant la Premiè Guerre Mondiale', Roman Rossfield, Thomas Buomberger and Patrick Kury (eds), *14/18 La Suisse et la Grande Guerre*, Baden, 2014, pp. 266-80.

Cotter, Cédric and Herrmann, Irène. 'Quand secourir sert se protéger: la Suisse et les ouvres humanitaires', Roman Rossfield, Thomas Buomberger and Patrick Kury (eds), *14/18 La Suisse et la Grande Guerre*, Baden, 2014, pp. 240–65.

Fuchs, Thomas. 'Interniert im Appenzellerland', Heidi Eisenhut und Hanspeter Spöri (eds), *Der Erste Weltkrieg und das Appenzellerland*, Appenzelische Jahrbuch, 2014, Heft 141, Heraugaben von der Appenzellischen Gemeinnützigen Gesellschaft, pp. 50–65.

Leu, Stéphanie. 'Visiting French Internees in Switzerland during the Frist World War: Women in the Construction of National States (1915-1918)', Lucia Aiello, Joy Charnley and Mariangela Palladino (eds), *Displaced Women: Multilingual Narratives of Migration in Europe*, Newcastle upon Tyne, 2014, pp. 149–62.

Radauer, Lena. 'Seite an Seite mit dem Feind – Deutsche Kriegsgefangene in Russland vor und nach 1917/1918', *Jahrbuch des Bundesinstituts für Kultur und Geschichte der Deutschen im Östlichen Europa*, Band 25, Oldenburg, 2017, pp. 219–34.

Walle, Marianne. 'Les Prisonniers de Guerre Français Internés en Suisse (1916-1919)', *Guerres mondiales et conflits contemporains*, 2014/1 (No. 253), 2014, pp. 57–72. DOI 10.3917/gmc.253.0057

Dissertations

Anderson, Julie. *The Soul of a Nation: a social history of disabledpeople, physical therapy, rehabilitation and sport in Britain, 1918-1970*, PhD Thesis, De Monfort University, Leicester, 2001.

Arnold, Franco. '*Unsere Kriegsgäste*' *oder* '*Verräter ihres Landes? Die Wahrnehmung der ausländischen Bevölkerung durch die Einheimischen im Oberwallis während des Ersten Weltkriegs*', Masterarbeit eingereicht bei der Philosophischen Fakultät der Universität Freiburg, 2011.

Draenert, Marcelin Oliver. *Kriegschirurgie und Kriegsorthopädie in der Schweiz zur Zeit des Ersten Weltkrieges*, Inauguraldissertation zur Erlangung der Doktorwürde der Philosophischen Fakultät der Universität Heidelberg, 2014.

Kühnis, Beni. *Deutsche Kriegsinternierte in Davos während des 1.Weltkriegs*, Maturaarbeit Schweizerische Alpine Mittelschule Davos, Davos, 2015.

Journal articles

Biernoff, Suzannah. 'The Rhetoric of Disfigurement in First World War Britain', *Social History of Medicine*, Vol. 24, Issue 3, December 2011, pp. 666-85.

Borgeaud, Charles. 'Switzerland and the War,' *The North American Review*, 1914.

Bürgi, Andreas. 'Die Tourismusmeile in Luzern', *Essen und Trinken unterwegs, Wege und Geschichte*, 1, 2013 , pp. 39-42.

Cotter, Cédric. 'The 1918 Bern Agreements: Repatriating Prisoners in a Total War', *Humanitarian Action*, 29 March 2018.

Durrer, Julia. 'Internierte während des Ersten Weltkriegs in Engelberg', *Engelbergerjahrbuch*, 2008, pp. 95-103.

Foreman, Lewis. 'In Ruhleben Camp', *First World War Studies*, Vol. 2, No. 1, 2011, pp. 27-40.

Lunn, Arnold. 'British Skiing During the War', *British Ski Yearbook for 1920*.

Koller, Christian. 'Sport Transfer over the Channel: Elitist Migration and the Advent of Football and Ice Hockey in Switzerland', *Sport in Society*, Vol. 20, No. 10, 2017, pp. 1390-404.

Waquet, Arnaud. 'Sport in the Trenches: The New Deal for Masculinity in France', *International Journal of the History of Sport*, Vol. 28, Nos. 3-4, March 2011, pp. 331-50.

Waquet, Arnaud. 'Wartime Football, a Remedy for the Masculine Vulnerability of Poilus', *International Journal of the History of Sport*, Vol. 29, No. 8, May 2012, pp. 1195-214.

Magazine and newspaper articles

Hoffmann, Walter K. 'Die Lehranstalt für internierte Kolonialdeutsche in Davos, Spätformen Kolonier Ausbildung', *Neue Züricher Zeitung*, 13/14 August 1977.

Makepeace, Clare. 'Just Like the Real Thing', *History Today*, Vol. 67, Issue 12, December 2017, pp. 44–55.

Messerli, Sylvaine. 'Dossier: Un Interné et sa Marraine de Guerre', *Passé Simple*, No. 32, February 2018, pp. 3–11.

Vuilleumier, Christophe. 'Dossier: La Suisse, asile de l'Europe, Dossier: Les Internés dans de la grande Guerre', *Passé Simple*, No. 21, January 1917.

Primary sources

Accords entre le Gouvernement de la République Français et le Gouvernemnt Impérial Allemand concernant les Prisonniers de Guerre et les Civils, Berne, 28 April 1918. Vieux Montreux Archives, Musé de Vieux Montreux.

Bach, Hugo. *Des Ausbildung der deutschen Internierten in der Region Davos*, 1917.

British Interned Magazine, Vol. 2, January 1918 to October 1918.

British Interned Mürren, Vol. 1, July 1917 to January 1918.

British Red Cross papers, IWM, Documents 8762.

Convention relative to the treatment of prisoners of war, Geneva, Chapter 4, Article 17, 27 July 1929.

Davoser Blätter.

Davoser Zeitung.

Deutsche Internierten Zeitung, 1917 to 1918.

Documents relating to internment of French and Belgian prisoners of war, Vieuz Montreux Archives, Musé de Vieux Montreux.

Favre, Major Eduard. *L'internement en Suisse*, 1917.

Grant Duff, Sir Evelyn. *The Reception of Wounded Prisoner Soldiers of Great Britain in Switzerland*, despatch from the British minister in Berne, 2 June 1916.

Jaccottet, G., Fourmestraux, Marcel de, Baud-Bovy, D. and Locking, John. *Au Soleil et sur les Monts, scènes de la vie des soldats alliés internés en Suisse*, L'Etape Libératrice, Geneva, 1918.

Kaisser, Isabelle. *Unserer deutschen Kriegsgäste am Vierwaldstädtersee*, 1916.

Kirmmse, Alexander. Photograph Album, Talmuseum Engelberg.

Le Journal de Internés Français, July 1917 to November 1918, Vieux Montreux Archives, Musé de Vieux Montreux.

Leicester, Leicestershire and Rutland Prisoners of War Committee 1914–1918, Records Office of Leicester, Leicestershire and Rutland, 14D35/24.

Leybourne family correspondence, on temporary loan to Durham County Record Office, (Durham at War).

Mission Catholique Suisse, 31-, Archives de l'Etat Fribourg.

Paillard, André. *Notes sur les événements politiques de 1914 à 1919 à Chateau d'Oex*, 1919.

Papers of Re R. Bulstrode, IWM, Documents 1276.

Photographs and documents relating to interned German prisoners, Dokumentationsbibliothek Davos.

Photographs, documents and artefacts, Talmuseum Engelberg.

Picot, Lt-Col. H. P. *The British Interned in Switzerland*, London, 1919.

Private papers of H. D. Munyard, IWM, Documents 10733.

Private papers of J. Gray, IWM, Documents 12469.

Private papers of Major E. R. Collins, IWM, Documents 15679.

War Office correspondence and reports concerning internment of wounded prisoners in Switzerland, The National Archive, London, FO 383/215, FO 383/216, FO 383/217, FO 383/218, FO 383/219, FO 383/325, FO 383/329, FO 383/330, FO 383/331, FO 383/357, FO 383/450, FO 383/451.

Index

Abiturientenexamen 90
absence of women 144
abuse of prisoners of war 36, 45–6, 49
accountancy 81, 90
accounts 205, 210
actors 142, 144
Ador, Gustave 17, 42
African soldiers 23–4, 209
agricultural labour 53, 82
Aigle 26
alcohol abuse 67–71, 79–80, 103, 128, 157, 183–4
Alexander, Major 184
all-male environment 144
Almendhubel 119, 123, 185, 187–8
Alpine Ski Club 117
Amstutz, Max and Walter 55
Anglican 148, 156, 158–9, 180
Anzac Day 154
Appenzellerland 26, 28, 47, 53, 82, 89, 109, 147
Armeesanitätsanstalt (ASA) 61–2
Armistice 26, 199, 201–4
army chaplain 158
Arosa 26, 53
Asian soldiers 23, 41, 160, 209
Asquith, Herbert 21
Association Franco-Belge 109
Ateliers Nationaux 84–5
Australians 154
Austria 47
Austro-Hungarians 160, 201

babies 190–1
Babtie, Sir William 23
Baden Powell, General 40
Bad Sonder 34
Baptists 159
basket weaving 83
Basle 145
Bastille Day 113
Bates, Miss 70, 156, 168

Beatenburg 80, 85
Beffroi, Le 143
Beiden 83, 89
Belfort, Het 143
Belgian King 152
Belgian workshop 86
benefit concerts 147
Berlin 78
Berne 24, 38, 53–4, 83, 86, 106–7, 113, 143, 150, 152, 155, 177, 181, 188, 190, 191, 203–5
Berne Accords 24–5, 58, 131–2, 200–1
Berne Internees' Theatrical Group 144
Bernese Oberland 26, 29, 42, 53–4, 80, 107, 145, 203
Bertie, Lord 19, 21
Bertrand, Marius 71
Bex 54, 72, 203
Bezirks Hospital 61
Bien du Soldat 154
billiards 114, 154–5
births 191
bobsleighing 112, 116, 118, 123–6, 130
Boer War 77
book binding 81, 86
book-keeping 81, 89
boot and shoe making 83, 85, 87
Borgeaud, Charles 14
Boudry 146
Bourbaki Panorama 2
Bourke, Joanna 5, 104
boxing 101, 104, 109, 111–12, 151
Brände, Fabian 100
bread 20, 59, 188
Brienz 54, 72, 128
British colony 33
British Interned Mürren/Magazine 6, 82, 93, 104, 106, 111, 120, 127–8, 142, 143, 177, 180, 182, 186, 200
British Interned Mürren Ski Club 117
British Interned Variety Company of Chateau d'Oex 144–5

British Legation 38
British Red Cross 82, 86, 88, 143, 169–72, 174, 177
British Ski Year Book 118
British Soldiers' Club 155
British Standard Ski Tests 117–19
Brun, Hans 61
Brunnen 82
Bulle, Lieutenant 67
Bulstrode, Revd. 187
Burchard, Herr 33
Bürgisser, Thomas 7
Business Education School 89–90

Campbell Bell, Revd. 158
Canadians 50, 69, 82, 102, 116, 126
Cantonal FC 109
Carlyon, Captain Edward Tristram R. 116, 118, 120–2
carpentry 81, 83–4, 86, 89, 95
Castres, Edouard 2
categories of illness or injury 18
categorisation of work capability 80–1, 84
Cattani, Herr 55
Caux 126–7
Cecil, Lord Robert 18–19, 23
Central Switzerland 26–7
Centre Sportif des Internés de Spiez 108
Cercle des Alliés 154
Chamberlain, Mrs Neville 170
Chapman, Private N. 65
charity 147
Charley, Major 93
Chateau d'Oex 19, 26, 29, 37–42, 47–8, 50, 53, 60, 62, 65, 69–70, 82–3, 87–8, 93, 95, 105, 107, 109–14, 123, 126–7, 130–1, 144–6, 148–9, 155–8, 160, 168, 170–3, 178, 189, 199, 200, 202–3, 205
children 151, 178, 186, 189, 190 –194
Christmas 150-2, 191–2
Christmas, John de 46
Christmas Eve 112, 150, 192
Chur 26, 53
church 148, 156, 180
Church of England Missionary Society 157, 159
cinema 147
civilian internees 78–9, 204, 208

class divisions 37–8
Clement, Doctor 62
coal 28, 42, 59–60, 204, 210
Collins, Major Ernest 59, 116, 127–8, 132, 147, 173, 185, 190, 201–2, 207
Collins, Private J. T. 37–8, 44
Collins, Tony 100
Colonial and Continental Church Society 156
Colonial Germans 90–1
comedy 142
Commission for Employment of Internees 81
Commission Romande des Internés 150, 155, 192
Commonwealth War Graves Cemetery 205
concert 131, 145–7, 150, 193
Concordia Hut 120–1
conscription 29
Constance 16, 24, 36–7, 46, 203
convalescence 61, 104, 107, 143
Cooke Daniels, Mrs 151, 154, 193
Cotter, Cédric 7
cricket 100–1, 103, 105, 109–11, 115, 130
cross-dressing 144, 208
Cubitt, Sir Bernard 21
curfew 154
curling 127, 129

daily routines 57
dancing 154, 189
Darmstadt 24
Dartford 23
Davos 2, 8, 18, 26, 33–4, 53, 89–90, 126, 132, 147–8, 181, 193, 200, 205
Davos Courier 143, 148
death 65–6, 205
demonstrations 202
dentistry 62–3, 131
Department of Gas and Heating 92
Derby Prisoners' Aid Committee 149
Derbyshire Prisoner of War Help Committee 174
Deutsche Internierten Zeitung 60, 126, 129, 142–3, 181, 193
Diableret 85–6
disability 79–80, 93–4, 130–2, 208, 209

discipline 209
Döberitz Camp 49, 142
Dolf, Doctor 91
Dorchester 23
Draenert, Marcelin Oliver 7
drawing 89, 93
drill 103
driving lessons 81, 87–8, 209
Dunant, Henry 14

Eales, Bombardier 199
Earle, Colonel 65, 105, 110, 157, 189
Easter 154
education 8, 44, 78–81, 90, 92, 96, 193, 209
Eiger Hotel 106–7, 109
employment 8, 70
employment regulations 81, 84
Engadine Express 143
Engelberg 8, 26–7, 35, 55, 60, 93, 108, 112, 114, 116, 123–5, 131, 146, 152, 176, 190
English Channel 24, 171–2
Entente 26
entertainers 8, 142, 144, 146–7, 193
Evans, Ralph du Boulay 116, 118–22, 143
examinations 90, 95
exchange of prisoners 200
exemption from work 81, 83
exhibitions 86, 94
export ban 203

Faljambe, Captain 72
Famille du Soldat 166
Fancy Leather Goods Manufacturers' Association 94
Favre, Major Eduard 24, 167
Favrod-Coune, Monsieur 39
FC Au 109
FC Berne 107
FC Comète 109
FC Lucerne 108, 114
Federal Polytechnic of Zurich 91–2
Feldgraue 34
female impersonation 144
fertilizers 28
Fête National 152, 190
Finnern, Johannes 47
food 45, 58–60, 132

food supplies 28, 42, 203
football 99–112, 114–16, 131
foreign languages 81, 83, 88, 90, 92
Foreign Office 6, 8, 204
Foreman, Lewis 3
Foyers du Soldats 70, 112, 151, 154–6, 209
Franco-Prussian War 2, 15
French Switzerland 13, 15, 19, 28–9, 53, 82, 153
Frey, Emil 46
Fribourg 26, 42, 53, 61–2, 92, 150, 152, 159, 203
Fribourg Allies' Hospital 62
Fridericianum 89–90
funerals 65, 160–1
funicular 119, 123, 132, 185, 187–8
Furse, Katherine 171, 173

gardening 81, 87
Gazette de Döberitz 112, 142–3
Geneva 15, 26, 92, 99, 145–6, 148, 179
Geneva Convention 15–17, 36, 77, 133
Geneva Society for Public Welfare 14–15
German Foreign Office 79
Gibbs, Private Alf 54, 149
gifts 34–5, 37, 203
Gillies, Midge 3, 132
Gimel 71
Glarus 26
golf 115
Grant Duff, Sir Evelyn 18, 21–2, 29, 40–3
Graubunden 53
Gray, Private James 99, 111
Grayzel, Susan 6
Grey, Sir Edward 20–2, 24, 29, 166
Grey Hut 155
Grindelwald 29, 119–20, 128, 146, 191
Gruyères 26, 150
Gstaad 47, 131, 160
Gunten 193
Gurkha 24, 41, 160–1
gymnasium 90
gymnastics 100, 103, 111–12, 114–15, 132

Hague Convention 17, 44, 77–8, 204
Hanbury Williams, General 204
Hauser, Colonel Doctor Carl 23–4, 26, 50, 53, 59, 61

Heiden 46–7
Herisau 67, 183
Herrmann, Irène 7
Hertslet, Sir Cecil 29
Hesse, Hermann 142
higher education 92, 209
hiking 116, 128, 131–2
Hilfsverein 34
Hindu 160–1, 209
Hobbs, Lieutenant 143
hockey 106
Hoffmann, President 14
Hoggarth, Henry 45
Holzminden 102
homosocial environment 208
horse riding 130
hospitals 60–2, 70, 72, 79, 131, 180, 210
Hotel des Alpes, Mürren 55, 59, 104–5, 110, 116
hotels 27, 29, 39–40, 45, 48, 54–6, 58–61, 104, 154, 208, 210
Hotel Signal du Bougy 71–2
Howard, Henry 20
humanitarianism 7, 28, 33, 55, 210
Hume-Williams, W. R. Ellis 110, 168

ice carnival 127
ice skating 104, 112, 116–26
identity card 54
imports 28, 59, 210
Indian soldiers 23, 41, 160, 209
indiscipline 66–7, 71, 95, 157, 202
influenza epidemic 65, 161
Interlaken 59–61, 65, 69, 81, 147, 154–5, 185, 187, 190–1
International Prisoner of War Agency 15
internee numbers 90, 210
internment camps (civilian) 3–4, 8, 28, 78–9, 101–2
Isle of Man 79, 102
Italy 13, 47

Jersaillon, Captain 89
Jones, Heather 6, 8, 36–7
Jones, Lieutenant Colonel 61
Jones, Major 110
Journal des Internés Français 6, 35, 46, 80, 92, 94–5, 106, 108, 142–4, 154–5, 180, 184, 191–2

Jung, Carl 65
Jungfraubahn 119–20, 129

Kaiser, Isabelle 183
Kaiserfeier 153
Kaiser Wilhelm II 13
Ketchum, J. Davidson 78, 101, 141
kilts 41, 144–5
Kirkup, Constance 130–1, 146, 177–8, 189
Kirmmse, Alexander 116
Kitchener, Lord 18, 169
Kleine Scheidegg 119
Koller, Christian 100
Kriegsgefangener 3

labour unions 81, 86, 210
Ladies' Workrooms 190
Lake Lucerne 54, 114
Lampen, Revd. Ernest Dudley 19, 156–8
Lausanne 40–2, 49, 53, 62, 86, 91–2, 108, 145, 203
Lauterbrunnen 42–2, 65, 152–3, 160, 192
law 92
leagues 107
leather work 81, 89, 93–5
Leckie, Isabelle 155
lectures 78, 149–50
Le Havre 36, 171–2, 174
Leicester 44–5, 165, 169, 180, 211
Leicester and Rutland Prisoner of War Committee 44–5, 165, 169, 211
Lens, Marguerite de 166
Les Avants 129, 180
lessons 44–5
letters 4, 44–6, 72
Leybourne, E. Angus 130–1, 146, 177–8
Leysin 18, 26–7, 33, 35, 45, 47, 53–4, 62–3, 86, 124, 146, 148, 155, 158, 160–1, 184, 203, 206
Lister, Captain 111
literacy and numeracy 81, 90
Llopart, Captain Doctor 54, 60, 154
Lofthouse Park 79
London 174, 177, 185
Lord Kitchener's Memorial Fund 169
Lucerne 2, 26, 29, 54, 60–2, 114, 153, 155, 176, 203

luge   125, 131
Lunn, Arnold   105, 116–23, 150, 179, 189
Lunn, Mabel   117–18, 154, 189
Lunn, Sir Henry   55–6, 116
Lyon   16, 22, 24, 36, 172, 190

MacSwinney, Elsie   171, 173
magazines   6, 8
Makepeace, Clare   3–4, 142
Malcolm, Ian   20
Manor Farm   61, 87, 156
Marchetti, Monsignor   20–2
marraines de guerre   166
marriage   176–85
Marshall, Corporal D.   71
Martin, Miss   151, 154, 193
masculinity   5–6, 96, 104, 132–3
Mason, Tony   103
Medical Commissions   35
medical convoys   16
medical delegation   17–18, 23, 46
medical staff   7, 16, 60, 63
medical treatment   60–1, 208
Meieringen   54, 87, 89, 120, 128, 149, 155, 186, 188
Merton Club   105
Middleditch, Lieutenant Robert Henry   116, 118, 120–1, 179
mimesis   144
misbehaviour   66–7, 71, 79–80
Mission Catholique Suisse   159–60
mobilization   2
Montana   26, 33, 58, 63, 114, 117
Montreux   8, 26, 38–9, 41–2, 89, 99, 115, 122, 145, 147–8, 150–1, 155, 200, 203
Montreux F.C.   105
moral regeneration   80, 103
motor mechanics   81, 87–9, 209
Motta, Guiseppi   17
mountain guides   120–1
Mount Pilatus   128–9
Moynier, Gustave   14
Müller, Doctor   60
Munyard, Corporal H. D. 'Bert'   109, 111, 177
Mürren   26, 29, 42–5, 47, 49, 54–6, 59–61, 69, 81, 87, 93, 105–7, 110–11, 113, 116, 118–19, 123, 126, 131, 143, 146–8, 150, 154–6, 159, 160, 168, 170, 177, 179, 180, 186–8, 199–200, 203

Mürren Temperance Society   128
musicians   142, 145–9, 152, 182, 193
Muslims   161, 209

name days   152
Napoleonic Wars   77
national identity   7, 28, 210
Naville, Edouard   18
Neish, Lieutenant Colonel   93, 199
Netley   23
Neuchatel   92, 109, 112, 180
neutrality   1, 2, 4, 7–8, 13, 20, 28, 60–1, 95, 207, 210
Newton, Lord   29, 43
New Year   151–3
New Zealanders   154
Northcliffe, Lord   167
Norway   21
number of prisoners of war   165, 201
nurses   60, 63

Oberegg   46–7, 82–3, 146–7
Oeuvre de la Colonie Suisse de France   175
Oeuvre Universitaire Suisse des Etuduants Prisonniers de Guerre   91
Office du Travail des Internés Français   84–5
orchestra   146–8, 154
Orchestre Symphonique des Internés Alliés   148, 150
Ormorod, Mrs   122, 174, 187–9
orthopaedic apparatus   83
Ourbil Haid   112

Paillard, André   40, 82, 93, 111, 202
Palace Hotel, Mürren   55, 59, 104–7, 116, 147, 189
Panayi, Panikos   3–4, 78–9, 102, 141
parcels   44–5, 49
Paris   19, 171–2, 174, 185
partiality   14–15, 28, 40
passports   168, 175, 190
Pau, General   153
Père Noël   151
physiotherapy   83
piano building   89
Picot, Lieutenant Colonel Henry Philip   8, 18, 40, 50, 65, 106, 110, 161, 167, 170, 178, 193

plastic surgery 63
Plunkett, Bombardier P. 95
Plüschow, Gunther 4
Poilu 100, 150
Poilu F.C. Berne 107
Polytechnic Touring Association 55–6, 61, 89
Pope Benoit XV 17, 19
ports 204
postal service 44
postcards 4, 44, 62
potatoes 28
pre-fabricated huts and shelters 85–6
Presbyterians 158
prime minister 21
printing 81, 87
prisoner-of-war camps 3–6, 8–9, 23–4, 35, 37, 44, 46, 49, 54, 72, 78, 100, 102, 141–4, 194, 200, 205
Prisoner of War Department 193
Prisoner of War Help Committee 20
prisoners of war 9, 19–20, 46
Pro Captivis 83
protestant 83, 160
proxy marriage 178
Prussian Ministry of Education 79
Public Schools Alpine Sports Club 116
punishment 66–7, 69–72, 95–6, 185, 203, 209

quarantine 161

Radauer, Lena 3
Ragaz-Pfäffers 26
Ranse, Marc de 148
Rastatt 24
rates of pay 57
rationing 1–2, 59, 132, 202–3
reception committees 37–8, 40, 46, 48
recuperation 5–6
Red Cross 2, 4, 7–9, 14–16, 18, 38, 40, 42, 46, 57, 83, 87, 110, 115, 122, 169, 171, 174, 177–8, 187, 194
refugees 145, 191
rehabilitation 80–1, 85, 89, 93–4, 103, 209
relatives 22, 70
relatives' visits 167–78, 186–9, 194, 208
religion 156–8
repatriation 25, 199–201, 204–7

Ricklin, Captain 65
Riedi, Eliza 103
Rivière, Jacques 175, 176
roll call 54
Rollier, August 35
Roman Catholics 83, 158–60, 180
Roper, Michael 4
Rosey 126
Rossinière 95
Roth, Frau Minister 34
Rougemont 40, 168
rowing 114
Royal Army Medical Corps 61
Royal Army Temperance Society 128, 158
rugby 100–1
Ruhleben Camp 3, 78, 101, 106, 109, 141
Rumbold, Sir Horace 204
Russians 3, 9, 19, 86

St Gallen 26, 34
St Moritz 27
St Peter's Church, Chateau d'Oex 156–7, 159, 205
Salvan 112
sanatoria 7, 27, 33, 35, 60, 63, 65, 72, 91, 126, 132, 205, 208
Schinznach in Aargau 26
schools 191–2
Scottish dancers 144–5, 209
seasonal celebrations 150–4, 190–2
Seeburg 54, 56, 61, 87, 89, 93, 113–14, 154
Seehof 205
separation allowances 178
Servette, la 107
Sewell, Revd. Archibold 158
sewing 190
sexual assault 185
ships 190
Simpkin, Miss 61
Simpson, Major 95
Ski Club of Great Britain 8
ski jumping 131
ski lessons 117
sledging 124–6, 188
slide shows 149–50
slipper making 82
Smith, Eric Lieutenant 81
smoking 155

Society for the Propagation of the Gospel 158
Soldiers' and Sailors' Families' Association 168
Solferino, Battle of 14
Soltau Camp 54
Sonderegger, Hermann 47
Southampton 171–2
Spanish flu 65–6, 161
Spiez 108, 151, 190
sport 8, 70, 99–133, 208–9
Sporting Club Franco-Belge des Internés d'Engelberg 108, 114, 125
Sports Committee 110, 141
Stanley, Arthur 18
Stans 60
Stella F.C. de Fribourg 109
Stobs 102
Stock, Harry 123, 185, 188
strikes 202
Stube 156
students 81
study 154
Sturzenegger, Lieutenant Colonel 23
submarine 24, 168, 171–2
Suchard 149
suicide 65, 79
Suisse Romande 13, 15
supply lines 210
surgery 61
swimming 114
Swiss Accident Insurance Hospital (SUVA) 61
Swiss Army 8, 13, 29, 33, 65–6, 152
Swiss Army Medical Corps 23–4, 35, 54
Swiss brides 184, 185, 202
Swiss Federal Council 202, 204
Swiss Federal Government 14–17, 21, 29, 33, 66
Swiss-German 13, 28, 40–3, 72
Sylvesterfeuer 152

tailors 86–7, 93–4
Taylor, Jack Perry 25, 180, 181
teachers 88–90, 92
technical college 87
technical education 91–6
tennis 102, 104–5, 111
Teufen 34, 69, 82–3, 183
Thapa, Dalbahadar 161

theatre 142, 144–6, 208
Théatre des Internés d'Engelberg 147
Thomas Cook and Son 56
Ticino 13
Timms, Private R. 54
Tipperary 155
tobogganing 110, 116, 118, 123–4, 126, 131–2, 185, 188
tombola 150
Tommies 37–8
Toogood, Mrs M. E. 23
Total Abstinence Rambling Club 128
tourism 1, 26–7, 29, 54, 148, 208, 210
toy making 83–4
trade 28
trains 24, 34, 36–7, 40, 42, 53, 66, 124, 129, 132, 171, 175, 187, 190, 203–6
trauma 79
Travail Internés Militaires 84
travel pass 54
Tsharner, Louis de 17
tuberculosis 7, 17–18, 33, 35, 58, 63, 205
tug of war 109

Union Chrétiennes de Jeunes Gens 86
United States 25–6, 49
universities 91

Valais 26
Vallorbe 172
Vansittert, Colonel and Mrs Eden 167
Varley, Edward 184
Vatican 20, 22
Vaud 40, 53
Vevey 26, 54, 66, 84, 87, 90, 110, 143, 179, 190, 205
Villars 53–4
Villingen 24
Vines, Edward 45
visitor numbers 1, 148
vocational training 81, 83, 87–96 209
Voluntary Aid Detachment 193
volunteers 144
Vuilleumier, Christophe 7

wages 80
Waldstatt 47
walking 114, 128, 131–2
Walzenhausen 47, 92
Waquet, Arnaud 100, 104

War Office   8, 19–21, 29, 43, 55, 106
War Pensions Scheme   94
watch repair   81, 89, 93
weddings   160, 176, 179–85
welcoming committees   37–8, 40, 46, 48
Wengen   128, 153, 160
Wesleyans   159
Western Jura   26
Whiteley's   60
Wiesen   26
Wilkinson, Oliver   2, 3
winter sport   115–28, 209
Wipers Times   143
Witzvil   72, 95
Wives' visits   167–78, 186–9, 194, 208
women   23, 67, 69, 71, 114, 144–5, 166–7, 170, 178, 182–3, 190, 194
Woods, Joseph A.   62

work   8, 29, 70, 72, 77, 80, 83, 93
work discipline   81, 93, 95, 209
work experience   209
work placements   89
workshops   82, 84–6, 88–9, 193
wounds   5, 8, 16, 18, 37, 42, 56, 61

YMCA Hut   69, 146, 156, 209
Young Boys Berne F.C.   107
Younger, Sir Robert   169
Young Men's Christian Association (YMCA)   69, 86, 147, 155–6, 209
Young Women's Christian Association (YWCA)   168, 174
Yverdon   147, 180, 203

Zeppelin   172, 181, 189
Zurich   37, 40, 53, 190, 203

www.ingramcontent.com/pod-product-compliance
Lightning Source LLC
Chambersburg PA
CBHW052038300426
44117CB00012B/1875